Microsoft

Start Here!™

Learn
HTML5

Faithe Wempen

Published with the authorization of Microsoft Corporation by:
O'Reilly Media, Inc.
1005 Gravenstein Highway North
Sebastopol, California 95472

ISBN: 978-0-7356-6982-6

1 2 3 4 5 6 7 8 9 LSI 7 6 5 4 3 2

Printed and bound in the United States of America.

Microsoft Press books are available through booksellers and distributors worldwide. If you need support related to this book, email Microsoft Press Book Support at mspinput@microsoft.com. Please tell us what you think of this book at http://www.microsoft.com/learning/booksurvey.

Microsoft and the trademarks listed at http://www.microsoft.com/about/legal/en/us/IntellectualProperty/ Trademarks/EN-US.aspx are trademarks of the Microsoft group of companies. All other marks are property of their respective owners.

The example companies, organizations, products, domain names, email addresses, logos, people, places, and events depicted herein are fictitious. No association with any real company, organization, product, domain name, email address, logo, person, place, or event is intended or should be inferred.

Acquisitions and Developmental Editor: Russell Jones

Production Editor: Melanie Yarbrough

Editorial Production: Box Twelve Communications

Technical Reviewer: John Meuller

Indexer: WordCo Indexing Services

Cover Design: Jake Rae

Cover Composition: Zyg Group

Illustrator: Rebecca Demarest

To Margaret

Contents at a Glance

Contents

What do you think of this book? We want to hear from you!

Microsoft is interested in hearing your feedback so we can continually improve our books and learning resources for you. To participate in a brief online survey, please visit:

microsoft.com/learning/booksurvey

What do you think of this book? We want to hear from you!

Microsoft is interested in hearing your feedback so we can continually improve our
books and learning resources for you. To participate in a brief online survey, please visit:

microsoft.com/learning/booksurvey

Introduction

Hypertext Markup Language (HTML) is the basic programming language of the World Wide Web. It's the common thread that ties together virtually every website, from large-scale corporate sites like Microsoft's to single-page classroom projects at the local grade school.

In simple terms, a **webpage (or HTML document)** is a plain text file that has been encoded using HTML so that it appears nicely formatted in a web browser. Here's what HTML means, word-by-word:

- **Hypertext** Text that you click to jump from document to document. This is a reference to the ability of webpages to link to one another.

- **Markup** Tags that apply layout and formatting conventions to plain text. Literally, the plain text is "marked up" with the tags.

- **Language** A reference to the fact that HTML is considered a programming language.

Don't let the phrase "programming language" intimidate you. Creating a webpage with HTML is much simpler than writing a computer program in a language like Microsoft Visual Basic or C++. You can create a simple webpage in just a few minutes.

> **Tip** When people think of computer programming, they usually think of writing a *compiled* program. A compiled programming language runs the human-readable programming code through a utility that converts it to an executable file (usually with an *.exe* or *.com* extension), which is then distributed to users. In contrast, HTML is an *interpreted* programming language. That means the program is distributed in human-readable format to users, and the program in which it is opened takes care of running it. The HTML code for webpages resides in files. Each time your web browser opens a webpage, it processes the HTML code within the file.

This book teaches beginner-level HTML in a rather fundamentalist way: by creating plain text files in Notepad. There are so many good website creation programs on the market nowadays that you may be wondering why this book takes this approach.

Simply put, it's because doing your own coding is the best way to learn HTML. In this book you'll build a website from the ground up, writing every line of code yourself. It's slower and not as much fun as a fancy graphical program, but it's great training.

The last chapter of this book shows how to use Microsoft Expression Web to create web content, and you may eventually choose to move to a program like that. However, you will be a much better web designer—and understand what is going on in design programs much better—if you tough it out with Notepad in the beginning.

Who Should Read This Book

This book is designed for non-programmers who are brand-new to HTML. It doesn't assume any previous web design or programming knowledge of any kind, so it's perfect for home hobbyists and self-educators, as well as high school and college classrooms.

Assumptions

This book expects that you have basic computer literacy skills and you can use the operating system on your PC. The detailed procedures for this book were written with Windows developers in mind, but the general information applies to building webpages on any operating system. You should know how to manage files, run programs, and access the Internet.

I'm also assuming that if you're reading this book, you are actually interested in learning HTML and not just knocking out a quick webpage only to never think about HTML again. This book provides you with a solid foundation in HTML that you'll be able to draw from for years to come.

Who Should Not Read This Book

This book is not for experienced programmers who already have significant HTML knowledge and are just interested in updating their skills for HTML5. This book doesn't cover many of HTML5's advanced features that experienced web developers are likely to be interested in learning about; instead, it provides a solid foundation for the beginner.

Organization of This Book

This book is divided into three sections, each of which focuses on a different aspect of webpage development. Part I, "Getting Started with HTML," explains how HTML works and helps you set up the structure of a page and place basic text elements on it such as headings, paragraphs, and lists. Part II, "Style Sheets and Graphics," explains how to use cascading style sheets (CSS) to apply formatting to a page or a group of pages and how to include graphic elements on a page. Part III, "Page Layout and Navigation," explains how to create intuitive page layouts and navigational aids as well as how to add special elements such as forms and multimedia.

Conventions and Features in This Book

This book presents information using conventions designed to make the information readable and easy to follow.

- Each exercise consists of a series of tasks, presented as numbered steps (1, 2, and so on) listing each action you must take to complete the exercise.

- Boxed elements with labels such as "Note" provide additional information or alternative methods for completing a step successfully.

- Text that you type displays in **boldface**. For example, if you are instructed to type some text to an existing block of code, the text you are to type is displayed in bold.

- Glossary terms marked in the text are explained in the glossary at the end of the book.

System Requirements

You will need the following hardware and software to complete the practice exercises in this book:

- A computer running the operating system of your choice. The examples in this book use Windows 8, but you can use any Windows, Mac, Linux, or UNIX operating system.

- A text-editing program. The examples in this book use Notepad, which comes with all Windows versions.

- One or more web browsers. The examples in this book use Internet Explorer 10. You will probably want at least one other browser in which to check your work, because different browsers might display content in different ways.

- An Internet connection to download the practice files.

Code Samples

Each chapter includes exercises that let you interactively try out new material learned in the main text. All files you will need to complete these exercises can be downloaded from the following page:

http://go.microsoft.com/FWLink/?Linkid=263540

Follow the instructions to download the *9780735669826_files.zip* file.

Installing the Code Samples

Follow these steps to install the code samples on your computer so that you can use them with the exercises in this book.

1. Unzip the *9780735669826_files.zip* file that you downloaded from the book's website (name a specific directory along with directions to create it, if necessary).

2. If prompted, review the displayed end user license agreement. If you accept the terms, select the accept option and then click Next.

> **Note** If the license agreement doesn't display, you can access it from the same webpage from which you downloaded the *9780735669826_files.zip* file.

Using the Code Samples

The folder created by the Setup.exe program contains subfolders for each chapter. Within a chapter's folder are additional subfolders that hold the files for each exercise. Each time you begin an exercise, make sure that you are using the files provided specifically for that exercise.

Each chapter folder contains a *_Solutions* subfolder, which contains samples of the finished files for that chapter's exercises. You can use these to check your work.

Acknowledgments

Thank you to my editorial team at O'Reilly for a job well done, including Russell Jones (Acquisitions/Development), John Mueller (Technical Editor), Jeff Riley (Copy Editor), and Melanie Yarbrough (Production Editor). It is a pleasure to work with a professional team of editors who make the complex process of producing a book go as smoothly as possible.

Errata & Book Support

We've made every effort to ensure the accuracy of this book and its companion content. Any errors that have been reported since this book was published are listed on our Microsoft Press site at oreilly.com:

http://go.microsoft.com/FWLink/?Linkid=263542

If you find an error that is not already listed, you can report it to us through the same page.

If you need additional support, email Microsoft Press Book Support at *mspinput@microsoft.com*.

Please note that product support for Microsoft software is not offered through the addresses above.

We Want to Hear from You

At Microsoft Press, your satisfaction is our top priority, and your feedback our most valuable asset. Please tell us what you think of this book at:

http://www.microsoft.com/learning/booksurvey

The survey is short, and we read every one of your comments and ideas. Thanks in advance for your input!

Stay in Touch

Let's keep the conversation going! We're on Twitter: *http://twitter.com/MicrosoftPress*

Getting Started with HTML

Chapter 1

HTML Basics: The Least You Need to Know

In this chapter, you will:

- Learn how HTML tags work

- Open a webpage in Notepad

- Preview a webpage in Internet Explorer

- Make, save, and view changes

- Learn how to publish your pages to a server

As you work through this book's exercises, you'll learn HTML by creating and editing text files in Notepad (or any plain text editor), and then viewing them in a web browser to check your work. This chapter teaches the important basic skills you need in order to work in these programs.

Important Before you can use the practice files provided for this chapter, you need to download and install them from the book's companion content location. For more information, see "Code Samples" at the beginning of this book.

Understanding HTML Tags

An HTML file (also known as a webpage file or document) is a plain-text file. That's why you can use a plain-text editor like Notepad to edit an HTML file. Within that file is literal text (that is, text that will literally appear on the screen when you display the page in a browser) plus tags that tell the browser how to format and arrange the text.

HTML tags are codes inside angle brackets, like this: *<p>*. There are dozens of tags defined in the HTML5 standard. You can use these tags to specify where formatting should be applied, how the layout should appear, what pictures should be placed in certain locations, and more.

For example, suppose you wanted a certain word to appear in bold, like this:

Save up to **50%** on clearance items.

In HTML, there's no Bold button to click (like there is in a word-processing program). Therefore, you have to "tag" the word or characters that you want to be bold. The tag to turn on bold is *<b>*, and the code to turn bold off is *</b>*. Your HTML code would look something like this:

```
Save up to <b>50%</b> on clearance items.
```

That's an example of a *two-sided tag*, which encloses text between an opening tag and a closing tag, in this case *<b>* and *</b>*. Note the forward slash (/) in the closing tag (*</b>*). That slash differentiates an opening tag from a closing tag. With a two-sided tag, there is always a corresponding closing tag for every opening tag.

To understand how this system of tagging came about, you need to know that back in the early days of the Internet, nearly everyone connected to it by using dial-up modems at speeds ranging from 2400 bps to 28.8 Kbps. That's really slow. Text files transfer much faster than binary files, so for any type of information-sharing system to be popular, it had to be text-based. Otherwise, people would doze off while waiting for a page to load.

People designing webpages also wanted their pages to be attractive. They couldn't just format pages in a word processor, though, because every word processor handled formatting differently and it was impossible to know which word processor a visitor might be using. Word-processing files are also much larger than plain-text files.

The web's creators developed an elegant solution. Instead of sending the formatted pages over the Internet, they created an application—a web browser—that could interpret plain-text code (HTML tags) as formatting instructions. The text could be sent quickly and efficiently in plain-text format, and then be processed and displayed attractively and graphically on the local PC.

HTML worked great all by itself for all kinds of text formatting, but some web designers wanted to include graphics on their pages. To accommodate this, the *<img>* tag was created, which designers use to refer to a graphic stored on a server. When the web browser gets to that tag, it requests that the image file be downloaded from the server and displayed on the page. (You'll learn how to insert images in Chapter 9, "Inserting Graphics.")

The *<img>* tag is different in several ways from the *<b>* tag. It is one-sided, meaning it does not have a closing tag, and it takes attributes. An *attribute* is text within the tag that contains information about how the tag should behave. For example, for an *<img>* tag, you have to specify a source (abbreviated *src*). Here's an example:

```
<img src="tree.gif">
```

This *<img>* tag uses the *src=* attribute and specifies that the file *tree.gif* be displayed.

Many tags accept attributes, either optional or required. You'll see many examples throughout the exercises in this book. Attributes are usually written in pairs in the form *name=value*, where the name of the attribute is on the left side of the equals sign, and the value on the right.

With HTML, you can also create hyperlinks from one page to another. When a visitor clicks a hyperlink, the web browser loads the referenced page or jumps to a marked section (a "bookmark") within the same page. You will learn to create hyperlinks in Chapter 5, "Creating Hyperlinks and Anchors."

The tag for a hyperlink is *<a>*, a two-sided tag, but most people wouldn't recognize it without the attribute that specifies the file or location to which to jump. For example, to create a hyperlink with the words Click Here that jumps to the *index.htm* file when clicked, the coding would look like this:

```
<a href="index.htm">Click Here</a>
```

There's a lot more to HTML, but that's basically how it works. You mark up plain text with tags that indicate where you want to apply elements such as formatting, hyperlinks, and graphics. Then a web browser interprets those tags and displays the page in its formatted state, a process called *rendering*. The trick, of course, is to know which tags to use, where they're appropriate, and what attributes they need. And that's the subject of this book. Starting in Chapter 2, you'll begin building a website from scratch, learning about each individual tag as you go. By the time you finish this book, you will have created a multi-page website using nothing but Notepad and the tags that you have personally learned about and typed. Talk about boot camp! There are professional web designers out there today who have never done this and who don't have the fundamental HTML coding skills that you'll have when you finish this book.

What is XHTML?

There is a language related to HTML called *Extensible Markup Language (XML)* that programmers use to create their own tags. It's widely used for web databases, for example, because it can define tags for each data field. Because XML can be so completely customized, programmers can create almost any other markup language within it just by re-creating all the officially accepted tags of that language.

XHTML, then, is HTML written within the larger language of XML. Because it is virtually identical to HTML in its functionality, the basic set of tags is the same and you can learn both HTML and XHTML at the same time. You can also use XHTML to create new tags and extensions, which is a valuable feature for advanced web developers.

There's just one thing about XHTML to watch out for: it's not tolerant of mistakes. For example, in HTML, technically you are supposed to begin each paragraph with *<p>* and end each paragraph with *</p>*. But in HTML you can leave out the closing *</p>* tag if you want (or if you forget it). That won't work in XHTML. There are lots of little ways that XHTML is picky like that. I'll point out some of them along the way in this book.

At one point, it was thought that XHTML would eventually replace HTML 4, but due to interoperability problems, that has not happened; instead HTML5 is poised to succeed HTML 4. This book doesn't explicitly cover XHTML, but most of what you will learn can be applied to XHTML coding.

Opening a Webpage in Notepad

The rest of this book assumes that you will be working in Notepad or some other text editor, so you'll need a basic understanding of whatever text editor you select. Notepad is included with all versions of Windows. It's a simple text editor that saves only in plain-text format. That's ideal for HTML editing because you don't need to worry about any extra word-processing formatting being included in the file.

> **Note** You are welcome to use a different text editor application to complete the exercises in this book. Notepad is just a suggestion.

When saving or opening files in Notepad, the default file extension is *.txt*. The Save dialog boxes and Open dialog boxes are set by default to filter file listings so only those files with .txt extensions appear. That means each time you browse for a file, you need to change the file type to All Files so you can browse for webpages (which have *.htm* or *.html* extensions).

Note You may run into various extensions on webpage files on the Internet, such as *.php*, *.asp*, and *.jsp*. Those are all special formats designed for use with specific server technologies. This book covers developing only the basic type of webpage: the type with an *.htm* extension.

In the following exercise, you will open a webpage in Notepad and examine its text and tags.

Open a Webpage in Notepad

1. In Windows 8, press the Windows key to display the Start screen. Begin typing Notepad, and when you see Notepad at the left, click it.

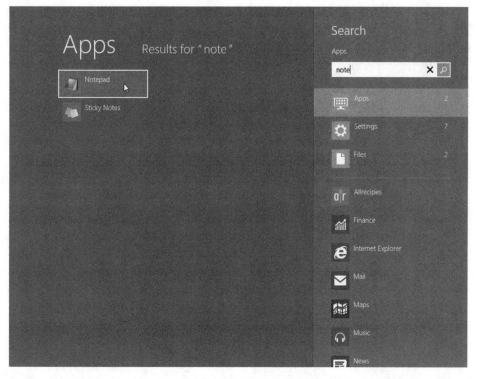

Or, if you're working in an earlier Windows version, from the Start menu, click All Programs | Accessories | Notepad.

Note Because you will be using Notepad extensively in this book, you might want to create a shortcut for Notepad on the taskbar. To do so in Windows 8, after locating the Notepad app as shown in the previous figure, right-click its tile, and then click Pin to Taskbar. Or, in an earlier Windows version, after locating Notepad on the Accessories submenu, right-click it there and then click Pin to Taskbar.

2. In the untitled Notepad window, click File | Open.

3. Navigate to the folder containing the practice files for this chapter. To do so, on the Places bar, click Documents (or My Documents if you are using Windows XP). In the Open dialog box, double-click Microsoft Press, double-click HTML 5 Start Here, and then double-click 01Basics.

 Note You won't see any files in the list at this point. The only thing that you should see is a _Solutions folder. (That folder contains the solution files for the lesson, but you don't need those now.)

4. Click the Files Of Type drop-down arrow and then click All Files.

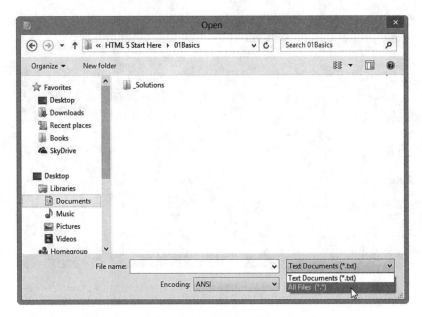

5. In the Open dialog box, click *welcome.htm* and then click Open.

The *welcome.htm* file opens in Notepad.

Note The *.htm* extension might not appear on the welcome file in the Open dialog box. By default, file extensions for known file types are turned off in Windows. To turn them on, open File Explorer (Windows 8), Computer (Windows Vista or 7), or My Computer (Windows XP). In Windows 8, on the View tab, select the File name extensions check box. In earlier Windows versions, click the Tools menu (press Alt for the menu bar if you don't see it) and then click Folder Options. On the View tab of the Folder Options dialog box, clear the Hide Extensions For Known File Types check box and then click OK.

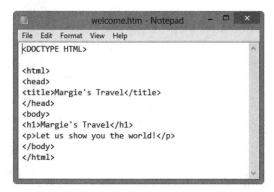

6. Locate the *<html>* and *</html>* tags.

   These tags signify the beginning and end of the HTML. They are typically the first and last tags in document, with the exception of the DOCTYPE, which you'll learn about later.

7. Locate the *<body>* and *</body>* tags.

   These tags signify the beginning and end of the visible portion of the webpage when viewed in a browser.

8. Locate the *<p>* and *</p>* tags.

   These tags signify the beginning and end of a paragraph.

   Leave Notepad open for later use. You don't have to save your work because you didn't make any changes.

Other Ways of Opening Webpages in Notepad

A quick way to open most file types in their default applications is to double-click them from any File Explorer (or Windows Explorer) window. However, the problem with doing that for HTML files is that the default application is your web browser, not Notepad. So when you double-click an HTML file, the file doesn't open in Notepad; the file opens in your web browser. One way to get around this is to right-click a file in File Explorer, point to Open With, and then click Notepad (see Figure 1-1). This opens Notepad and loads the file.

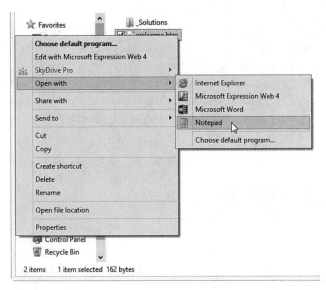

FIGURE 1-1 You can open a file with Notepad by right-clicking the file, pointing to Open With, and then clicking Notepad.

 Note File Explorer is the file management interface in Windows 8. In earlier versions of Windows, that same interface is called Windows Explorer.

Here's another method: You can create a shortcut to Notepad on your desktop and then drag-and-drop individual HTML files onto that shortcut whenever you want to open an HTML file in Notepad. To create a desktop shortcut for Notepad in Windows 8, locate Notepad from the Start screen, right-click its tile, and then click Open File Location. In the File Explorer window that displays, right-click Notepad, point to Send To, and then click Desktop (Create Shortcut). See Figure 1-2. In earlier Windows versions, locate Notepad on the Start menu (Start | All Programs | Accessories), right-click it, point to Send To, and then click Desktop (Create Shortcut).

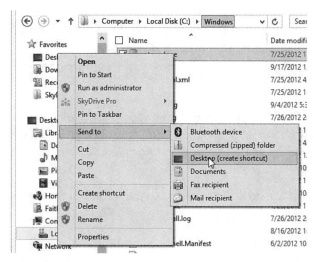

FIGURE 1-2 To copy the Notepad shortcut to the desktop, right-click it, point to Send to, and then click Desktop (create shortcut).

> **Caution** Theoretically, you could set Notepad as the default application for opening files that have an *.htm* or *.html* extension. But that would cause more problems than it's worth, because then *all* your HTML content would open in Notepad not just the pages you are using for these lessons.

Adding a Location to the Favorites List

While working through this book, you will open many files in Notepad. To save yourself the trouble of navigating to the data file folder each time, you might want to add that folder to your Favorites bar, which displays in the navigation pane in the Open dialog box.

In the following exercise, you learn how to add a shortcut that brings you directly to the HTML 5 Start Here folder from the Favorites list.

Add a Location to Your Favorites List

1. In Notepad, click File | Open.

Note You can actually do this in almost any application (especially the Microsoft ones), but Notepad is handy because you worked with it in the preceding exercise.

2. Navigate to the folder containing the practice files for this book.

   On the Places bar, click Documents (or click My Documents if you are using Windows XP). In the Open dialog box, double-click Microsoft Press. The HTML 5 Start Here folder displays as an icon. Depending on your View setting, the icon might be a different size than shown here. The icon size is not important for the task at hand.

3. Drag the HTML 5 Start Here folder icon to the Favorites list on the left side of the window.

   A shortcut for that folder displays on the Favorites list.

Drag the
folder here

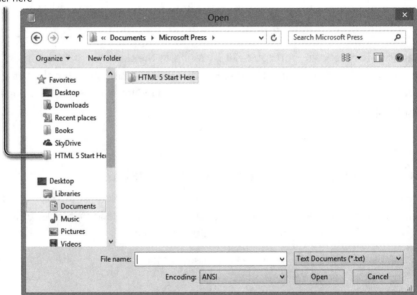

Now, the next time you want to open a file in the Open dialog box, you can click that short-cut, and then double-click the folder for the chapter you are working on, which is much more convenient!

Previewing HTML Files in a Web Browser

Because Notepad is not a WYSIWYG ("What You See Is What You Get") program, you won't be able to immediately see how the tags you type will look in the finished product. To work around this, most people like to keep a browser window open next to Notepad so they can see their work by looking at their browser.

You can preview your work in any browser; you do not need to use Internet Explorer 10 (although that's what I use in this book's examples). In fact, as you progress with your web development skills, you will probably want to acquire several different browsers in which to test your pages, because each browser might display page elements a little differently. For beginners, though, Internet Explorer is a good choice because it's one of the most popular browsers—one that a large percentage of your target audience is likely to be using. Other popular browsers include Google Chrome, Firefox, Safari, and Opera.

If you are using Windows 8, you have two different versions of Internet Explorer: the regular desktop version and the customized Windows 8 app version. You can start the desktop version of Internet Explorer from the Internet Explorer icon that's pinned to the left of the taskbar on the desktop. You can start the custom version from the Internet Explorer tile on the Start screen. This book uses the desktop version of Internet Explorer, but you might want to check your work in the custom version when you start developing your own sites.

Caution Versions of Internet Explorer prior to version 10 do not support some of the HTML5 features. (Internet Explorer 9 supports most of the features, but not all.) You will probably want to test your webpages in an earlier version of Internet Explorer to make sure that people who use those versions will be able to view your pages. But don't use an early version of Internet Explorer as you work through this book's examples; you won't get the full effect of the new HTML5 features.

Tip If the video card in your computer has two monitor connectors on it, or if you have an additional video card that you could install in your system, you might want to set up two monitors side-by-side. That way you can work on your HTML code in Notepad on one monitor and display the page full-screen in Internet Explorer in the other. All recent versions of Windows support at least two monitors, and some versions support many more.

In the following exercise, you will display an HTML file in Internet Explorer. I use the desktop version of Internet Explorer 10 for the examples in this book. To see the displayed file and the underlying code at the same time, open the file in Notepad and then arrange the windows so that both are visible at once.

Open a Webpage in Internet Explorer

1. Using File Explorer (or Windows Explorer), open *Documents\Microsoft Press\HTML 5 Start Here\01Basics* and then double-click *welcome.htm*. The file opens in Internet Explorer (or your default browser, if you're not using Internet Explorer).

Note If Internet Explorer is not your default browser but you want it to be, from within Internet Explorer, click Tools | Internet Options, click the Programs tab, and then click Make Default.

That's by far the easiest way if File Explorer is already open and displaying the file's location. Follow the next steps to learn another way that might be preferable when Internet Explorer is already open but File Explorer (or Windows Explorer) isn't.

2. In Internet Explorer, click File | Open.

The Open dialog box displays.

Note If the menu bar does not display in Internet Explorer, press the Alt key to display it.

3. Click the Browse button and then browse to *Documents\Microsoft Press\HTML 5 Start Here\01Basics*.

Tip If you created the shortcut in the Favorites bar earlier in the chapter, you can use that to save a few clicks when browsing for the location.

4. Click *welcome.htm* and then click Open.

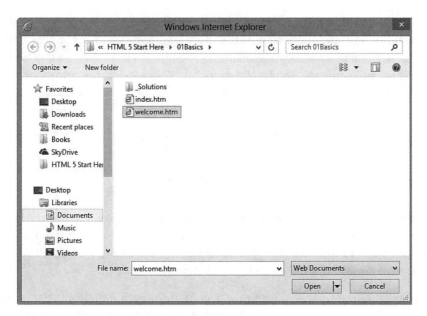

The path to the file displays in the Open dialog box.

5. Click OK.

The file opens in Internet Explorer. Leave Internet Explorer open for the next exercise.

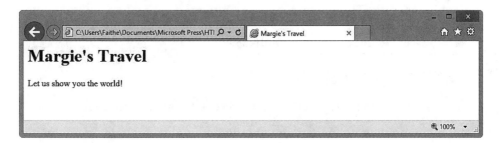

Tip Remember, not all web browsers display pages the same way. For example, one browser's idea of what text should look like might be different from another. It's a good idea to check your pages in multiple web browsers, such as Firefox, Netscape, and Opera. These are available as free downloads from *www.firefox.com*, *www.netscape.com*, and *www.opera.com*, respectively.

Making, Saving, and Viewing Changes

After you've made a change to a webpage, you will probably want to see how that change looks in a browser. If you set up your Internet Explorer and Notepad windows side by side in the preceding two exercises, it's easy to view those changes. Simply save your work in Notepad and then refresh the display in Internet Explorer by clicking the Refresh button or pressing F5.

In the following exercise, you will change *us* to *me* in the *welcome.htm* file and then preview that change in Internet Explorer. This exercise builds on the previous two, so make sure you have completed them before starting this exercise. You can use this procedure throughout the rest of the book to preview your work from each exercise.

Make and View Changes to an HTML File

1. In both Notepad and Internet Explorer, reopen the *welcome.htm* file (if it is not still open) located in the *Documents\Microsoft Press\HTML 5 Start Here\01Basics* folder.

    Remember, if you're using Windows 8, we're using the desktop version of Internet Explorer. In earlier versions of Windows that's not an issue because there is no custom version.

2. In Notepad, locate the word *us* and change it to *me*, as shown in the bold text in the following code:

    `<p>Let **me** show you the world!</p>`

3. Save your work (File | Save).

4. Switch to Internet Explorer and click the Refresh button (or press F5).

    The webpage now displays *me* rather than *us*.

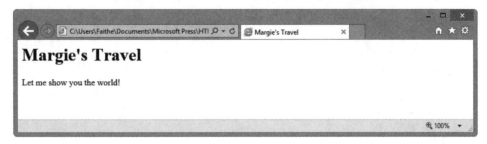

5. Close Internet Explorer and close Notepad.

Key Points

In this chapter, you explored HTML and you were introduced to some basic skills that will be essential in following along with the exercises in upcoming chapters. Here are the key points to remember from this chapter:

- Any plain text editor, including Notepad, can be an HTML editor.

- Most webpages have an *.htm* or *.html* extension. You can open these pages in Notepad, but first you need to change the Files Of Type setting in the Open dialog box to All Files. You must change this setting each time you use the Open dialog box.

- An alternative way to open a webpage in Notepad is to right-click it in File Explorer, point to Open With, and then click Notepad.

- To preview a page in a web browser, click File | Open from the browser's menu.

- You can double-click an *.htm* or *.html* file in File Explorer to open it automatically in your default web browser.

- To see the changes you make in Notepad reflected in your web browser, save your work in Notepad and then, with the file already displayed in your browser, click Refresh in the browser window.

Chapter 2

Setting Up the Document Structure

In this chapter, you will:

- Specify the document type

- Create the HTML, head, and body sections

- Create paragraphs and line breaks

- Specify a page title and keywords

Every society needs an infrastructure with certain rules that everyone agrees to for the general public good. For example, we have all agreed that a red light means "stop" and a green light means "go." Everyone who wants to participate in the transportation system must play by those rules. If not, chaos ensues.

HTML is the same way. You can get creative with your web content, but there must be an underlying structure in place for web browsers to read and render your webpages properly. That means the document must contain certain tags that identify its major sections and that indicate to the browser what type of coding the document uses.

In this chapter, you'll learn how to structure a document with the correct underlying tags. You'll learn how to specify the type of HTML you are writing and how to create Head sections and Body sections. You'll also learn how to create paragraph breaks and line breaks, how to specify a page title, and how to enter hidden keywords by which your page can be found in search engines.

Important Before you can use the practice files provided for this chapter, you need to download and install them from the book's companion content location. See "Code Samples" at the beginning of this book for more information.

Specifying the Document Type

The *document type* tells the browser how to interpret the tags. Including a document type tag is not strictly necessary, but if you're trying to get into good HTML habits from the get-go, you'll want to make sure it's included.

When creating an HTML5 document, the first line of the document should be this tag:

```
<!DOCTYPE html>
```

The *DOCTYPE* tag always begins with an exclamation point and is always placed at the beginning of the document, before any other tag. Most HTML tags are not case-sensitive, but the word *DOCTYPE* should always be uppercase.

Using the *DOCTYPE* tag is like signing a contract. It is an optional tag, but when you use it, you are promising that your coding will conform to certain standards. When a web browser encounters a *DOCTYPE* tag, it processes the page in standards mode. When it doesn't encounter the *DOCTYPE* tag, it can't assume that the page conforms to a standard, so it processes the page in quirks mode. When the browser sees the tag *<!DOCTYPE html>*, it assumes you are using HTML5.

The distinction between *standards mode* and *quirks mode* came about in earlier days, when there were problems with standardization between web browsers. With some browsers, to display pages properly, you needed to get a little creative with the HTML code. Modern HTML coding does not allow that, but some older pages still include these obsolete workarounds. By using the *DOCTYPE* tag, you are making a promise to the web browser that there is nothing but pure HTML code in the page. (And, since I'm teaching you to do everything the *right* way, that's a reasonable promise you can make.)

Earlier versions of HTML used more complex *DOCTYPE* tags. If you were using HTML 4.01, for example, the syntax for the tag would be:

```
<!DOCTYPE HTML PUBLIC "-//W3C/DTD HTML 4.01 Transitional//EN" "http://www.w3.org/TR/
html4/loose.dtd">
```

And, if you were using XHTML, the syntax for the tag would be:

```
<!DOCTYPE HTML PUBLIC "-//W3C/DTD XHTML 1.0 Transitional//EN" "http://www.w3.org/TR/
xhtml1/DTD/xhtml1-transitional.dtd">
```

 Note If you are writing XHTML code, the *DOCTYPE* tag is required.

Creating the HTML, Head, and Body Sections

All your HTML coding—except the *DOCTYPE* tag—should be placed in an *<html>* section. Recall from Chapter 1 that when a tag is two-sided, as *<html>* is, it requires a corresponding closing tag that is identical to the opening tag but contains a slash immediately after the opening angle bracket (for example, *</html>*). The tags *<html>* and *</html>* serve as a "wrapper" around all the other tags in the document except the *DOCTYPE* tag.

In addition, your HTML file should have two sections: a Head section and a Body section. The *Head section* is defined by the two-sided tag *<head>*. The Head section contains the page title, which is the text that will display in the title bar or page tab of the web browser. It also includes information about the document that is not displayed, such as its metatags (which you'll learn about later in this chapter). You can also include lines of code that run scripts, like Javascript.

The *Body section* is defined by the two-sided *<body>* tag and it contains all the information that displays in the web browser when you view the page.

Note The *<html>*, *<head>*, and *<body>* tags are all optional in HTML, but you should still use them because it's a good design practice. They are required in XHTML. In addition, in XHTML you must add an argument to the *<html>* tag that declares its XML namespace, a reference to the fact that XHTML is created within XML (as you learned in Chapter 1). Here's how the opening *<html>* tag should look in an XHTML document: *<html xmlns="http://www.w3.org/1999/xhtml">*.

In the following exercise, you will create an HTML5 template file that you can reuse later for your own work. That way you don't have to retype those same *DOCTYPE*, head, and body tags every time you want to create a new webpage.

Create an HTML5 Template

1. Open Notepad and then click the Format menu. Word Wrap should have a check mark next to it. If it does not, click it to enable the Word Wrap feature.

Tip Using Word Wrap makes it easier to see long lines of HTML coding without scrolling.

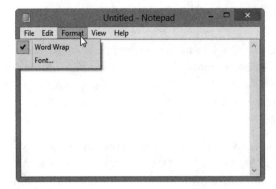

2. In the Notepad window, type the following:

```
<!DOCTYPE html>
```

3. Press Enter and then type:

```
<html>
<head>
```

4. Press Enter two or three times to insert some blank lines and then type:

```
</head>
<body>
```

5. Press Enter two or three times to insert some blank lines and then type:

```
</body>
</html>
```

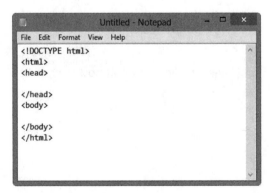

6. Save the file as *HTML5.htm* on your Windows desktop (or to any other location that is convenient for you).

Note Most of the files you work with in this book will be stored elsewhere, but you might find it helpful to keep the templates created in this exercise handy for reuse. The desktop is a convenient place to store them. Of course, you can store them anywhere you like.

7. Close Notepad.

You now have a template for creating any HTML documents you like. You can reopen this template file and save it under different names.

Tip If you want to avoid accidentally editing the template in the future, make it read-only. To do so, in Windows Explorer, right-click the file and then click Properties from the contextual menu. In the Properties dialog box, select the Read-Only check box. When you try to save changes to a read-only file, an error message displays and a Save As dialog box prompts you to save a copy of it with a new name.

Creating Paragraphs and Line Breaks

Within the *<body>* section of the document, you type the text that will display on the webpage. Each paragraph of text should be enclosed in a two-sided tag that indicates its type.

The most basic paragraph type is the body paragraph, indicated by the *<p>* tag. It is a two-sided tag, so the paragraph text is placed between a *<p>* and a *</p>*.

Note In HTML, the code will still work even if the *</p>* is omitted; in XHTML, however, it won't work without a closing tag. Even if you never plan on coding in XHTML, it is a good practice to include the *</p>* tag. This way, you won't fall into any sloppy habits.

When a browser displays a webpage, it inserts vertical white space between paragraphs (see Figure 2-1).

FIGURE 2-1 The browser inserts a blank vertical space between each paragraph.

That spacing is usually convenient, but it can be a problem when the extra space between lines is unwanted, such as with an address (see Figure 2-2).

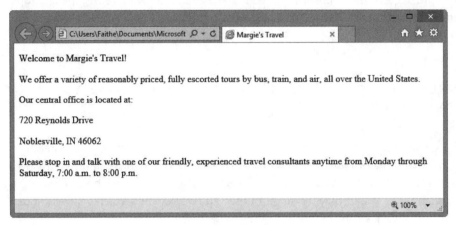

FIGURE 2-2 Sometimes you do not want extra space between each line, as shown in this example.

To create a line break without officially starting a new paragraph (and thereby adding that extra white space), use the line break tag: *
*. This is a one-sided tag placed within a paragraph, at the end of each line, like this:

```
<p>720 Reynolds Drive<br>
Noblesville, IN 46062</p>
```

> **Note** In XHTML, the line break tag is *
*. The end slash (and the space preceding it) is necessary to indicate that it's a self-closing tag. Notice that the slash is placed after the letters, not before, as with the closing end of a two-sided tag. In XHTML, one-sided tags must end with a slash to indicate that they are self-closing. The space between the text and the final slash is also required, so the tag will be recognized in HTML.

In the following exercise, you will add text to an HTML file template and then preview it in Internet Explorer.

Add Text to an HTML File

1. Open the *HTML5.htm* file located in the *Documents\Microsoft Press\HTML 5 Start Here\02Structure\CreatingParagraphs* folder.

2. Save the file as *index.htm* in the *Documents\Microsoft Press\HTML 5 Start Here\02Structure* folder.

Note It is customary to name the opening page of a website *index.htm*, *index.html*, *default.htm*, or *default.html*. When users type a URL in their web browsers but omit the file name (like typing *www.microsoft.com* rather than *www.microsoft.com/filename.htm*), most servers will automatically respond with the index or default page (if one exists).

3. In Internet Explorer, open the *index.htm* file and arrange the Notepad window and the Internet Explorer window so that both are visible.

    The index file displayed in Internet Explorer is currently blank.

4. In the Notepad window, type the following text between the *<body>* and *</body>* tags:

```
<p>Welcome to Margie's Travel!</p>
<p>We offer a variety of reasonably priced, fully escorted tours by bus,
train, and air, all over the United States.</p>


<p>Our central office is located at:<br>
720 Reynolds Drive West<br>
Noblesville, IN 46062</p>
<p>Please stop in and talk with one of our friendly, experienced travel
consultants anytime from Monday through Saturday, 7:00 a.m. to 8:00 p.m.</p>
```

5. Save your work and then switch to Internet Explorer and press F5 or click the Refresh button to see the result of the changes. Leave both windows open for the next exercise.

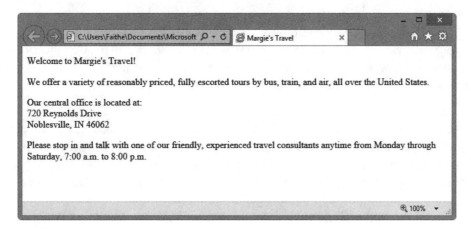

6. Close Notepad and Internet Explorer.

Note Your screen might look slightly different, depending on the settings you have configured in your browser.

Specifying a Page Title and Metatags

Perhaps you noticed in the preceding exercise that the complete path to the file displayed in the page tab or in the browser title bar (depending on the browser you are using). Usually when you view a webpage, a friendly, descriptive title displays in that spot instead. That text is specified by a *<title>* tag placed in the *<head>* section (also called the header). Here's an example:

```
<head>
<title>Margie's Travel</title>
</head>
```

Troubleshooting Make sure you place the *<title>* tag in the *<head>* section; don't place it in the *<body>* section.

Another element you can place in the header is the *<meta>* tag. The *<meta> tag* has several purposes. One of these is to identify keywords related to your page. Placing appropriate keywords on your page can make it easier for people to find your page when they are searching the web using a search engine. When some search engines index your page, they rely not only on the full text of the page, but also on any keywords they find in the *<meta>* tag area.

Note Not all search engines refer to *<meta>* tags. Google does not, for example; it indexes only the text contained in the *<body>* area. Because of the potential for abuse of the system, such as web developers packing their pages with unrelated keywords, fewer and fewer search engines these days are using them.

For example, suppose the Margie's Travel site would be useful to people who are searching for guided travel tours and vacations that are customized for senior citizens. Perhaps the phrase "senior citizen" is not mentioned on the main page, but you want people who search for that phrase to be directed to the main page anyway. You could place the following in the *<head>* section:

```
<meta name="keywords" content="senior, senior citizen, travel, tours">
```

Notice that the *<meta>* tag in this code is a single-sided tag that contains two attributes: name and content. The values for each of those arguments follow the equals sign and are contained in double quotation marks.

Note If you are coding in XHTML, you would add a space and a / at the end of *<meta>* tag because it is a one-sided (self-closing) tag. This is not necessary in HTML.

The *<meta>* tag can also be used to redirect visitors to another page. For example, suppose you told everyone the address of your website and then you needed to move it to another URL. You could place a "We've Moved" page at the original address and use the *<meta>* tag to redirect users to the new address after five seconds, like this:

```
<meta http-equiv="refresh" content="5; url=http://www.contoso.com/newpage.htm">
```

Here's yet another common use: the *<meta>* tag can specify a character encoding scheme. This is not a big issue if you are coding only in English (or in a language like English that uses a Roman character set), but it is considered a tidy coding practice to include anyway. If you want, you can add *<meta charset="utf-8">* to the *<head>* section of your document to explicitly spell out that your page is in English.

In the following exercise, you will add a page title and some keywords to the index.htm page you created in the preceding exercise.

Specify a Page Title and Metatags

1. In Notepad, open the *index.htm* file from the previous exercise. If you have not completed the previous exercise, open the *index.htm* file located in the *Documents\Microsoft Press\HTML 5 Start Here\02Structure\SpecifyingTitle* folder.

2. Between the *<head>* and *</head>* tags, type the following text to create the page title:

   ```
   <title>Margie's Travel</title>
   ```

3. After the title, type the following *<meta>* tag:

   ```
   <meta name="keywords" content="senior, senior citizen, travel, tours">
   ```

   Press Enter to start a new line and then type the following *<meta>* tag:

   ```
   <meta encoding="utf-8">
   ```

4. Save your work and then view the file in Internet Explorer.

   The tab displays the site name, but notice that the inclusion of the *<meta>* tags caused no apparent difference in the displayed text of the page. This is because the keywords and encoding specification do not display on the webpage itself.

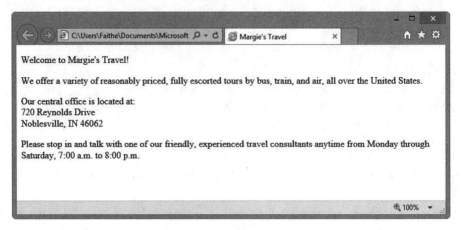

5. Close Notepad and Internet Explorer.

Key Points

In this chapter, you learned how to create the overall structure of a document and how to divide it into head and body sections. You learned how to create paragraphs and how to add a page title. Here are the key points to remember from this chapter:

- To specify HTML5 as the document type, type *<!DOCTYPE html>* at the beginning of the file.

- All the HTML coding in a document (except the *DOCTYPE*) is enclosed within a two-sided *<html>* tag.

- The *<html>* and *</html>* tags enclose the *<head>* and *<body>* sections.

- The *<head>* area contains the page title (*<title>*) and any *<meta>* tags. The *<body>* area contains all the displayable text for the page.

- Enclose each paragraph in a two-sided *<p>* tag. Most browsers add space between paragraphs when displaying the page.

- To create a line break without starting a new paragraph, use the one-sided *
* tag.

- When coding for XHTML, end one-sided tags with a space and a slash (/). The space is required for recognition in HTML, and the slash is necessary for recognition in XHTML.

- Use the *<title>* and *</title>* tags to enclose the text that should display in the browser's title bar. Place these in the *<head>* section of the file.

- Use *<meta>* tags in the *<head>* section to indicate keywords and the document encoding language.

Chapter 3

Formatting Text with Tags

In this chapter, you will:

- Create headings

- Apply bold and italic formatting

- Apply superscript and subscript formatting

- Use monospaced and preformatted text

- Format a block quotation

- Configure Internet Explorer view settings

Creating webpages is not word processing. It's important to keep that in mind as you learn HTML because I'm going to ask you to be patient for a few chapters as you learn HTML the *right* way—that is, the standards-compliant way.

When most people think of formatting text, the first thing that pops into their minds is choosing a font—a typeface, size, and color. That's easy to do in a word-processing document, but in HTML it's more complicated. Early versions of HTML used a *<font>* tag to specify a particular typeface, size, or color. If it were a decade ago, I would be happy to teach you that tag in this chapter, but the *<font>* tag has been removed from HTML5. Even though most browsers still recognize the *<font>* tag, you shouldn't use it; it's obsolete. Therefore, rather than teach you bad habits with old tags, I'm going to teach you how to apply typefaces, sizes, and colors to text with *styles*—but not in this chapter. Although using styles is a superior way of applying fonts to text, it is a little more advanced than you're ready for just yet. You'll learn all about using fonts in HTML code in Part II, "CSS Style Sheets and Graphics."

This chapter introduces several important tags that format text according to its purpose. In Chapter 2, "Setting Up the Document Structure," you learned about the *<p>* tag for regular paragraphs, but there are many other tags that are used for headings, programming code, quotations, and more.

Most of the tags discussed in this chapter are *semantic tags*; they describe the *function* of the text, rather than provide directions for formatting. For example, the *<h1>* heading tag specifies that the text within it should be formatted as a major heading, but it provides no specifics as to what that formatting should be.

The formatting specifics for semantic tags can come from a variety of sources:

- **Styles** As you will learn in Part II of this book, you can specify the font families and sizes to use throughout your entire website. For example, you can select a font family that will be suggested to the browser whenever a certain tag is applied.

- **The web browser in use** Each web browser has defaults for the standard HTML tags. For example, in Internet Explorer (and most other browsers), *<h1>* is left-aligned, 18-point Times New Roman. Most browsers use the same defaults for the very basic tags, but non-standard browsers, such as those on phones, often display text very differently.

- **Individual user customization** A user can customize his web browser to suit his preferences. Later in this chapter, you'll get to play with these settings in Internet Explorer so you'll know what your potential audience might be doing.

Keep in mind as you practice using tags that their formatting is not fixed. The results you see when previewing the exercise pages in Internet Explorer represent the default settings for your version of Internet Explorer (or whatever browser you are using to preview them); the style is not intrinsic to those tags themselves. That will become important in Part II of the book, when you learn how to define more specific formatting for tags.

 Important Before you can use the practice files provided for this chapter, you need to download and install them from the book's companion content location. See "Downloading the Companion Content" at the beginning of this book for more information.

Creating Headings

Headings in webpages function the same way as they do in printed documents--they separate text into sections. The HTML standard defines six levels of headings, *<h1>* through *<h6>*, each one progressively smaller in font size.

As previously noted, there are no *specific* sizes or fonts assigned to the heading tags; their appearance can vary depending on the browser and its settings. But the heading levels connote *relative* sizes; the higher the heading number, the smaller the size in which it will render on the screen. In Internet Explorer 9, for example, using the default settings, these six heading levels look as shown in Figure 3-1.

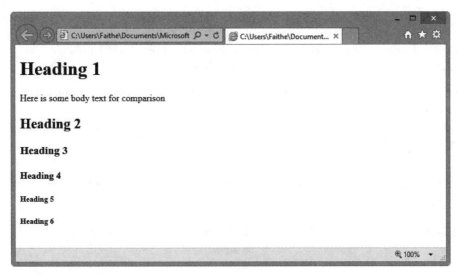

FIGURE 3-1 Headings using the default formatting in Internet Explorer 10.

Perhaps you noticed that headings 5 and 6 are actually smaller than body text. Keep in mind, though, that these are just the default settings; you can redefine these headings to display any size you want.

Many screen-reader programs use the heading codes *<h1>* through *<h6>* to help visually impaired users navigate a document, and some page structures rely on headings for outlining, too. (HTML5 has a new way of outlining documents, but that's beyond the scope of this book.) In some cases, though, you might have a stack of headings that collectively should take up only one spot in an outline, like this example:

```
<h1>Margie's Travel</h1>
<h2>Travel for the young at heart!</h2>
```

HTML5 introduces a new tag to deal with this situation: *<hgroup>*. When you enclose a stack of headings within *<hgroup>*, only the first heading in the stack displays in an outline; other headings will be ignored by screen readers and other outlining tools.

```
<hgroup>
<h1>Margie's Travel</h1>
<h2>Travel for the young at heart!</h2>
</hgroup>
```

Browsers that do not support this tag simply ignore it, so there is no harm in using it when appropriate.

In the following exercise, you will create some headings for the opening page of Margie's Travel's website.

Create Headings

1. In both Notepad and Internet Explorer, open the *index.htm* file located in the *Documents\Microsoft Press\HTML 5 Start Here\03Format\CreatingHeadings* folder.

2. Immediately below the *<body>* tag, edit the first line to use the *<h1>* tag instead of the *<p>* tag, like this:

   <h1>Welcome to Margie's Travel!**</h1>**

3. Click at the end of the line you just edited, press Enter to start a new paragraph, and then type the following:

   <h5>Leave the details to us, and leave your worries behind</h5>

 Note Some coding purists will tell you that you should use an *<h2>* heading instead of *<h5>* for the subtitle above and then apply a style to make the text look like you want, but because it is a few chapters yet until you will learn about styles, I'm taking a shortcut. For now, the default appearance of the *<h5>* heading is much closer to the desired look we want for this exercise.

4. Use a two-sided *<hgroup>* tag to enclose the two paragraphs you just worked with, like this:

   <hgroup>
   <h1>Welcome to Margie's Travel!</h1>
   <h5>Leave the details to us, and leave your worries behind</h5>
   </hgroup>

5. Immediately above the line containing the text *Our central office is located at:*, type the following:

   <h2>Come See Us</h2>

6. Save the file and then refresh Internet Explorer to check your work.

   The new heading displays in the body of the page.

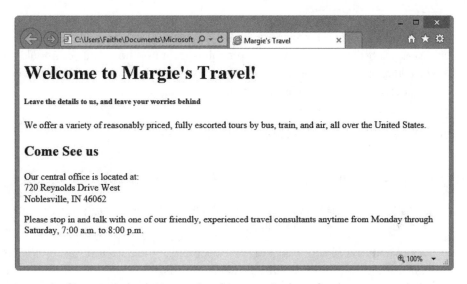

7. Leave the file open in both Notepad and Internet Explorer for the next exercise.

Applying Bold and Italic Formatting

Applying bold and italic styles are two ways of making text stand out and attract attention. You generally use these styles in paragraphs rather than in headings, but it's perfectly acceptable to use them anywhere.

For simple **boldface** and *italics*, use the ** tag or the *<i>* tag, respectively. Each is a two-sided tag that encloses the text to be formatted. For example:

```
<p>I had a <i>great</i> time at the party.</p>
<p>The reception will be held at <b>The Arbor Arch</b> in Plainfield.</p>
```

If you want to apply both bold and italic formatting, you can nest one tag inside the other. Don't mix up their order, though. When nesting tags, the rule is: *first in, last out*. So this is correct:

```
<p>The next book we will read is <b><i>The Catcher in the Rye</i></b></p>
```

In contrast, the following example is wrong, because the order of the ending ** and *</i>* tags are reversed:

```
<p>The next book we will read is <b><i>The Catcher in the Rye</b></i></p>
```

Even though the tags in the preceding example are improperly nested, most browsers will still display them correctly, provided you are using HTML as the document type. In an XHTML document, however, this type of tag reversal is not accepted.

Note HTML also allows the *<strong>* tag as a substitute for *<b>* and the *<em>* tag (emphasis) as a substitute for *<i>*. You will probably never use those, but you should know what they are in case you come across them. You can also define bold attributes and italic attributes for styles, as you will learn in Part II.

In the following exercise, you will make text bold and italic.

Apply Bold and Italic

1. If they are not already open, open the *index.htm* file (that you worked with in the previous exercise) in both Internet Explorer and Notepad.

    Alternately, you can use the i*ndex.htm* file located in the *Documents\Microsoft Press\HTML 5 Start Here\03Format\ApplyingBold* folder.

2. In Notepad, locate the *<h5>* heading near the top of the document and then enclose its text in an *<i>* tag:

    `<h5><i>Leave the details to us, and leave your worries behind</i></h5>`

3. In the first body paragraph, enclose *fully escorted* in a *<b>* tag:

    `<p>We offer a variety of reasonably priced, <b>fully escorted</b> tours by bus, train, and air, all over the United States.</p>`

4. Enclose the office hours in *<b>* and *<i>* tags:

    `<p>Please stop in and talk with one of our friendly, experienced travel consultants anytime from Monday through Saturday, <b><i>7:00 a.m. to 8:00 p.m.</i></b></p>`

Note Remember the "first in, last out" rule. If you begin with *<b><i>*, end with *</i></b>*.

5. Save the file and then refresh Internet Explorer to view the results.

    Leave the file open in both Notepad and Internet Explorer for the next exercise.

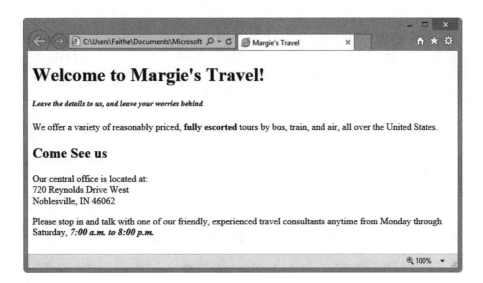

Applying Superscript and Subscript Formatting

Superscript formatting makes text smaller and raises it off the *baseline*. You'd typically use superscript to format exponents in math equations (for example, the 2 shown in X^2+1) and for footnote numbers and symbols (like this**). You can also use superscript to format ordinal numbers (such as 1st, 2nd, and 3rd) to make your page look more polished.

Subscript makes text smaller and moves it below the baseline. The most common use for subscripts is in chemical formulas (for example, H_2SO_4).

Note How much the text shifts up or down, or how much smaller the font size becomes, depends on the browser. In some browsers, using superscript or subscript changes the line spacing so that a paragraph that contains them can seem unevenly spaced.

In the following exercise, you will apply superscript formatting to create a footnote and an ordinal.

Apply Superscript Formatting

1. If they are not already open, open the *index.htm* file that you worked with in the previous exercise in both Internet Explorer and Notepad.

Alternately, you can use the *index.htm* file located in the *Documents\Microsoft Press\HTML 5 Start Here\03Format\ApplyingSuperscript* folder.

2. At the end of the last line of text, between the *</b>* and the *</p>* tags, type **¹**, as shown in the following:

```
<p>Please stop in and talk with one of our friendly, experienced travel
consultants anytime from Monday through Saturday, <b><i>7:00 a.m. to 8:00
p.m.</i></b><sup>1</sup></p>
```

This creates a superscript number for a footnote.

3. Immediately before the *</body>* tag, type the following:

```
<p><sup>1</sup>Closed the 1<sup>st</sup> Saturday in January</p>
```

4. This creates the footnote itself, which includes an ordinal number.

5. Save the file and then refresh the page in Internet Explorer to view the results.

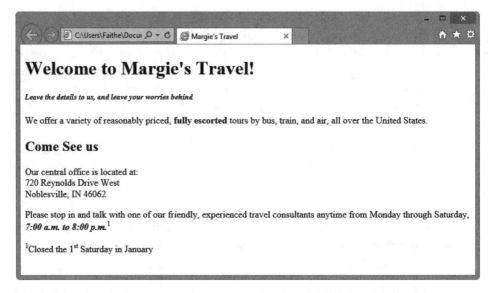

6. Close Notepad and Internet Explorer. The next exercise uses a different file.

Using Monospace and Preformatted Text

Most of the text in this book is set in a *proportional font*. This means that individual characters take up varying amounts of space horizontally, depending on the size of the individual character. For example, the letter *M* takes up more space than the letter *I*, so a string of Ms occupies more space than a string of Is.

As a demonstration, let's take a look at 10 of each character to see the difference:

MMMMMMMMMM

IIIIIIIIII

Most webpages that we're accustomed to viewing use proportional fonts; they are attractive, professional-looking, and easier to read.

In contrast, a *monospace font* is one whose characters occupy exactly the same amount of horizontal space, regardless of the actual size and shape of the individual character. Back in the days of the typewriter, all type was monospaced because of the way the typewriter worked: as you typed, the carriage moved exactly the same amount of space to the right, no matter which letter was keyed. Here are those same 10 Ms and Is in a monospace font:

MMMMMMMMMM

IIIIIIIIII

Some common uses for monospaced text include:

- Lines of programming code (like the HTML lines in this book)

- Text that you are instructing a user to type

- ASCII art (artwork created by using text characters)

It is uncommon to use monospaced text on a website, but for special situations it's nice to have that capability. To apply monospace style, you can use any of the tags outlined in Table 3-1. Most browsers do not make a formatting distinction between these tags by default, but you can define them differently in your styles if you like.

TABLE 3-1 Tags that Apply Monospace Style

Tag	Description
<kbd>	(Keyboard) The tag used for monospaced text to indicate something a user should type on a keyboard
<code>	(Code) The tag used for monospaced text applied to programming code
<samp>	(Sample) The tag used for sample text, which is largely the same thing as <code>

Note The <tt> tag was widely used for monospace text in a document in earlier HTML versions, but is not supported in HTML5.

These tags work nicely if you just want to make certain that characters appear in a monospaced font, but they don't change the fact that HTML omits extra spacing and line breaks that the text might include. When formatting something that requires the verbatim inclusion of white space (such as spaces or line breaks), you must use the *<pre>* tag, which stands for "preformatted." The *<pre>* tag not only displays the text in monospace, but also preserves all the spaces and line breaks that the web browser would usually ignore, so the text will look very similar to the original.

> **Note** There are many different monospace fonts. Most browsers use Courier (or a variant) unless you specify otherwise. Later in this chapter, you will learn how to specify a plain text font in Internet Explorer by changing the setting in the browser that controls the font used for monospace.

The *<pre>* tag can also come in handy when text that you copied and pasted from another source contains a lot of line breaks and paragraph breaks. You could manually enter a *
* for every line break and a *<p>* for every paragraph break, but that is pretty labor-intensive for a large file with a lot of breaks. Using the *<pre>* tag is a shortcut. One common use for the *<pre>* tag is in poetry archives, for example, where line breaks and spacing add meaning to the poems.

In the following exercise, you will add monospaced text to an existing page and you will create a new page containing a poem and an ASCII graphic.

Use Monospaced and Preformatted Text

1. In both Notepad and Internet Explorer, open the *instructions.htm* file located in the *Documents\Microsoft Press\HTML 5 Start Here\03Format\UsingMonospace* folder.

2. Enclose *club* in step 2 and enclose *margie* in step 4 in *<kbd>* tags:

   ```
   <p>1. Click in the Login box.<br>
   2. Type <kbd>club</kbd>.<br>
   3. Click in the Password box.<br>
   4. Type <kbd>margie</kbd>.</p>
   ```

3. Save the file and then refresh Internet Explorer (F5) to check your work.

   The text is now monospace, but it doesn't stand out very well. Let's make it more noticeable by formatting it as bold.

4. Enclose the two monospace words in *<b>* tags (on the inside of the *<kbd>* tags):

```
<p>1. Click in the Login box.<br>
2. Type <kbd><b>club</b></kbd>.<br>
3. Click in the Password box.<br>
4. Type <kbd><b>Margie</b></kbd>.</p>
```

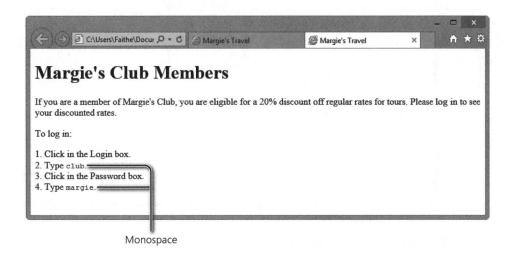

Monospace

Note You can place the *<b>* tags either inside or outside the *<kbd>* tags as long as you apply the first-in, last-out rule consistently. For example, you could write *<b><kbd>customer</kbd></b>* or you could write *<kbd><b>customer</b></kbd>*, but you should not mix up the tag order like this: *<b><kbd>customer</b></kbd>*. Improperly nested codes usually render properly in HTML, but not in XHTML

5. Save your work and then refresh Internet Explorer to see the changes. Now the monospace text displays in boldface.

6. Close the *instructions* file and close Internet Explorer.

7. Open the *poem* file in Notepad and Internet Explorer.

8. In Notepad, in the *<head>* section, create the following title:

```
<title>Song of the Open Road by Walt Whitman</title>
```

9. Open another copy of Notepad, and in it, open the *poemtext* file.

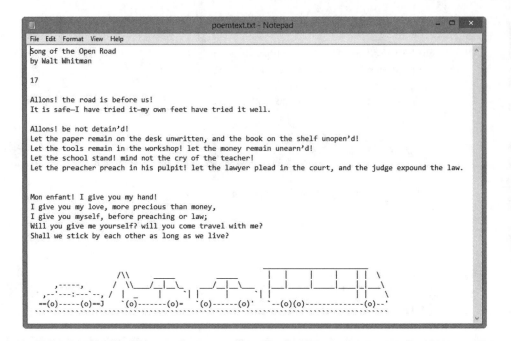

 Note The ASCII art at the end of the poem might not look right if the Notepad window is narrow; widen the Notepad window as needed if you want to see the picture as it was intended to display. How it looks in Notepad has no bearing on how it will look in Internet Explorer, however.

10. Select all the text in the *poemtext* file (Ctrl+A is one way to do so) and press Ctrl+C to copy it to the Clipboard.

11. Close the *poemtext* file.

12. In the *poem* file, click below the *<body>* tag and press Ctrl+V to paste the copied text between the *<body>* and *</body>* tags.

13. Apply the *<h1>* tag to the poem title within the *<body>* section:

<h1>Song of the Open Road**</h1>**

14. Apply the *<h4>* tag and the *<i>* tag to the attribution:

<h4>by Walt Whitman**</h4>**

Note Because this webpage is so simple, the *<hgroup>* tag you learned about earlier in the chapter would be superfluous here. Avoid using tags for their own sake; this makes your code needlessly bloated.

15. Apply the <h5> tag to the stanza number:

    <h5>17**</h5>**

16. Apply the *<pre>* tag to the rest of the poem and to the graphic below it:

```
<pre>Allons! the road is before us!
It is safe—I have tried it—my own feet have tried it well.


Allons! be not detain'd!
Let the paper remain on the desk unwritten, and the book on the shelf
unopen'd!
Let the tools remain in the workshop! let the money remain unearn'd!
Let the school stand! mind not the cry of the teacher!
Let the preacher preach in his pulpit! let the lawyer plead in the court, and
the judge expound the law.


Mon enfant! I give you my hand!
I give you my love, more precious than money,
I give you myself, before preaching or law;
Will you give me yourself? will you come travel with me?
Shall we stick by each other as long as we live?
```

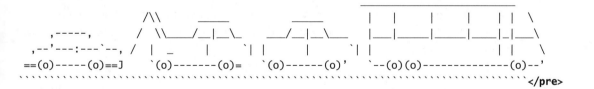

17. Save the *Poem* file and then refresh Internet Explorer to check your work.

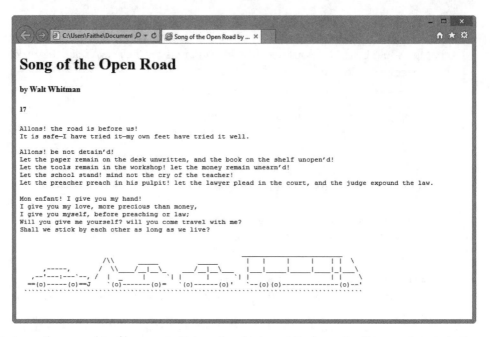

18. Leave the *poem.htm* file open in Notepad and Internet Explorer; it will be used again in the next exercise.

Formatting a Block Quotation

When quoting blocks from other sources, it is customary, both on webpages and in print, to indent those blocks from the main body of the text. The *<blockquote>* tag does exactly that. And don't feel constrained about using it; you can use *<blockquote>* for any text that you want to indent. You don't have to use it only for quotations.

The *<blockquote>* tag has a *cite="URL"* attribute, but most browsers don't do anything with it. If you happen to know the URL for the source you are citing, it is good practice to include it in the tag for browsers that do support the attribute and also as an aid to anyone who might be viewing or editing your raw HTML code later.

Note There is also a *<q>* tag, which is used for formatting inline quotations. Its only functionality is to place quotation marks around the text that it encloses. Most people don't use this tag because it is much easier to simply type the quotation marks.

In the following exercise, you will add a block quotation to a webpage.

Use a Block Quotation Tag

1. In Notepad, open the *bio.txt* file located in the *Documents\Microsoft Press\HTML 5 Start Here\03Format\FormattingBlock* folder.

2. Select all the text (Ctrl+A) and copy it to the Clipboard. Then close *bio.txt*.

3. Open the file *poem.htm* in both Notepad and Internet Explorer if they are not already open from the preceding exercise. You can use the copy of *poem.htm* you used previously in the chapter or you can open the copy located in the *Documents\Microsoft Press\HTML 5 Start Here\03Format\BlockQuote* folder.

4. In the *poem* file, click between the *</pre>* and *</body>* tags to move the insertion point there, and then press Ctrl+V to paste the copied text.

5. Enclose the text *Brief Bio from Wikipedia.org:* in an *<h4>* tag:

   <h4>Brief Bio from Wikipedia.org:**</h4>**

6. Enclose the biographical note in a *<p>* tag:

   <p>Walter "Walt" Whitman (1819-1892) was an American poet, essayist, and journalist. A humanist, he was part of the transition between transcendentalism and realism, incorporating both views in his works. Whitman is among the most influential poets in the American canon, often called the father of free verse.**</p>**

7. Immediately before the opening *<p>* tag in the previous example, type this opening *<blockquote>* tag:

   <blockquote cite="http://en.wikipedia.org/wiki/Walt_whitman">

> **Note** Don't remove the *<p>* tags for the quoted paragraphs; place the *<blockquote>* tags around the outside of them.

8. At the end of the paragraph, after the *</p>* tag, type the closing *</blockquote>* tag:

   </blockquote>

9. Save the *poem* file and then display it in Internet Explorer to check your work.

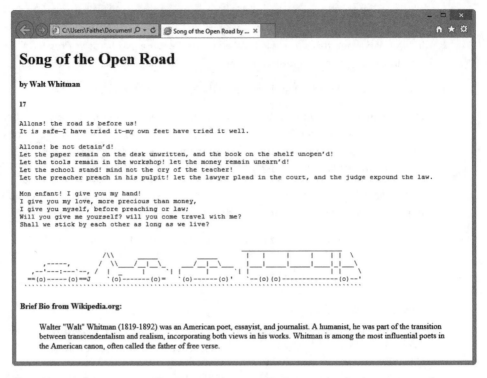

10. Close Notepad. Leave *poem.htm* open in Internet Explorer to use in the next exercise.

Configuring View Settings in Internet Explorer

At the beginning of the chapter, I mentioned that users can customize how certain tags are displayed on their own computers by setting the viewing preferences in their browsers. To understand what people might be doing with your pages, take a few moments to examine the settings in Internet Explorer 9. The customization capabilities in other browsers, including previous versions of Internet Explorer, are similar.

In the following exercise, you will view HTML pages in Internet Explorer 10 and then specify a variety of settings.

Configure Internet Explorer View Settings

1. If *poem.htm* is not already open in Internet Explorer, open it. A copy of *poem.htm* is available in *Documents\Microsoft Press\HTML 5 Start Here\03Format\ConfiguringSettings*.

2. If the menu bar doesn't display in Internet Explorer, press Alt to make it visible.

3. Choose View | Text Size | Largest.

All the text on the page increases in size.

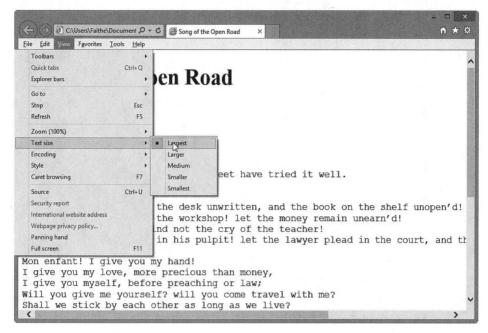

4. Choose View | Text Size | Smallest.

All the text on the page decreases in size.

5. Choose View | Text Size | Medium.

The text returns to its default size.

6. Choose Tools | Internet Options.

The Internet Options dialog box displays.

7. On the General tab, click the Fonts button.

The Fonts dialog box displays.

8. In the Webpage font list, click Arial.

Note Windows comes with a basic set of fonts and you get more fonts when you install some applications, such as Microsoft Office. Arial is included with Windows, and Lucida Console is included with Office.

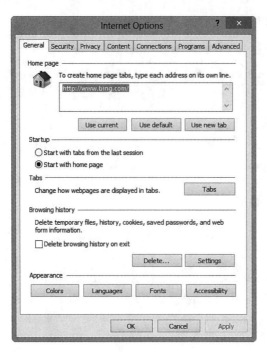

9. In the Plain text font list, click Lucida Console (if you have it; otherwise select another font). Plain text means monospace in this context.

Your choices are immediately reflected in the sample text below the font lists.

10. Click OK to apply your changes and to close the Fonts dialog box.

11. Click OK to apply your changes and to close the Internet Options dialog box.

   The page now displays in Arial font for regular text and in Lucida Console for monospace text. Your font choices are now overriding Internet Explorer's defaults.

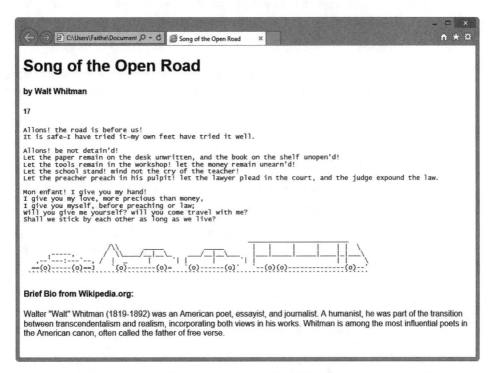

12. Repeat steps 6-11 to change the webpage font back to Times New Roman and the plain text font back to Courier New.

 Note You do not need to perform step 12 if you prefer the new font choices, but it is generally a good idea to preview your webpages in the same font that most people will be using to view them.

13. Close Internet Explorer.

Key Points

- Most tags are semantic. They specify that text has a certain function, such as a heading or quotation, rather than specifying a certain way it should appear.

- The exact formatting (the appearance) applied to tagged text is controlled by the default settings of the browser, by individual user customization, or by styles.

- Define headings by using the tags *<h1>* through *<h6>* (largest to smallest).

- When one heading immediately follows another as a subheading, you might want to group them with *<hgroup>* so that screen readers and outlines show them as a single unit. This is optional.

- To make text bold, use the *<b>* tag; to italicize it, use the *<i>* tag.

- The tag for superscript is *<sup>*; the tag for subscript is *<sub>*.

- Monospaced text uses a font whose characters all occupy the same amount of horizontal space, no matter the specific character; its opposite is proportional text.

- By default, most web text appears in a proportional font. To specify a monospaced font, use the *<kbd>*, *<code>*, or *<samp>* tag. HTML5 no longer supports the obsolete *<tt>* code for monospaced text.

- By default, a web browser strips out any extra spaces and ignores paragraph breaks (except for those created when using the *<p>* tag). To force the browser to render spaces and line breaks in text, enclose that text in a *<pre>* tag.

- To set off a block quotation, use the *<blockquote>* tag. The tag can take a *cite="URL"* attribute, but most browsers do not make use of it.

- In Internet Explorer, you can choose a default text size from the View menu. This affects only your copy of Internet Explorer, not the page itself.

- In Internet Explorer, you can choose a default text font by opening the Internet Options dialog box, clicking Fonts, and specifying the fonts to use for various purposes.

Chapter 4

Using Lists and Backgrounds

In this chapter, you will:

- Create bulleted and numbered lists

- Create definition lists

- Insert special characters

- Insert horizontal lines

- Choose background and foreground colors

- Specify a background image file

Suppose you're studying for an important test or gathering information for a big project at work. There's a lot of data and very little time in which to digest it. Which would you rather browse through: a long report on the topic, or a list of the important points?

If you're like most people, you would probably prefer a list. Lists make text easier to skim. English teachers might wring their hands over this (and I can say this because I *was* an English teacher), but we've become a society of skimmers and browsers. People don't like to read paragraph after paragraph of plain text. They like their information divided up into easily digestible chunks.

In this chapter, you'll learn to create several types of lists with HTML, including bulleted lists, numbered lists, and definition lists. You'll learn how to create nested lists within lists, how to use styles to specify the bullet character or numbering style, and how to create horizontal lines (which in HTML-speak are called *rules*) that further help divide a page.

You'll also learn about entity codes that make it possible to insert special characters or symbols that are not on your keyboard as well as symbols such as greater than (>) and less than (<) that would ordinarily be interpreted as HTML tag markers.

Finally, this chapter takes a quick look at webpage backgrounds, both solid color and graphics. Most professional web designers do not use background colors or background graphics, but some hobbyists find them fun. In addition, when you learn about using divisions in Chapter 11, "Creating Division-Based Layouts," you'll see how understanding backgrounds can come in handy for creating a navigation bar that contrasts with the main page.

 Important Before you can use the practice files provided for this chapter, you need to download and install them from the book's companion content location. See "Code Samples" at the beginning of this book for more information.

Creating Bulleted and Numbered Lists

In Chapter 3, "Formatting Text with Tags," you worked with a file that contained a numbered list, but it was set up as a regular *<p>* paragraph with *
* breaks for each line, such as the following:

```
<p>1. Click in the Login box.<br>
2. Type <b>club</b>>.<br>
3. Click in the Password box.<br>
4. Type <b>margie</b>.</p>
```

Tagging the list this way worked in this instance because the lines were short and simple, but HTML has tags designed specifically for creating lists, and it's better to use those tags when possible. They accept attributes that you can use to control formatting and they create hanging bullets and numbers (that is, bullets and numbers that "hang" off the left margin of the paragraph).

The tag for a numbered list is *<ol>*, which stands for ordered list. For a bulleted list, the tag is *<ul>*, which stands for unordered list. Each numbered or bulleted item within the list is tagged *<li>*, to denote that it's a list item. You start the list with the opening *<ol>* or *<ul>* tag, enclose each list item with *<li>* and *</li>* tags, and then finish the list with the closing *</ol>* or *</ul>* tag. Here's the numbered list from the previous example, this time using the proper tags:

```
<ol>
    <li>Click in the Login box.</li>
    <li>Type <b>club</b>.</li>
    <li>Click in the Password box.</li>
    <li>Type <b>margie</b>.</li>
</ol>
```

> **Note** The indentation is added to make the text easier for you to read, but the browser ignores extra spaces. In fact, if the *<ol>* tag had been placed on the same line as the first *<li>* item, it would not have made any difference.

You've probably noticed that what's missing here is the numbers themselves. That's because when creating an ordered list in HTML, you don't assign the numbers to the items yourself. You let HTML handle that for you as well as the paragraph alignment. The result is a standard, recognizable numbered list (see Figure 4-1).

1. Click in the Login box.
2. Type club.
3. Click in the Password box.
4. Type margie.

FIGURE 4-1 An ordered list.

A bulleted list works the same way, except you use *<ul>* tags. Here's an example:

```
<ul>
    <li>Bring in the mail</li>
    <li>Take out the trash</li>
    <li>Feed the dogs</li>
    <li>Stop the newspaper delivery</li>
</ul>
```

This produces a basic bulleted list on a webpage (see Figure 4-2).

- Bring in the mail
- Take out the trash
- Feed the dogs
- Stop the newspaper delivery

FIGURE 4-2 An unordered list.

Nesting Lists

You can nest lists within one another. In the following example, we have a bulleted list embedded within a numbered list. Notice how this nested list was constructed. The bulleted sublist (the *<ul>* tag) is placed within one of the *<li>* tags within the numbered *<ol>* list.

```
<ol>
   <li>Thursday: Do Algebra homework</li>
   <li>Friday: Housesit for neighbors:
      <ul><li>Bring in the mail</li>
      <li>Take out the trash</li>
      <li>Feed the dogs</li>
      <li>Stop the newspaper delivery</li></ul></li>
   <li>Saturday: Wash car</li>
</ol>
```

On a webpage, it would look like what's shown in Figure 4-3.

1. Thursday: Do Algebra homework
2. Friday: Housesit for neighbors:
   • Bring in the mail
   • Take out the trash
   • Feed the dogs
   • Stop the newspaper delivery
3. Saturday: Wash car

FIGURE 4-3 A multi-level list.

Changing the Bullet or Number Character

Bulleted lists and numbered lists can be styled by using a *list-style-type: type* attribute. This is a type of style-based attribute that you will be seeing a lot more of later in this book, but for now we're using it as a standalone technique for changing the bullet character or numbering style. You can use the values shown in Table 4-1 for the *list-style-type* attribute. (Table 4-1 isn't a comprehensive list, but it covers all the values you are likely to use.)

To apply the attribute, place it in the opening *<ul>* or *<ol>* tag. For example, to create a bulleted list that uses the square bullet character, start the list this way:

```
<ul style="list-style-type: square">
```

To create a numbered list that uses uppercase Roman numerals, start the list this way:

```
<ol style="list-style-type: upper-roman">
```

> **Note** Another way of specifying the bullet or number type is use a cascading style sheet (CSS); you'll learn more about CSS later in the book, starting in Chapter 6, "Introduction to Style Sheets."

TABLE 4-1 Common list style *type* Attribute Values

List Style	Value	Result
Bulleted	*Disc*	Filled circle (the default)
	Circle	Unfilled circle
	Square	Filled square
Numbered	*Decimal*	1, 2, 3, 4 (the default)
	decimal-leading-zero	01, 02, 03, 04
	lower-roman	i, ii, iii, iv
	upper-roman	I, II, III, IV
	lower-alpha	a, b, c, d
	upper-alpha	A, B, C, D
	None	(nothing)

Specifying the Start of a Numbered List

To start a numbered list at a number other than 1, use the *start="n"* attribute with the *<ol>* tag, where *n* is the starting number. For example:

```
<ol start="3">
```

You might want a different starting number if a list is continuing from an earlier list, but separated from the current list by some regular paragraphs, for example.

The starting number is always specified as an Arabic numeral in the *<ol>* tag, even if you have chosen a Roman numeral or letter style for the list.

You can use the *value="n"* attribute for an individual list item *<li>* if you want to change the numbering for one item only. For example, to force a particular list item to be numbered with a 5 (or in a list with Roman numerals, a V), insert the *value="n"* attribute, as shown here:

```
<li value="5">
```

Note The *start=* and *value=* attributes are both deprecated, but they still work in HTML5.

In the following exercise, you will create and nest ordered and unordered lists.

1. In Notepad and Internet Explorer, open the *destinations.htm* file in the *Documents\Microsoft Press\HTML 5 Start Here\04Lists\NestingLists* folder.

2. Create the following numbered list above the *</body>* tag:

```
<ul>
<li>Alaskan Salmon Fishing</li>
<li>The Vineyards of Northern California</li>
<li>Sedona and the Grand Canyon</li>
<li>Michigan Fall Festivals</li>
</ul>
```

3. Save the file and then refresh Internet Explorer to view your work.

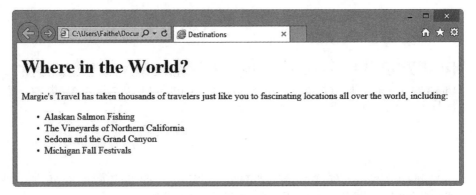

Immediately beneath the Alaskan Salmon Fishing line, create a nested ordered list as shown below, then save and check your work.

```
<ul>
<li>Alaskan Salmon Fishing</li>
<ol>
<li>Sitka Sound</li>
<li>Kenai Peninsula</li>
<li>Matanuska Susitna Valley</li>
</ol>
```

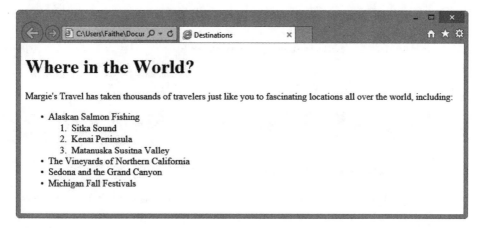

4. Immediately beneath the *Sedona and the Grand Canyon* line, create a nested ordered list as shown below, then save and check your work.

```
<li>Sedona and the Grand Canyon</li>
<ol>
<li>Sedona Red Rock Jeep Tour</li>
<li>Sedona Energy Vortex Exploration</li>
<li>Grand Canyon Photo and Sightseeing Motorcoach Tour</li>
<li>Grand Canyon Helicopter Adventure</li>
</ol>
```

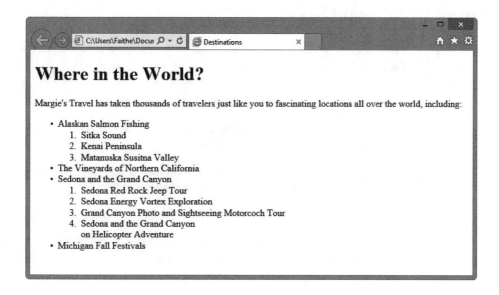

5. Change the opening tag of both ordered lists so that they use uppercase Roman numerals:

```
<ol style="list-style-type: upper-roman">
```

6. Save and then check your work. Close Notepad and Internet Explorer.

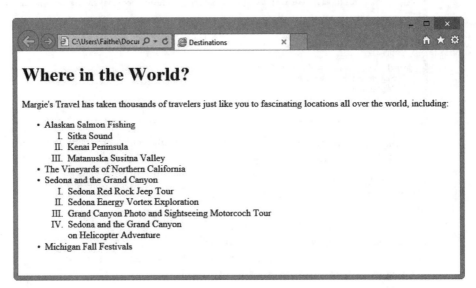

Creating Definition Lists

A definition list (see Figure 4-4) is just what it sounds like: a list that presents terms with their definitions, such as you would see in a glossary. The word being defined serves as a heading, and the definition paragraph is indented under it.

Moderate Hiking
> Up to 3 miles per day. Terrain may include moderately steep inclines, and may be narrow, twisting, and unpaved. Hiking boots are recommended.

Moderate Walking
> Up to 3 miles per day over flat terrain or small hills and valleys; paths are usually paved. There may be stairs. Not wheelchair accessible unless explicitly indicated.

FIGURE 4-4 An example of a definition list.

The complete list (headings and definition paragraphs) is contained within the *<dl>* and *</dl>* tags, which stands for *definition list*. Each word to be defined is contained in a *<dt>* (*definition term*) tag, and the definition paragraphs are contained in *<dd>* (*definition description*) tags. Here's the code for the example shown in Figure 4-4:

```
<dl>
<dt>Moderate Hiking</dt>
<dd>Up to 3 miles per day. Terrain may include moderately steep inclines, and may be
narrow, twisting, and unpaved. Hiking boots are recommended.</dd>
<dt>Moderate Walking</dt>
<dd>Up to 3 miles per day over flat terrain or small hills and valleys; paths are
usually paved. There may be stairs. Not wheelchair accessible unless explicitly
indicated.</dd>
</dl>
```

This example shows a one-to-one relationship between words and definitions (one definition for each word), but that's not a requirement. You can have multiple consecutive entries of either type. You might do this to accommodate situations in which a single word has two meanings or two words have the same definition.

Note HTML permits you to omit the closing *</dt>* and *</dd>* tags, but you should get into the habit of using them anyway. XHTML requires them.

In the following exercise, you will create a glossary of terms on a webpage.

Create a List of Definitions

1. In Notepad and Internet Explorer, open the *definitions.htm* file located in the *Documents\Microsoft Press\HTML 5 Start Here\04Lists\CreatingDefinitions* folder.

2. Above the *</body>* tag, type the following:

```
<dl>
<dt>Light Hiking</dt>
<dd>Up to 2 miles per day over gentle hills and valleys in a natural setting.
Trails may be narrow, uneven, and unpaved. Athletic shoes or hiking boots are
recommended.</dd>


<dt>Light Walking</dt>
<dd>Up to 2 miles per day over mostly flat, paved terrain. Not wheelchair
accessible unless explicitly indicated.</dd>
```

```
<dt>Moderate Hiking</dt>
<dd>Up to 3 miles per day. Terrain may include moderately steep inclines, and
may be narrow, twisting, and unpaved. Hiking boots are recommended.</dd>


<dt>Moderate Walking</dt>
<dd>Up to 3 miles per day over flat terrain or small hills and valleys; paths
are usually paved. There may be stairs. Not wheelchair accessible unless
explicitly indicated.</dd>
</dl>
```

3. Save the file and then refresh Internet Explorer to view your work. Close Notepad and Internet Explorer.

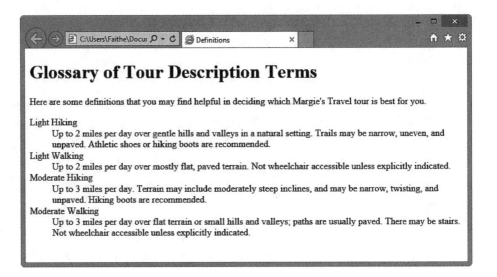

Inserting Special Characters

Special characters are characters that are not included on a standard English keyboard. Examples include letters with accent marks over them (such as in the word résumé) or an ownership symbol (such as © or ™). In HTML, these special characters are referred to as *entities*. You create them by using codes beginning with an ampersand (&), followed by an entity name or an entity number, and then ending with a semicolon. The entity names and entity numbers both represent the same thing; you can use either one. For example, * * or * * each renders as a non-breaking space.

In addition to the non-keyboard symbols, certain other symbols must be created as entities in HTML because they have a specific meaning in HTML. The most common are the ampersand (&), the greater than sign (>), and the less than sign (<). You can't just type those symbols in HTML code because a browser will interpret them as tags or entities rather than characters to display.

Table 4-2 lists the most common entities. For a more complete list, refer to the *entities.htm* file included with the data files for this book.

TABLE 4-2 Common Entities

Symbol	Entity Name	Entity Number
& (ampersand)	&amp;	&#38;
< (less than)	&lt;	&#60;
> (greater than)	&gt;	&#62;
(nonbreaking space)		
¢ (cent)	&cent;	&#162;
£ (pound)	&pound;	&#163;
¥ (yen)	&yen;	&#165;
© (copyright)	&copy;	&#169;
® (registered trademark)	&reg;	&#174;
° (degree)	&deg;	&#176;
± (plus or minus)	&plusmn;	&#177;
†(dagger)	&dagger;	&#8224;
™ (trademark)	&trade;	&#8482;

Note The nonbreaking space entity * * is very popular for creating spaces, and in fact, many WYSIWYG web site creation programs like Microsoft Expression Web and Adobe Dreamweaver insert them for you when you press the spacebar. Don't use nonbreaking spaces instead of good layout techniques, though. For example, if something needs to be indented a certain amount, use the correct HTML tags and styles for indenting it, don't just "space over" with a half-dozen * * codes.

In the following exercise, you will add copyright and trademark symbols to a webpage using entities.

Insert Special Characters

1. In Notepad and Internet Explorer, open the *index.htm* file located in the *Documents\Microsoft Press\HTML 5 Start Here\04Lists\InsertingSpecial* folder.

2. Add copyright and trademark symbols to the copyright notice at the bottom of the file:

```
<p>Copyright &copy; Margie's Travel&trade;<br>
No material may be reproduced without written permission</p>
```

3. Save the file and then refresh Internet Explorer to check your work. Leave Notepad and Internet Explorer open for the next exercise.

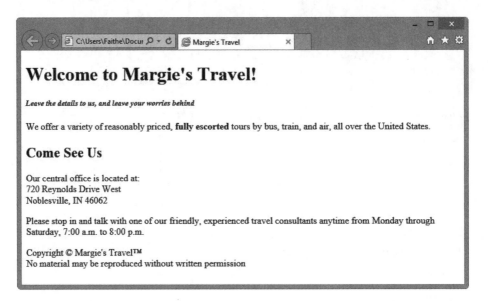

Inserting Horizontal Lines

Horizontal lines—which HTML calls *horizontal rules*—can be useful as dividers between sections of text in a webpage. For example, in the preceding exercise, you created a copyright notice that blends in perhaps a little too well with the rest of the text on the page; it would stand out more if it were separated from the rest of the document by a horizontal line. You might also want to add another horizontal line between the first headings and the rest of the document (see Figure 4-5).

To add a horizontal line, simply add the following one-sided tag where you want the line to appear:

```
<hr>
```

Note In XHTML, you must add a space and closing slash, like this: *<hr />*. HTML5 also recognizes that syntax as an optional alternative. The slash is required for XHTML compatibility, while the space preceding the slash enables older browsers to read the tag correctly.

By default, the line runs the entire width of the browser window, is two pixels in height, and is black with a chiseled effect. You can change these characteristics by applying attributes within the tag.

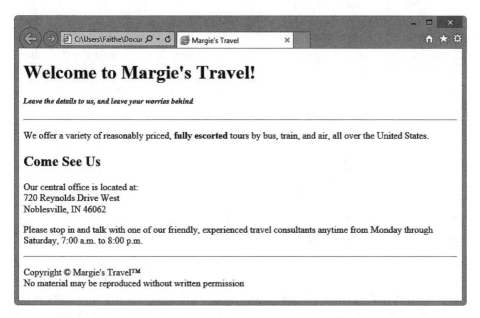

FIGURE 4-5 Horizontal lines separate sections of the page content.

Most of the original attributes for the *<hr>* tag were deprecated in HTML 4.01; attributes such as *align*, *color*, *size*, and *width* are not supported at all in HTML5. You now set the rendering characteristics for a horizontal line using styles, as you will learn in Chapter 6, "Style Sheets and Graphics."

It's best to specify a uniform appearance for all lines by using a cascading style sheet, as you'll learn to do in Chapter 6, but you can also add styling directly to the *<hr>* tag by simply including the *style="attributes"* attribute, which is what we'll do here in this chapter. After you learn the other methods, you may choose to use these methods instead in your own work.

The style attributes you can set for a horizontal line are *border*, *color*, *background-color*, *width*, and *height*. When you combine two attributes in a single *style=* statement, you separate them with semicolons. For example, to create a red line that is 3 pixels thick and spans 50% of the window's width, you would write:

```
<hr style="color: red; background-color: red; height: 3px; border:none; width: 50%">
```

Why two different color specifications? Some browsers use *color* to assign a color to the line, others use *background-color*; therefore, you should include both tags and assign the same color for both. The browser will read whichever one it needs and ignore the other one.

For a solid line with no border, you should include *border:none*, as shown in the previous example. Otherwise the horizontal rule will have a thin black border around it.

Note: In Chapter 8, "Formatting Paragraphs with CSS," you'll learn more possibilities for using the border attribute, including creating solid borders, dotted borders, and dashed borders.

HTML recognizes these 16 basic color names. You can also specify a color by its hexadecimal number, like #f00 for red.

- Aqua
- Black
- Blue
- Fuchsia

- Gray
- Green
- Lime
- Maroon

- Navy
- Olive
- Purple
- Red

- Silver
- Teal
- White
- Yellow

Note To see full-color samples of these colors, refer to Documents\Microsoft Press\HTML 5 Start Here\Reference\colors.htm. See the section "Understanding How Colors are Specified on Webpages" later in this chapter to find out how you can use other colors than the ones listed above.

In the following exercise, you will add two horizontal rules to a webpage.

Add Decorative Horizontal Lines

1. Start with the *index.htm* file still open in Notepad and Internet Explorer from the previous exercise. Or open *index.htm* in Notepad and Internet Explorer in the *Documents\Microsoft Press\ HTML 5 Start Here\04Lists\CreatingRule* folder.

2. Immediately above the copyright notice, add this tag:

    ```
    <hr style="color: green; background-color: green; height: 3px">
    ```

3. Save the file and then refresh Internet Explorer to check your work.

4. Use the Change Zoom Level control in the bottom-right corner of the Internet Explorer window to zoom in to 400% and look at the horizontal rule. Notice that it has a border around it.

5. The color and style of the border depend on the browser; in Internet Explorer 10, it's a dark gray border on the top and left and a light gray border on the bottom and right.

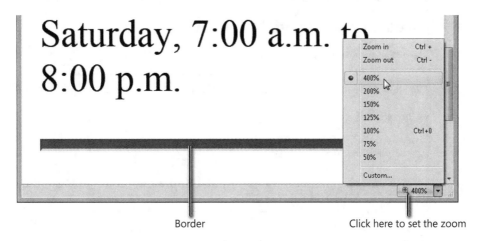

Border   Click here to set the zoom

6. In Notepad, add *border:none* to the style:

   `<hr style="color: green; background-color: green; height: 3px; border:none">`

7. Save the file in Notepad and then refresh Internet Explorer to check your work. Notice that the horizontal rule is now solid, with no border.

8. In Notepad, change the color of the horizontal rule to red and then set its width to 85%:

   `<hr style="color: red; background-color: red; height: 3px; border:none; width: 85%">`

9. Select the entire *<hr>* tag and then press Ctrl+C to copy it to the Clipboard.

10. Paste the copied tag immediately below the *</hgroup>* tag. Save the file.

11. In Internet Explorer, reset the zoom to 100% and then refresh Internet Explorer to check your work. Leave Notepad and Internet Explorer open for the next exercise.

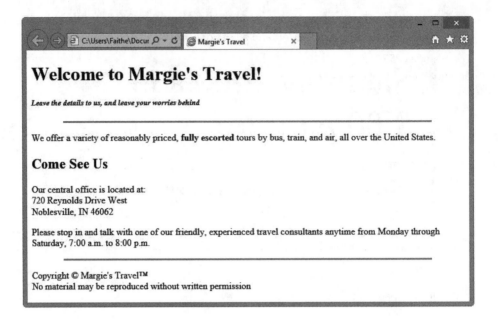

Choosing Background Colors and Foreground Colors

Many web design experts caution against using dark or patterned backgrounds on webpages because these backgrounds can make it difficult to read the text. Some designers go so far as to say that you should not use *any* background color at all; they prefer that black text on a white background be the norm. A quick look at a few major commercial websites will confirm the near-universality of this opinion. Look at high-traffic sites like *www.msn.com*, *news.google.com*, and *www.microsoft.com*; you'll find that the body text is almost exclusively black (or another dark color) on a white (or other pale) background.

Rules are made to be broken, however, and you might find situations in which a colored or patterned background is perfect for a certain page (or set of pages). For example, you might assign a background color to a webpage that you want to differentiate from other pages of a website.

Understanding How Colors are Specified on Webpages

The 16 basic colors presented in the preceding section are the best colors to use on webpages because they are universally accepted. Every browser interprets these colors the same way. However, you will probably find many situations in which none of those 16 colors is appropriate. For example, you might find that they are all too dark or too vivid to make an attractive page background. Therefore, you will sometimes need to rely on other ways of specifying colors.

One way to specify a color is by its RGB (red-green-blue) value. Using this method, you can describe a color using a series of three numbers, from 0 to 255. Each number represents the component of red, green, or blue that makes up the color. For example, pure red is *255,0,0*; that is, maximum red (255), no green (0), and no blue (0). You can create a large range of colors using these three values. For example, *255,153,0* represents a particular shade of orange—full red, a little more than half green, and no blue.

Another way to express color values in HTML is by using a hexadecimal value. The hexadecimal values represent the RGB values converted to the base-16 numbering system. For example, the value 255 converts to FF, so the RGB value *255,255,0* can also be expressed as the hexadecimal value *#FFFF00*.

The problem with defining colors by using RGB or hexadecimal values is that not every display supports that many colors. Any unsupported colors appear as *dithered* (that is, formed with a cross-hatch pattern of two colors blended together). Therefore, most web designers try to stick with what are called *web-safe colors*. A web-safe color is one that exactly matches one of the colors in a standard 8-bit color display. Web-safe colors use only the following numeric values for red, green, and blue: 0, 51, 102, 153, 204, and 255. To see full-color samples of all the web-safe colors, refer to *My Documents\Microsoft Press\HTML 5 Start Here\Reference\websafe.htm*.

Yet another way to express color values is by using extended names. These are similar to the basic color names, but there are a lot more of them. Officially they are supported only by Internet Explorer, but most browsers recognize them. To see full-color samples of all the extended colors, refer to *My Documents\Microsoft Press\HTML 5 Start Here\Reference\extended.htm*.

 Note Not all named colors in the extended set are web-safe; in fact, most of them aren't. Colors from the extended set are convenient because they are named, but web-safe colors are often a better choice.

Applying a Background Color

To specify a background color for an entire page, insert the *style="background-color: color"* attribute into the opening *<body>* tag. For example, to make the background of an entire page yellow, use the following:

```
<body style="background-color: yellow">
```

You can use the color name, the RGB value, or the hexadecimal value. Therefore, the following are equivalent to the code just shown:

```
<body style="background-color: #FFFF00">
<body style="background-color: rgb(255,255,0)">
```

Applying a Foreground Color

The foreground color is the default text color for the page. You can set the foreground color by using the *style="color: color"* attribute. It can be combined with the attribute for the background color in a single *style=* statement. For example, to set yellow text on a navy blue background, use the following:

```
<body style="background-color: navy; color: yellow">
```

> **Note** Just like with the horizontal rule earlier in this chapter, we are using styles here to format the body of the page. You will learn more about styles in Chapter 6.

In this exercise, you will change the foreground and background colors of a webpage.

Apply Background and Foreground Colors

1. Start with the *index.htm* file still open in Notepad and Internet Explorer from the previous exercise. Or open *index.htm* in Notepad and Internet Explorer in the *Documents\Microsoft Press\ HTML 5 Start Here\04Lists\ApplyingBackground* folder.

2. Add the following style attribute to the *<body>* tag:

    ```
    <body style="color:navy; background-color:#FFFFCC">
    ```

3. Save the file and then refresh Internet Explorer to check your work.

    The webpage text should now be navy blue, and the page background should be pale yellow.

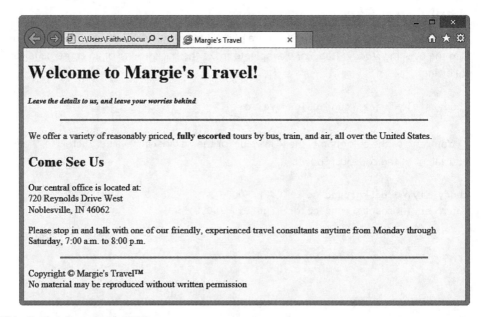

4. Leave the file open in Notepad and Explorer for the next exercise.

Specifying a Background Image File

A background image displays behind the text on a page. By default, the image is tiled to fill the page and scrolls with the page.

Unfortunately, there are plenty of examples of ineffective or distracting backgrounds on the web. Here are some tips for making yours better than those.

First of all, choose images that are designed to be tiled, so each copy blends smoothly into the next. When the image's edges blend well, it will look like a single large image. In Figure 4-6, the edges do not blend well.

FIGURE 4-6 This background image is distracting and you can see where the copies begin and end.

On the other hand, the edges of the tiled copies shown in Figure 4-7 blend together well in both directions.

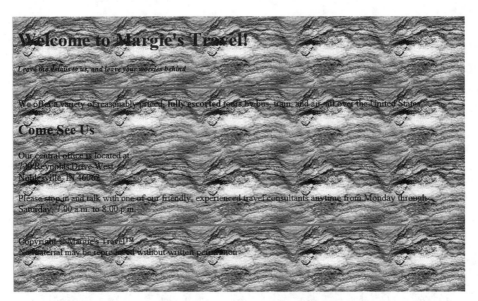

FIGURE 4-7 This background is also distracting, but the edges of each copy blend together well.

Use subtle patterns that don't distract from the text. The preceding examples fail that test; they impede readability in a big way. Figure 4-8 shows a better one.

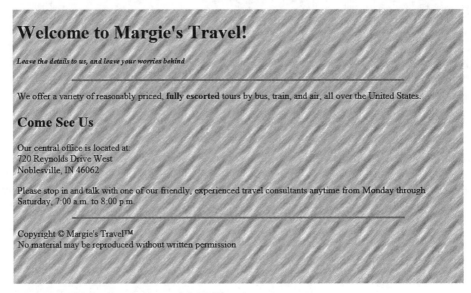

FIGURE 4-8 This background image is less distracting.

If you specify a background image, you should also specify a background color. The color will not be visible unless the image fails to display for some reason or unless the image has transparent areas in it. The background color is especially important if you use a dark background image and a light foreground color; if the image does not display, the text still must display on a dark background to be readable.

To use a background image file, use a *style="background-image: url(image)"* attribute in the opening *<body>* tag, as you did for foreground and background colors in the preceding section. For example, to use the background image file called *granite.gif* that is located in the same folder as the HTML file, you would write:

```
<body style="background-image: url(granite.gif)">
```

Notice that you must enclose the image file name in parentheses following the *url*. You do not need to specify a path to the image as long as it is stored in the same folder as the HTML file.

The *<body>* tag can hold many style specifications in a single *style=* attribute. Separate them with semicolons, as you did previously with the foreground and background colors. For example, to combine the background image, background color, and foreground color in a single attribute, do the following:

```
<body style="background-image: url(granite.gif); color: navy; background-color:
#FFFFCC">
```

By default, the background image is repeated both horizontally and vertically to fill the window. You can force it not to repeat by adding the *background-repeat=* attribute to the *<body>* tag and specifying *repeat-x* (repeat horizontally only), *repeat-y* (repeat vertically only), or *no-repeat*. For example, to prevent any repeating, use the following:

```
<body style="background-image: url(granite.gif); color: navy; background-color:
#FFFFCC; background-repeat: no-repeat">
```

By default, the background image scrolls with the text when the user scrolls down the page. To force the image to stay fixed, add the *background-attachment=fixed* attribute to the *<body>* tag, as follows:

```
<body style="background-image: url(granite.gif); color: navy; background-color:
#FFFFCC"; background-attachment=fixed">
```

In the following exercise, you will display an image as a webpage background.

Use a Graphic as a Background

1. Start with the *index.htm* file still open in Notepad and Internet Explorer from the previous exercise. Or open *index.htm* in Notepad and Internet Explorer in the *Documents\Microsoft Press\ HTML 5 Start Here\04Lists\SpecifyingImages* folder.

2. Replace the existing opening *<body>* tag with this one:

    ```
    <body style="background-image: url(ripplez.gif); background-color: #FFFFCC">
    ```

Note To avoid having to specify a path to the image file, place the image file and the HTML file in the same folder. If you are using your index.htm file from the previous exercise, copy the *ripplez.gif* file into the folder where the active copy of *index.htm* is stored.

3. Save the file and then refresh the Internet Explorer display to check your work. Close the Notepad and Internet Explorer windows.

Key Points

- To create a numbered (ordered) list, use the *<ol>* tags. For a bulleted (unordered) list, use the *<ul>* tags.

- Within the *<ol>* or *<ul>* tags, use *<li>* tags for each list item. These tags are all two-sided. HTML does not require the closing *</li>*, but XHTML does.

- Ordered and unordered lists can be nested. Enclose the second-level *<ul>* or *<ol>* list within a *<li></li>* tag inside the main list.

- To use a different bullet character or numbering style, use the *style="list-style-type: type"* attribute in the *<ul>* or *<ol>* opening tag.

- To create a definition list, use the *<dl></dl>* tags. Within the *<dl>* tags, enclose each term in a *<dt></dt>* tag, and enclose each definition in a *<dd></dd>* tag.

- You can display special characters on a webpage by using HTML character entity references.

- To insert a horizontal line (rule), use the *<hr>* tag. This is a one-sided tag. Put any style specifications for the line within it, such as border, color, height, and width.

- You can specify colors by using basic or extended names, RGB values, or hexadecimal values.

- To assign a background color to a page, insert a *style="background-color: color"* attribute into the *<body>* opening tag. For a foreground color, use *style="color: color"*. These attributes can be combined into a single statement with a semicolon separator, like this: *style="background-color: red; color: white"*.

- To assign a background image to a page, insert a *style="background-image: image"* attribute into the *<body>* opening tag.

Chapter 5

Creating Hyperlinks and Anchors

In this chapter, you will:

- Hyperlink to a webpage

- Hyperlink to an email address

- Create and hyperlink to anchors

- Hyperlink to other content

The web is based on hyperlinks. Each webpage contains active links to other pages, which in turn link to even more pages, until presumably the entire web (or at least a great chunk of it) is bound together. In fact, that's where the name "web" comes from. Hyperlinks can connect to other places on a webpage, to other pages within your website, to pages outside your site, and to many types of web and non-web content.

You activate a *hyperlink* by clicking a designated bit of text or a graphic that, depending on the link, takes you to a different location on the page, opens a different webpage, starts an email message, downloads a file, lets you view a movie or listen to a sound clip, starts a web-based program, and so on. You have probably clicked thousands of hyperlinks, perhaps without thinking much about the coding behind them. After reading this chapter, you'll understand *how* they work, and you'll be able to create your own.

In this chapter, you'll learn about the <*a*> tag, which is used to create various types of hyperlinks. You'll find out how to create hyperlinks to webpages and email addresses, how to create anchor points within a document, and how to hyperlink directly to an anchor point. I'll also show you how to hyperlink to non-web content, like a Microsoft Word document or a Microsoft Excel spreadsheet.

Important Before you can use the practice files provided for this chapter, you need to download and install them from the book's companion content location. See "Code Samples" at the beginning of this book for more information.

Hyperlinking to a Webpage

No matter what type of hyperlink you want to create, the basic syntax is the same. It starts with the *<a>* tag and then uses an *href=* attribute (short for "hyperlink reference") which provides the URL or the path to the destination. For example, an opening tag might look like this:

```
<a href="http://www.microsoft.com">
```

This is followed by the text that will be underlined as the link text that you click, or by a reference to the image that will serve as a hyperlink. (You'll learn more about images in Chapter 9, "Inserting Graphics.") After that text is the closing *</a>* tag. Here's a complete example:

```
Visit <a href="http://www.microsoft.com">Microsoft.com</a> for the latest
information.
```

When viewed in a browser, this produces a text-based hyperlink (see Figure 5-1).

Visit <u>Microsoft.com</u> for the latest information

FIGURE 5-1 A text hyperlink is usually underlined.

Hyperlinks are underlined by default. You can specify alternative formatting for hyperlinks by using styles, as explained in Chapter 6, "Introduction to Style Sheets."

Using Partial Paths and Filenames

In some cases, you do not need to provide a file name or a complete path to the destination in a hyperlink. It depends on the context and the file's name.

If you do not link to a specific page, the server that hosts the website responds by displaying the default page for that site (if one is available). If a browser does not request a specific page when accessing a server, most servers will send the default page, which is usually named either *index* or *default*. Perhaps you wondered why the main page of Margie's Travel's website is called *index.htm*—and now you know.

In Internet Explorer, type the following URL in the Address bar:

http://www.microsoft.com/en/us

Campbell 416-396-8890

to Public Library

D: 2 ********** 6522

ormat: DD/MM/YYYY

er of Items: 3

D:37131200320026
The personal tax planner guide
'018
due:18/08/2018

D:37131146284112
CSS3 for dummies
due:18/08/2018

D:37131139729214
Learn HTML5
due:18/08/2018

hone Renewal# 416-395-5505
torontopubliclibrary.ca
day, July 28, 2018   9:44 AM

The opening page of the US version of the Microsoft website opens. Now type this URL instead:

http://www.microsoft.com/en/us/default.aspx

The same page loads. The first time, when you omitted the file name, the web server responded by sending the default file, which is named *default.aspx*.

 Note The URL in this example points to a page named *default.aspx*. *ASP* stands for Active Server Pages, which is an advanced technology used for commercial web development. Pages created with ASP typically have .asp or .aspx extensions. For your own pages, you should continue to use the .htm extension.

If you want to link to a specific page, you must specify the complete file name. For example, if you wanted to provide a direct link to the page where users can download Windows Media Player, you would use this tag:

```
<a href="http://www.microsoft.com/windows/windowsmedia/player/
download/download.aspx">Download Windows Media Player</a>
```

Using Relative and Absolute Paths

Paths that contain a complete address that anyone can use to get to that page are called *absolute paths*. Absolute paths are very reliable, but they are also long and awkward to type. For example:

```
<a href="http://www.margiestravel.com/travel/images/london.htm">London Tours</a>
```

When you are linking to files in the same website as the link itself, you do not need to include the complete path to the file; you can simply provide its name. When the file is in the same folder, you need only supply the file name. For example, if the *index.htm* and *london.htm* pages of the Margie's Travel site were in the same folder, in the *index.htm* file, you could refer to *london.htm* like this:

```
<a href="london.htm">London Tours</a>
```

This is called a *relative path,* because the destination file is relative to the current file's location. Relative paths make it easier to develop and test your website in a different file location than the one where it will eventually be stored. For example, in this book, you'll be doing most of your development in the *Documents\Microsoft Press\HTML 5 Start Here* folder, which would typically not be the final destination for a site you are developing. By making as many relative references as possible, you avoid the need to re-code every URL when your site is moved to its final destination.

When creating a link to a file that's stored in a subfolder of the current one, you can point to that subfolder but otherwise leave the path relative. For example, suppose that *index.htm* is stored in a folder called *c:\main* and *london.htm* is stored in *c:\main\destinations*, which would be considered a subfolder (or *child folder*) of it. To refer to *london.htm* from within *index.htm*, you would use a tag like this:

```
<a href="destinations/london.htm">London Tours</a>
```

You can also create a link to a file that is up one level (a *parent folder*) with a relative reference. For example, suppose you wanted to refer to *index.htm* from within *london.htm* (both in the same locations as before). You would precede the reference with *../* to indicate that the file is one level up:

```
<a href="../index.htm">Home</a>
```

Setting a Target Window

By default, a hyperlink opens the referenced page in the same browser tab. That means the new page replaces the previous page. Usually this is fine, but in some cases you might want the hyperlink to open in a new tab (or window, if the browser you are using does not support multiple tabs). For example, perhaps you want to recommend that visitors check out a page on another site, but you don't want them to leave your site.

To direct the hyperlink to open a page in a new tab, add the attribute *target="_blank"* to the *<a>* tag. For example, to open the *london.htm* file in a new window, the tag would be structured like this:

```
<a href="london.htm" target="_blank">London Tours</a>
```

Note The *target=* attribute is not allowed in XHTML. W3C suggests that you use JavaScript for such situations.

In the following exercise, you will create hyperlinks to other files.

Create Hyperlinks to Files

1. In Notepad and Internet Explorer, open the *swdestinations.htm* file located in the *Documents\Microsoft Press\HTML 5 Start Here\05Links\CreatingHyperlinks* folder.

2. In Notepad, locate the text *Sedona* and enclose it with an *<a>* tag that refers to *sedona.htm*:

```
<li><a href="sedona.htm">Sedona</a></li>
```

3. Locate the text *Back to Home page* and enclose it with an *<a>* tag that refers to *index.htm*:

```
<p><a href="index.htm">Back to Home page</a></p>
```

4. Locate the text *Arizona State Tourism Guide* and enclose it with an *<a>* tag that refers to *www.arizonaguide.com* and opens in a new window:

```
<p><a href="http://www.arizonaguide.com" target="_blank">Arizona State
Tourism Guide</a></p>
```

5. Save the file and then refresh Internet Explorer.

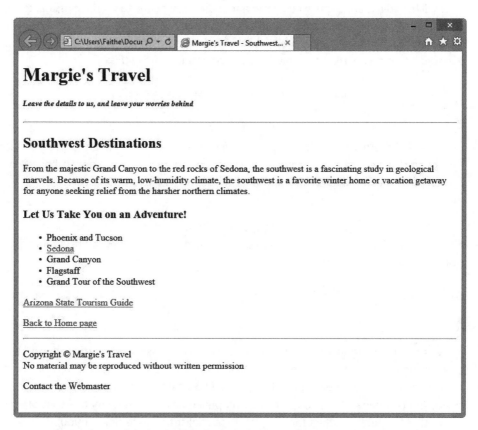

6. In Internet Explorer, click the Sedona hyperlink. The Sedona page displays.

7. Click the Back button in the browser window to return to the Southwest page.

8. Click the Back to Home page hyperlink. The Index page displays.

9. Click the Arizona State Tourism Guide hyperlink. That site opens in its own tab.

10. Click the Back button to return to the Southwest page. Close all open files.

inking to an Email Address

...inks can point to anything, not just to webpages. For example, you can create email hyperlinks that start the user's default email program, create a new message, and insert the recipient's address. (You can also set it to fill in the message subject if you like, which can be useful in helping you organize incoming messages and direct them appropriately.)

Email hyperlinks are useful when you want to direct someone to send a message to a particular person. For example, it is common to include a link that, when clicked, emails a site's webmaster. To create a hyperlink to an email address, use the same *href=* attribute as you did previously, but instead of a web address, type *mailto:* followed by the email address, like this:

```
<a href="mailto:support@margiestravel.com">Contact Us</a>
```

> **Note** Not everyone who has web access also has an appropriate email program set up to take advantage of a *mailto:* hyperlink. You might prefer to set up a web-based contact form, which you will learn about in Chapter 14, "Creating User Forms."

Not all browsers support live email hyperlinks. It's a good idea to also include the actual email address in text form on the page, in case someone cannot use your hyperlink. In such a case, the text would mirror the address as follows:

```
Contact <a href="mailto:support@margiestravel.com">support@margiestravel.com</a>
```

> **Caution** Including an email address on a publicly accessible webpage is bound to generate a certain amount of incoming junk mail (also known as *spam*). For this reason, do not put your main email address on a public page. If you have your own domain, or if your ISP or hosting company allows you to have multiple email addresses, create a special account to be used for public contact (or ask your IT specialist to create one for you). That way if you get too much junk mail, you can delete that address and start over with a new one without disrupting your main email account. If you don't have access to multiple email accounts, consider a free web-based account.

To add a default subject line to the email, add *?subject=Comment* (or whatever you want the text in the subject line to be) after the email address, like this:

```
<a href="mailto:support@margiestravel.com?subject=Comment">Contact Us</a>
```

The person using the hyperlink to contact you can change the subject line in her email program before sending the message.

Tip Even if all email from the site is directed to the same person, you might still create multiple email hyperlinks, each one with different default subject lines.

Another option, *title=*, specifies a ScreenTip for the hyperlink. This attribute displays a message when the user hovers the mouse pointer over the hyperlink and also reports its information to screen reading programs. By default, the ScreenTip for a hyperlink shows the address of the link, but you can make it display anything you like.

In the following example, because the text is the same as the hyperlink, it would be a waste for the ScreenTip to repeat the same hyperlink yet again:

```
Contact <a href="mailto:support@margiestravel.com">support@margiestravel.com</a>
```

A ScreenTip should ideally be succinct and clearly state the purpose of the hyperlink. For example, to display the message *Please contact us with questions or comments* in the ScreenTip, add the following to the code:

```
<a href="mailto:support@margiestravel.com" title="Please contact us with questions
or comments">support@margiestravel.com</a>
```

You can also use the *title=* attribute to omit extraneous portions of the complete hyperlink so visitors do not see them in the ScreenTip. For example, creating a title that contains only the email address, and not the subject or title parts of the tag, makes it easier to read.

In the following exercise, you will create a *mailto:* hyperlink.

Create a mailto: Hyperlink

Note Use the practice file provided for this exercise rather than the file created in a previous exercise.

1. In Notepad, open the *swdestinations.htm* file located in the *Documents\Microsoft Press\HTML 5 Start Here\05Links\LinkingEmail* folder.

2. Locate the text *Contact the Webmaster* at the bottom of the document and enclose it in a hyperlink that sends email to *webmaster@margiestravel.com*:

   ```
   <p><a href="mailto:webmaster@margiestravel.com">Contact the Webmaster</a></p>
   ```

3. Add a subject line of *Question/Comment* to the hyperlink:

    `<p><a href="mailto:webmaster@margiestravel.com?subject=Question/Comment">Contact the Webmaster</a></p>`

4. Add a title to the hyperlink that will display *webmaster@margiestravel.com* as a ScreenTip:

    `<p><a href="mailto:webmaster@margiestravel.com?subject=Question/Comment" title="webmaster@margiestravel.com">Contact the Webmaster</a></p>`

5. Save the file and then check your work in Internet Explorer.

6. In Internet Explorer, point to the <u>Contact the Webmaster</u> hyperlink at the bottom of the page.

    The ScreenTip displays.

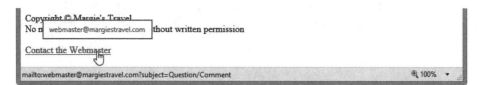

Note The full text of the hyperlink is visible either in the status bar or in a separate pop-up, depending on the browser and whether the status bar is displayed. To toggle the status bar on/off in Internet Explorer, choose View (Alt+V) | Toolbars | Status Bar.

7. Click the <u>Contact the Webmaster</u> hyperlink.

    Your default email program starts (if it was not already running) and a new email message opens with the specified information in the To: and Subject: lines. (Microsoft Outlook 2010 is shown in the graphic.)

Information provided from hyperlink

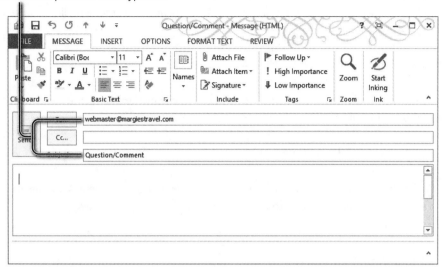

8. Close the email message window without sending the message and then close the Notepad and Internet Explorer windows.

Creating and Hyperlinking to Anchors

An *anchor* is a marker within an HTML document, roughly analogous to a bookmark in a Word document. You define a specific location in the document with an anchor name and then you can hyperlink directly to that anchor.

Anchors are most valuable in long documents with multiple sections. They provide a means for users to jump directly to whatever section they want rather than having to read or scroll through the entire document. You can do this internally by creating a list of hyperlinks at the top of the document, or you can do this externally by including an anchor name in a hyperlink to another document. There are two parts to the process:

1. Mark the anchor location.

2. Create a hyperlink that refers to it.

To define an anchor, create an *<a>* tag around the destination text and include a *name=* attribute. For example, suppose you have a heading that reads *Conclusion* and you want to create an anchor point with that same name:

```
<a name="conclusion">Conclusion</a>
```

To refer to the anchor point, include its name in the *href=* attribute. Precede the anchor name with a pound sign (#). If the anchor point is in the same document as the hyperlink, you can use a relative reference like this:

```
<a href="#conclusion">View the Conclusion</a>
```

Otherwise, you must include the name of the file in which the anchor is located. For example, if the anchor were in a file called *report.htm*, it would look like this:

```
<a href="report.htm#conclusion">View the Conclusion</a>
```

The same rules apply to the file name as they do with regular hyperlinks. If the document is not in the same folder, you must refer to the folder either absolutely or relatively.

In the following exercise, you will create and link to anchor points in an HTML document.

Create an Anchor Point

1. In Notepad and Internet Explorer, open the *canyon.htm* file located in the *Documents\Microsoft Press\HTML 5 Start Here\05Links\CreatingAnchors* folder.

2. In Notepad, locate the following tag. Make sure you get the copy that is in a *<h3>* tag, not the copy that is in the list.

   ```
   <h3>Grand Canyon Indian Country West Rim Bus Tour<h3>
   ```

3. Enclose the tag in an anchor tab and include *bus* with the *name=* attribute:

   ```
   <h3><a name="bus">Grand Canyon Indian Country West Rim Bus Tour</a></h3>
   ```

> **Note** You can nest the *<a>* tags within the *<h3>* tags or vice versa, but be consistent at both ends.

4. Repeat steps 2-3 for the other *<h3>* level headings in the document, using the names *bike* and *copter* for them, respectively:

   ```
   <h3><a name="bike">Grand Canyon South Rim Hermit's Rest Bike Ride</a></h3>
   ...


   <h3><a name="copter">Deluxe Grand Canyon Helicopter Tour</a></h3>
   ```

5. In the bulleted list at the top of the document, create a hyperlink from the bus tour anchor to the heading:

`<li><a href="#bus">`Grand Canyon Indian Country West Rim Bus Tour`</a></li>`

6. Repeat step 5 for each of the other list items:

`<li><a href="#bike">`Grand Canyon South Rim Hermit's Rest Bike Ride`</a></li>`

`<li><a href="#copter">`Deluxe Grand Canyon Helicopter Tour`</a></li>`

7. Save the file and then refresh Internet Explorer.

8. Click each of the hyperlinks in the bulleted list; click the Back button after each one to return to the top of the page.

As you click each link, the browser scrolls down the page to display the corresponding heading at the top of the window. The exception is the last one, which does not display at the very top because it is so near the bottom of the page; instead, the lower portion of the page displays when its link is clicked.

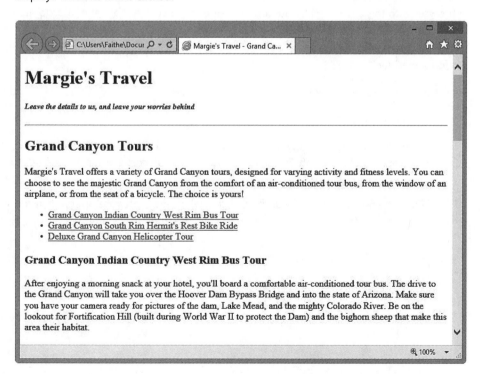

Hyperlinking to Other Content

A hyperlink can reference any file, not just a web document. You can take advantage of this to link to other content such as Microsoft Office documents, compressed archive files such as .zip files, and even executable program files such as setup utilities for programs you want to provide to your visitors. The procedure for linking to other content is the same as for linking to a webpage; the only difference is the file name you enter in the hyperlink.

 Note You can create hyperlinks to pictures, but linking to a picture by using the *<a>* tag opens the picture in its own window rather than displaying it on the webpage. In Chapter 9, "Inserting Graphics," you will learn how to place pictures on the pages themselves.

Before you create a link to non-HTML content, you need to remember that not everyone has the same software. At first, it might seem like a great idea to provide a set of reports as Word documents, for example, but what about people who don't have Word installed? Some browsers have a feature that automatically tries to download an appropriate viewer, player, or plug-in (an extension to the browser for handling a certain type of file) for anything it can't display as native content. That's a great feature when it works, but it's not reliable because not all your web visitors will have a browser with this capability. If you don't provide an HTML alternative for a proprietary-format file, you should at least provide a hyperlink to a free viewer that can display that file type. This is especially important with audio and video clips, which you will learn about in Chapter 15, "Incorporating Sound and Video."

Here are some of the popular viewers and the addresses where they can be downloaded:

- Adobe Reader: *get.adobe.com/reader*

- Microsoft Download Center, offering Microsoft Office viewers (PowerPoint, Excel, Word) and trial versions of Microsoft Office: *http://www.microsoft.com/downloads/default.aspx*

 Tip After the 60-day trial period, the Office trial version software operates in reduced functionality mode that still allows users to view documents created with Word, Excel, and PowerPoint.

In the following exercise, you will create a hyperlink to a Word file and to the Microsoft Download Center page.

1. In Notepad and Internet Explorer, open the *swdestinations.htm* file located in the *Documents\Microsoft Press\HTML 5 Start Here\05Links\LinkingOther* folder.

2. In Notepad, on the Grand Canyon line of the list, add the following:

```
<li>Grand Canyon (Brochure also available in XPS format)</li>
```

3. Add a hyperlink that makes the words *XPS format* a hyperlink to the file *brochure.xps:*

```
<li>Grand Canyon (Brochure also available in <a href="brochure.xps">XPS
format</a>)</li>
```

4. Save the file and then refresh Internet Explorer.

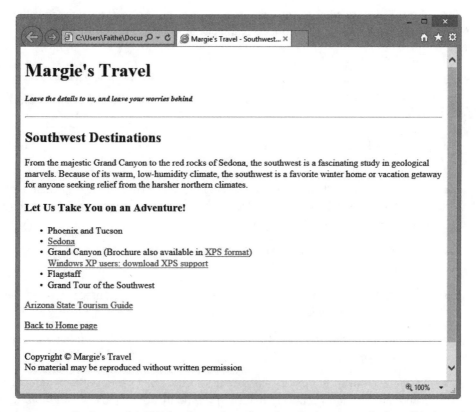

5. In Internet Explorer, click XPS format and confirm that the brochure displays. If it doesn't, check your typing on the hyperlink and make sure that you have an XPS viewer installed.

Note In order to display XPS format, you must have an XPS viewer; the viewer is included with Windows Vista and later. Users of Windows XP can get XPS capabilities by installing the Microsoft XML Paper Specification Service Pack, found at *http://www.microsoft.com/download/details.aspx?id=11816*.

6. In Notepad, add a line break at the end of the Grand Canyon list item, and then add a hyperlink that points people to the Microsoft page where they can download the XPS viewer:

```
<li>Grand Canyon (Brochure also available in <a href="brochure.xps">XPS
format</a>)<br><a href=" http://www.microsoft.com/download/en/
details.aspx?id=11816">Windows XP users: download XPS support</a></li>
```

7. Save your work in Notepad and then refresh Internet Explorer.

8. Test the new hyperlink to confirm that it displays the Microsoft page for downloading XPS support. If it doesn't, check your typing in Notepad.

9. Close Notepad and Internet Explorer.

Key Points

- To create a hyperlink, use the *<a>* tag with the *href=* attribute. The *<a>* tag is two-sided, so add *</a>* after the text that you use as the hyperlink.

- Use absolute paths (that is, paths containing the full location of the file) when referring to content outside your own website. Use relative paths when referring to files in the same folder as the current page or files in a parent or child folder.

- To open a hyperlink target in a new window, include the *target="_blank"* attribute in the *<a>* tag.

- To create hyperlink that opens a pre-addressed email message, precede the address with *mailto:* (for example, *mailto:support@microsoft.com*).

- To create an anchor point, use the *name=* attribute with the *<a>* tag (for example, *<a name="equipment">*).

- To reference an anchor point, reference the anchor point name, but remember to precede the name with a pound symbol (#) in the *href=* attribute (for example, *<a href="#bike">*).

- You can create hyperlinks to other types of content besides webpages, but you should include hyperlinks to viewers for any content types that might not be supported by all browsers (and/or make HTML or plain-text alternative versions available).

- To provide a viewer for a type of content, create a hyperlink that points to a site from which it can be downloaded or store the viewer on your own website and provide a link to it.

PART II

Style Sheets and Graphics

Chapter 6

Introduction to Style Sheets

In this chapter, you will:

- Construct style rules
- Create styles for nested tags
- Create classes and IDs for applying styles
- Apply styles to hyperlinks
- Create and link to external style sheets

After you learn about cascading style sheets, you will wonder how anybody ever had the patience to create large websites without them. Cascading style sheets can save you a tremendous amount of time by standardizing the formatting of an entire webpage or group of pages.

A *cascading style sheet* (CSS) is code that specifies formatting based on styles. You can store the CSS code in the *<head>* section of the webpage to which you want it to apply, or you can store it in a separate file with a .css extension (for situations in which you want the same CSS to apply to more than one webpage). The formatting then "cascades" down to the individual instances of each tag. You can also place a style directly within an individual tag if desired, as you did in Chapter 4, "Using Lists and Backgrounds."

In this chapter, you'll learn how to construct style sheets and how to attach them to a document, either by placing them within the document itself or by linking to them as a separate file. You'll learn how to define a style and how to apply it. The next several chapters will include further opportunities to practice with various style types.

Important Before you can use the practice files provided for this chapter, you need to download and install them from the book's companion content location. See "Code Samples" at the beginning of this book for more information.

Understanding Styles

In simplest terms, a *style* is a formatting rule. That rule can be applied to an individual tag, to all instances of a certain tag within a document, or to all instances of a certain tag across a group of documents.

In Chapter 4, you saw how to use the *style=* attribute for ordered and unordered lists. For example, to use a square bullet character in an unordered list, you would use the *style=* attribute with the *<ul>* tag like this:

```
<ul style="list-style-type: square">
```

But suppose you have several unordered lists in your document and you want them all to use the same square bullet character. You could type the style attribute into the opening *<ul>* tag for each one, but that's a lot of work. Instead, you can create a *<style>* section within the *<head>* section that creates a global style rule for all *<ul>* tags in the document. The *<style>* section might look like this:

```
<style type="text/css">
ul {
    list-style-type: square
}
</style>
```

Don't worry about the line breaks; they are simply a means of making your code more readable. Many third-party CSS editing programs format style rules with the extra line breaks for that reason. However, the preceding code could also be written like this:

```
<style type="text/css">ul {list-style-type: square}</style>
```

Notice that the *<ul>* tag does not have angle brackets. Also, note that the rules for the tag display in curly braces. Other than those two minor differences, the syntax is exactly the same as when applied directly to a specific *<ul>* tag. You don't need to include the *style=* attribute because the entire definition is enclosed in a *<style>* tag.

You can define multiple rules within one *<style>* section. For example, if you want to expand this example to also specify that ordered lists are labeled with lowercase letters rather than numbers:

```
<style type="text/css">
ul {
    list-style-type: square ;
}
ol {
    list-style-type: lower-alpha
}
</style>
```

Now further suppose that you want these specifications to apply to all the bulleted and numbered lists in all documents in your entire website. You can create an external cascading style sheet and then refer to that style sheet in the *<head>* section of each document to which it should apply. For example, here's the entire text of an external cascading style sheet (a plain text file with a .css extension) that would apply the specified rules.

```
ul {
    list-style-type: square;
}
ol {
    list-style-type: lower-alpha;
}
```

It's the same code that was enclosed within the *<style>* tag in the previous example. When style rules appear in a separate file, you don't need the *<style>* tag.

A cascading style sheet can get very complex if it includes a lot of rules, but the principles are always the same as in these examples. The remainder of this chapter explores how to construct style rules within both embedded and external style sheets.

Constructing Style Rules

An embedded style sheet consists of a two-sided *<style>* tag placed in the *<head>* section of a document. Between the *<style>* and *</style>* tags, you define the rules for the various styles.

A style rule begins with the name of the tag or other element to which the style applies. For example, if you are creating a rule that will apply to all instances of the *<h1>* tag, start the rule with *h1* (no brackets):

```
<style>
h1
</style>
```

No brackets are necessary around *h1* because it's already enclosed in the *<style>* tag.

Next, type a set of curly braces. (You can place them on separate lines for improved readability if you want.) Then place the rule inside the braces. For example, to create a rule that uses the color red for the text of a first-level heading, use the following:

```
<style>
h1 {
    color: red
}
</style>
```

If you have more than one rule to apply, such as a color plus a typeface, separate the rules with semicolons within the curly braces. It is customary but not required to write each rule on its own line. For example, to specify that the heading text must be both red and 14 pixels in height, include the following in your rule:

```
<style>
h1 {
    color: red;
    font-size: 14px;
}
</style>
```

If multiple tags should have the same rule applied to them, you can list them together and separate them by commas. For example, if all heading styles *<h1>* through *<h6>* should be red, you could write:

```
<style>
h1, h2, h3, h4, h5, h6 {
    color: red ;
}
</style>
```

In the following exercise, you will create an embedded style sheet governing the appearance of horizontal lines.

Create an Embedded Style Sheet

1. In Notepad and Internet Explorer, open the *index.htm* file located in the *Documents\Microsoft Press\HTML5 Start Here\06Styles\ConstructingRules* folder. Use the referenced version rather than a copy you worked with in an earlier exercise.

2. Examine the horizontal rules in Internet Explorer. Note that they are plain, gray, and run across the entire width of the page.

3. In Notepad, in the *<head>* section, modify the style so that the lines are blue, 75% of the browser window in width, 3 pixels in height, and left-aligned, as follows:

```
<style>
hr {
    color: blue;
    background-color: blue;
    height: 3px;
    width: 75%;
    text-align: left;
}
</style>
```

The horizontal lines are now blue and 3 pixels thick.

Note Notice that you use the text-align attribute to align the horizontal line even though it is not text. That's because there is no separate alignment attribute for elements that do not contain text. Not all browsers support this usage (notably some versions of Firefox), so if horizontal rule alignment is an Important part of your layout, be sure to test this in multiple browsers.

4. Save the file and then refresh the Internet Explorer display.

   The appearance of both lines has changed.

Horizontal rules now occupy 75% of the page width, are blue, are left-aligned, and are 3px thick.

5. In Notepad, delete the *text-align: left;* portion of the style rule so that the lines are center-aligned (the default).

6. Save your work in Notepad and then refresh Internet Explorer to see the change.

7. Close Internet Explorer and Notepad.

Creating Styles for Nested Tags

Sometimes you might want to apply a specific formatting only when one tag is nested within another. For example, perhaps you want a bulleted list that's nested within another bulleted list to use a different bullet character. If you simply created a rule for the entire tag, all text to which this tag has been applied would be formatted the same way. For example, if you created a style for the *<ul>* tag, all bulleted items would use the same bullet character. Instead, you must specify that you want to apply a rule only to the nested tag.

To do this, instead of using a single style name at the beginning of the rule, specify that the item is nested by listing the parent style name followed by the descendent (child) style name. For example, to use round bullets for all numbered lists that are nested within bulleted lists, specify the following:

```
ul ol {list-style-type: circle}
```

This technique works with multiple nested levels. For example, to apply this formatting only to bulleted lists nested within other bulleted lists that are in turn nested within numbered lists, specify the following:

```
ul ol ul {list-style-type: circle}
```

You can do this with any text attributes, not just those pertaining to the bullet or number type. For example, to make all the bold text that displays in unordered lists appear blue, specify the following:

```
ul b {color: blue}
```

In the following exercise, you will apply different bullet characters to a nested list by creating styles in the *<style>* area of a document.

Use Styles to Format a Nested List

1. In Notepad and in Internet Explorer, open the *destinations.htm* file located in the *Documents\Microsoft Press\HTML 5 Start Here\06Styles\CreatingNested* folder.

   Notice in Internet Explorer that the first-level bullet characters are black circles and the second-level bullets are white circles.

2. In Notepad, in the *<head>* section, type a two-sided *<style>* tag, and then within that, create a style rule specifying that first-level unordered lists have a square bullet character:

```
<style>
ul {
    list-style-type: square
}
</style>
```

3. Save your work in Notepad and then refresh Internet Explorer. All list items at all levels use the square black bullet character.

- Alaskan Salmon Fishing
    - Sitka Sound
    - Kenai Peninsula
    - Matanuska Susitna Valley
- The Vineyards of Northern California
- Sedona and the Grand Canyon
    - Sedona Red Rock Jeep Tour
    - Sedona Energy Vortex Exploration
    - Grand Canyon Photo and Sightseeing Motorcoach Tour
    - Grand Canyon Helicopter Adventure
- Michigan Fall Festivals

4. Create a style rule specifying that second-level unordered lists have a disc bullet character:

```
<style>
ul {
    list-style-type: square
}
ul ul {
    list-style-type: disc
}
</style>
```

Note The complete list of the valid values for *list-style-type:* includes *disc, circle, square, decimal, lower-roman, upper-roman, lower-alpha, upper-alpha,* and *none.*

5. Save the file and then refresh Internet Explorer. The bullet characters change.

- Alaskan Salmon Fishing
    - Sitka Sound
    - Kenai Peninsula
    - Matanuska Susitna Valley
- The Vineyards of Northern California
- Sedona and the Grand Canyon
    - Sedona Red Rock Jeep Tour
    - Sedona Energy Vortex Exploration
    - Grand Canyon Photo and Sightseeing Motorcoach Tour
    - Grand Canyon Helicopter Adventure
- Michigan Fall Festivals

6. Close Internet Explorer and Notepad.

Note There are other CSS styles you can use to format lists. For example, you can use a graphic as a bullet character by using the *list-style-image* attribute, like this:

```
ul { list-style-image: url("bullet.gif") }
```

where *bullet.gif* is the name of the graphic file to be used as a bullet character.

Creating Classes and IDs for Applying Styles

As you have just seen, style rules can modify the built-in tags in HTML by redefining their formatting. Styles don't stop there, however. You can make your own styles by creating classes and IDs.

Classes and *IDs* mark certain elements so that you can refer to them in your style sheet. A class can be applied to multiple selections, whereas an ID uniquely identifies a specific selection within a document. (Different documents can use the same ID.) Classes and IDs are the foundation of CSS formatting; you will use them extensively as you create your own websites.

For example, suppose you have an unordered list of items and you want the featured items to display in red. One way to do it would be to manually add the *style="color: red"* attribute to each list item:

```
<li style="color: red">The Wineries of Italy</li>
```

However, this method is not optimal because if you instead decide to make the new items blue, you would need to make the change manually for each instance. A better way is to create a class called *featured* and then define formatting for it in the *<style>* area. Then you could apply the *featured* class to each bullet point you want to spotlight.

To apply a class style, add a *class=* attribute to the opening tag for the element. For example, to make a list item part of the *new* class, use the following:

```
<li class="featured">The Wineries of Italy</li>
```

Then in the *<style>* area, add a style that defines the class as red. The only difference between defining a class and redefining a standard tag is that you put a period in front of a class name:

```
<style>
.new {
    color: red
}
</style>
```

IDs work the same way, except that you can apply them only once per document. For example, you might apply an ID to a unique heading. To create an ID, add an *id=* attribute to the tag:

```
<li id="special">Special Discounts Available</li>
```

Then define the ID in the *<style>* area, preceding the ID name with a hash symbol (#), like this:

```
<style>
#special {
    color: red
}
</style>
```

> **Note** Why would you create an ID just for one heading? Wouldn't it be easier to just apply the formatting to the individual heading's tag? Well, yes, if you are creating only one web-page. However, if you are creating multiple pages and each page has an instance of that special item that the ID defines, you can save yourself a lot of time by using an ID, especially if you store your styles in an external CSS file (which you'll learn later in this chapter).

In the following exercise, you will create a class and apply it to items in a list.

Create and Use Classes

1. In Notepad and Internet Explorer, open the *destinations.htm* file located in the *Documents\ Microsoft Press\HTML 5 Start Here\06Styles\CreatingClasses* folder.

2. In the *<style>* section, add a new class that makes sale items red:

   .sale {color: red}

3. In the *<body>* section, add the *class="sale"* attribute to the *<li>* opening tag for *Sitka Sound* and *Grand Canyon Helicopter Adventure*:

   ```
   <ul>
   <li>Alaskan Salmon Fishing</li>
   <ul>
   <li class="sale">Sitka Sound</li>
   <li>Kenai Peninsula</li>
   <li>Matanuska Susitna Valley</li>
   </ul>
   <li>The Vineyards of Northern California</li>
   <li>Sedona and the Grand Canyon</li>
   <ul>
   ```

```
<li>Sedona Red Rock Jeep Tour</li>
<li>Sedona Energy Vortex Exploration</li>
<li>Grand Canyon Photo and Sightseeing Motorcoach Tour</li>
<li class="sale">Grand Canyon Helicopter Adventure</li>
```

4. Add *Sale!* to the beginning of the tour names for each of the two lines you modified in step 3:

```
<ul>
<li>Alaskan Salmon Fishing</li>
<ul>
<li class="sale">Sale! Sitka Sound</li>
<li>Kenai Peninsula</li>
<li>Matanuska Susitna Valley</li>
</ul>
<li>The Vineyards of Northern California</li>
<li>Sedona and the Grand Canyon</li>
<ul>
<li>Sedona Red Rock Jeep Tour</li>
<li>Sedona Energy Vortex Exploration</li>
<li>Grand Canyon Photo and Sightseeing Motorcoach Tour</li>
<li class="sale">Sale! Grand Canyon Helicopter Adventure</li>
```

5. Save your work in Notepad and then refresh Internet Explorer to see the changes.

Note Each style rule here is run in as a single line, whereas in earlier examples rules were broken into multiple lines for readability. It makes no difference which way you do it. The one-line method is more compact, but the multi-line method is easier to browse when editing code. From this point on in the book, most style rules will be written in the more compact form to save space.

6. Modify the *sale* class so that the text displays in orange:

   ```
   .sale {color: orange}
   ```

7. Save the file and then refresh Internet Explorer. Note that the sale items are now orange.

8. Close Internet Explorer and Notepad.

Applying Styles to Hyperlinks with Pseudo-Classes

By default in most browsers, text hyperlinks display as underlined blue text and *visited* hyperlinks (that is, hyperlinks to pages you have already visited) display as underlined purple text. You have probably seen websites where this wasn't the case, though, and perhaps wondered how they did it.

You can control hyperlink formatting by placing attributes in the *<a>* tag for each link, although it's tedious to do so. For example, to make an individual hyperlink magenta:

```
<a href="foliage.htm" style="color: magenta">Monte Carlo Resorts</a>
```

You could apply a class to all hyperlinks, as you learned in the preceding section, but that method does not provide a way to distinguish between the visited links and the unvisited links. Ideally you would want them to be different colors, and that's not possible when you use a class to define them. To apply different colors, you can use *pseudo-classes*. A pseudo-class is a class that uses a variable to determine membership. HTML defines pseudo-classes called *link* and *visited* for unvisited and visited hyperlinks, respectively.

You do not need to apply anything to the individual hyperlink tags within the *<body>* section to use pseudo-classes. Simply create the style rule in the *<style>* section for the pseudo-classes and the browser will apply that rule throughout the document. For example, to make all visited links magenta and all unvisited links black:

```
<style>
a:link {color: black}
a:visited {color: magenta}
</style>
```

There are three additional pseudo-classes that you can use with hyperlink styles:

■ **focus** This is used for links that are selected by using the keyboard (that is, by using a keyboard shortcut to move the selection outline onto the hyperlink) but not yet activated (that is, the user hasn't pressed Enter to activate the selection). This is not an issue when you select a link with the mouse because clicking a link both selects it and activates it. This pseudo-class is not commonly used because so few people navigate pages by using the keyboard that it is not worthwhile to go to the trouble.

■ **hover** This is used to change the appearance of a link when the mouse is positioned over it. You can use this pseudo-class to make a link change color, become bold, and so on when the user points at it.

■ **active** This is used for a link when it is clicked. Immediately after being clicked, the link changes to the *visited* state. You might use this pseudo-class if you have set the link and visited states to the same value but want the link to change momentarily when clicked.

Caution A link can be in more than one state at once. For example, a link can be visited yet also in the hover state if a mouse pointer is positioned over it. Therefore, the order in which you list the style rules for links is significant, because later rules will override earlier ones. Define them in the following order to avoid any confusion: *link, visited, focus, hover, active.*

In the following exercise, you will create pseudo-class styles for various hyperlink states.

Use Pseudo-Classes to Define Hyperlink Formatting

1. In Notepad and Internet Explorer, open the *index.htm* file located in the *Documents\Microsoft Press\HTML 5 Start Here\06Styles\StylingHyperlinks* folder.

2. In Internet Explorer, click the Southwest hyperlink, and then click the Back button to return to *index.htm.*

   Different colors are used to identify visited and unvisited links.

3. In Notepad, in the *<style>* area, add these rules:

```
a:link {color: blue}
a:visited {color: green}
a:hover {color: lime}
a:active {color: red}
```

4. Save the file and then refresh Internet Explorer. The visited Southwest hyperlink now displays as green.

5. Position the mouse pointer over each hyperlink.

   Notice that hyperlink text is lime green when you position the mouse pointer over it.

6. Click the Southwest hyperlink.

   Notice that the hyperlink text color changes to red immediately before the Southwest Destinations page loads.

7. Click Back to return to *index.htm*.

8. Close Notepad and Internet Explorer.

Creating and Linking to External Style Sheets

Embedded style sheets work well for single-page websites, but to really take advantage of what cascading style sheets can do, you need to create an *external style sheet*. A single external style sheet can be linked to multiple documents, ensuring complete consistency even when used for a large site. An external style sheet also makes it easy to change the formatting of your site after the pages have been constructed. Rather than having to edit each page individually, you can simply change the style sheet.

An external style sheet is a plain-text file, just like an HTML file. The only difference is that you assign it a .css extension rather than an .htm extension. It contains anything you would place within the *<style>* tag if you were creating the style sheet internally. You do not need the *<style>* and *</style>* tags themselves.

After creating the style sheet, you create a link to it in the *<head>* area of each document that will use it. For example, if the style sheet is named *default.css*, you would link to it by inserting this code in the document's *<head>* area, as shown in the following:

```
<link rel="stylesheet" type="text/css" href="default.css" />
```

> **Note** The name *default.css* is common, but not required. You can name your style sheet anything you like, as long as the name ends with a .css extension.

An embedded style sheet takes precedence over an external one. For example, if your external style sheet specifies Roman numerals for ordered lists but your embedded style sheet specifies uppercase letters, ordered lists will be labeled with uppercase letters. Furthermore, any tag-specific styles you apply take precedence over both embedded and external style sheets. So if you add a style rule to an individual *<ol>* tag, that setting will override any style sheet settings.

> **Note** Since *<link>* is a one-sided tag, the space and the / at the end are used for XHTML compatibility; if you are not coding in XHTML, they are optional.

In the following exercise, you will create an external style sheet and link a webpage to it.

Create and Use an External Style Sheet

1. In Notepad and Internet Explorer, open the *index.htm* file located in the *Documents\Microsoft Press\HTML 5 Start Here\06Styles\CreatingExternal* folder.

2. In Notepad, select all the text between *<style>* and *</style>* but do not include those tags in the selection.

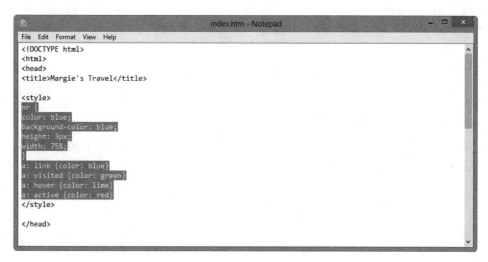

3. Press Ctrl+X to cut the text from the document and store it in the Clipboard.

4. Save the file and then start a new document in Notepad (File | New).

5. Press Ctrl+V to paste the text from the Clipboard into the new document).

6. Save the new document as *default.css* in the same folder as *index.htm* (*Documents\Microsoft Press\HTML 5 Start Here\06Styles\CreatingExternal*).

```
nr {
color: blue;
background-color: blue;
height: 3px;
width: 75%;
}
a: link {color: blue}
a: visited {color: green}
a: hover {color: lime}
a: active {color: red}
```

7. In Notepad, return to the *index* file and then delete the *<style>* and *</style>* tags.

8. Add this line to the *<head>* section:

```
<link rel="stylesheet" type="text/css" href="default.css">
```

9. Save the file and then refresh Internet Explorer.

    The file does not appear to change, but the styles are now defined in the external style sheet rather than in the embedded style sheet.

> **Note** One way to quickly check whether the style sheet is applied is to position the mouse pointer over a hyperlink. If the style sheet is working, the hyperlink text will display as lime green.

10. Close *index.htm* and then open *swdestinations.htm* in Notepad.

11. In *swdestinations.htm*, add the same line to the *<head>* section as in step 8.

12. Save the file and then close Notepad. Open *swdestinations.htm* in Internet Explorer to confirm that the external style sheet has been applied to this file too. (Look for green visited hyperlinks and blue horizontal rules.)

13. Close Internet Explorer.

Key Points

- Styles can define the formatting for specific instances of a tag, for all uses of a tag within a document, or for all uses of a tag within a group of documents.

- A cascading style sheet is a list of style rules applied to tags within an HTML document. This list can either be internal (embedded) or external to the document (a linked file).

- When rule conflicts occur, they are resolved as follows (from highest priority to lowest):

  - Styles applied to individual tags

  - Styles applied using an internal style sheet (with highest priority going to the entries nearest the bottom of that style sheet)

  - Styles applied using an external style sheet (again, with highest priority to the entries nearest the bottom)

- There are three ways to apply a style. You can use the *style=* attribute within an individual tag, you can create an embedded style sheet, or you can create an external style sheet.

- You place an embedded style sheet in the *<head>* section of the file and enclose it in a *<style>* tag. An external style sheet is a separate plain text file with a .css extension.

- A style sheet consists of one or more style rules. A style rule is the tag, class, or ID name followed by curly braces in which the specifications are placed.

- Each specification takes the format of *name*: *value*. For example, *list-style-type: square*.

- Use semicolons to separate multiple specifications within a rule. To define two or more tags the same way, include both tags (with a comma between them) before the opening curly brace, like this: *h1, h2 {color: black}*. If you omit the comma, two tag names in a row refer to nested styles in a rule. For example, *ol ul {color: green}* refers to unordered lists nested within ordered lists.

- You can assign a class to multiple elements. You can define a style based on a class. Precede a class's name in a style sheet with a period, like this: *.new {color: red}*.

- An ID must be uniquely assigned within a document. You can define a style based on an ID. Precede the ID in a style sheet with a hash symbol (#), like this: *#special {color: red}*.

- Apply a class or ID to a tag by including the *class=* or *ID=* attribute within its opening tag, like this: *<ol class="new">*.

- To apply styles to hyperlinks, use a pseudo-class of the hyperlink type. You can apply the *link*, *visited*, *hover*, *active*, or *focus* pseudo-class like this: *a:visited {color: red}*.

- To create an external style sheet, start a new Notepad document and then place all the style rules within it. Then refer to it from the *<head>* section of each document to which that style sheet should apply by using the tag *<link rel="stylesheet" type="text/css" href="default.css">*, where *default.css* is the name of your style sheet.

Chapter 7

Formatting Text with CSS

In this chapter, you will:

- Specify a font family

- Specify a font size and color

- Apply bold and italics

- Apply strikethrough and underlining

- Create inline spans

- Adjust spacing between letters

Learning how to create style rules opens up a whole new world in HTML formatting. Virtually anything that you can do in a word-processing program, you can do in HTML by using styles.

You might be wondering whether the simple text-formatting tags you learned about in Part I of the book, such as the *<b>* and *<i>* tags, are still relevant. They are—to a degree; however, the W3C is increasingly focused on applying text formatting by using styles, which means you should try to use the style-based formatting that you'll learn in this chapter (and the next). It's worth noting that the old formatting tags still work perfectly well when you create HTML5 documents, and web browsers will continue to support tag-based formatting for a long time. If you've already created an extensive website that uses formatting tags, there's no big rush to recreate your existing pages by using styles. As you create new pages, however, it's a good idea to do it "right" from the start by using styles for all your formatting.

In this chapter, you'll learn about character-based formatting—that is, formatting that makes individual characters look a certain way. You'll learn how to specify fonts, sizes, and colors; how to use styles to apply bold, italic, strikethrough, or underline styling to your text; and how to add a background to text and adjust the spacing between letters. In Chapter 8, "Formatting Paragraphs with CSS," you'll learn about paragraph formatting features such as line spacing, indentation, and alignment.

Important Before you can use the practice files provided for this chapter, you need to download and install them from the book's companion content location. See "Code Samples" at the beginning of this book for more information.

Specifying a Font Family

Specifying a certain font to display on a page can be tricky because not everyone has the same fonts installed. Even fonts that come with Microsoft Windows, such as Courier New and Arial, are not universally acceptable because not everyone who has access to the web uses a Windows-based computer.

To work around this issue, you can specify a *font family* rather than an individual font. A font family is a set of fonts listed in order of preference. If the computer displaying your page does not have the first font in the list, it checks for the second, and then the third, and so on until it finds a match. For example, here's how to specify a font family in a style rule:

```
p {font-family: "Arial", "Helvetica", sans-serif}
```

Although no font is universally available on all PCs, there are a few generic font types that are nearly so: serif, sans-serif, cursive, fantasy, and monospace. Those font types are not specified with quotation marks around them, as is the case in the preceding example. Figure 7-1 shows how each of those fonts renders on a webpage.

Serif

Sans-serif

cursive

FANTASY

monospace

FIGURE 7-1 Built-in font types in HTML, as rendered in Internet Explorer 10.

Note In the preceding example, the Cursive font does not display in a manner that you might expect from its name; it doesn't look like cursive handwriting. In most browsers, cursive displays as a rounded version of sans-serif.

By specifying a generic font type as the final font in the family, you can virtually guarantee that you'll at least get your last choice. If the browser can't use any of your preferences, it will simply render the text using its default font. Here are some common font families, grouped by their similar appearances:

- Arial Black, Helvetica Bold
- Arial, Helvetica, sans-serif
- Verdana, Geneva, Arial, Helvetica, sans-serif
- Times New Roman, Times, serif
- Courier New, Courier, monospace
- Georgia, Times New Roman, Times, serif
- Zapf-Chancery, cursive
- Western, fantasy

You can also add a *font-family* attribute to an individual tag to ensure that the text stands out. Here's how you might set an individual paragraph to the second font family from the preceding list:

```
<p style="font-family: Arial, Helvetica, sans-serif">
```

Notice that there are no quotation marks around any of the font names when applied in this way. Instead, the quotation marks are placed around the entire style rule.

In the following exercise, you will assign a default font to all the *<p>* tags in a document, and then you'll override that font choice on a specific paragraph.

Apply Fonts with Styles

1. Open *default.css* in Notepad and then open *index.htm* in Internet Explorer from the files located in the *Documents\Microsoft Press\HTML5 Start Here\07Text\SelectingFont* folder.

2. In *default.css*, add a style rule that defines a font family of Verdana, Arial, Helvetica, and sans-serif for the *<p>* tag and the *<li>* tag:

   ```
   p, li {font-family: "Verdana", "Arial", "Helvetica", sans-serif}
   ```

3. Save *default.css* and then refresh the Internet Explorer display for *index.htm*.

The font of all the text in paragraphs and lists changes.

4. Open the *index.htm* file in Notepad. Change the tag for the copyright notice at the bottom of the page to use the Times New Roman, Times, or serif font:

```
<p style="font-family: Times New Roman, Times, serif">Copyright &copy;
Margie's Travel<br>
No material may be reproduced without written permission<br>
<a href="mailto:webmaster@margiestravel.com">Contact the Webmaster</a></p>
```

5. Save the file and then refresh Internet Explorer.

Font determined by
style rule defined
in default.css

Font rule overridden
by style sttributes
in the <p> tag

Because each page of the website has a copyright notice, it might be better to create a class (as you learned in Chapter 6, "Introduction to Style Sheets") and change the font for the class. That's what we'll do next.

6. In the *index.htm* file in Notepad, remove the *style=* attribute you just applied to the copyright notice and instead apply a class called *copyright* to that paragraph:

```
<p class="copyright">Copyright &copy; Margie's Travel<br>
No material may be reproduced without written permission<br>
<a href="mailto:webmaster@margiestravel.com">Contact the Webmaster</a></p>
```

7. Save the file and then refresh Internet Explorer.

   The copyright notice has reverted to the default font set for *<p>* tags in the *default.css* style sheet because no special formatting has been defined for the copyright class.

8. In the *default.css* file in Notepad, define the copyright class to use the Times New Roman, Times, or serif font:

```
.copyright {font-family: "Times New Roman", "Times", serif}
```

9. Save the file and then refresh Internet Explorer.

10. Close Notepad and Internet Explorer.

Specifying a Font Size and Color

There are many ways to set the font size in HTML, but all the methods use one of two strategies: specify an absolute size or specify a size in relation to the parent tag.

To specify an absolute size, you use a number followed by a unit of measurement. The most common unit of measurement for webpages is *px*, which stands for pixels. (An average size for text is 10px.) Pixels are the native unit of measurement for computer monitor display modes. HTML also accepts inches (in), centimeters (cm), millimeters (mm), points (pt), and picas (pc), but those units are most appropriate when working with a page designed to be printed.

The size of a pixel depends on the display resolution of the monitor. For example, suppose someone views your page using a 17-inch monitor at 800 × 600 resolution. (That's a very low resolution, but it makes for a good example because small numbers are easier to work with.) The monitor's size is measured diagonally, so it's about 13.6 inches wide and 10.2 inches tall. If 10.2 inches high represents 600 pixels, there are about 60 pixels per inch vertically. Therefore, a 15-pixel character height translates into about 1/4 of an inch onscreen. Now suppose the display resolution is 1024 × 768. That means there are about 77 pixels per inch vertically; a 15-pixel character height translates into about 1/5 of an inch onscreen.

> **Note** HTML does not usually accept a numeric size without a unit of measurement. There are a few exceptions, though; one is the line-height style you will learn about in Chapter 8.

To specify a relative size, you use a relational description: xx-small, x-small, small, medium, large, x-large, or xx-large. The exact size of each of those specifications depends on the base size within the parent tag. Figure 7-2 shows some examples of fonts at those various sizes.

xx-small

x-small

small

medium (the default)

large

x-large

FIGURE 7-2 Samples of the built-in text sizes.

You can define a font size for an entire tag in the style sheet like this:

```
p {font-size: 12px}
```

Or you can embed it in a single paragraph's tag like this:

```
<p style="font-size: x-small">This text is extra-small.</p>
```

You can also specify relative sizing as a percentage of the base size, such as 120%. Another way to specify relative sizing is in ems. An *em* is a multiplier of the base font; for example, 2em is two times the base size, or 200%. It's called an em because it's the width of a capital M character.

For example, you could make text tagged as *<h3>* twice the size of the base font by including the following in the style sheet:

```
h1 {font-size: 2em}
```

Or you could set the size for an individual heading:

```
<p style="font-size: 2em">This text is twice the base size.</p>
```

To specify a font color, use the *color* attribute that you learned in previous chapters. For example, to make text in all *<p>* tags blue, place this style rule in the style sheet:

```
p {color: blue}
```

To include the *color* attribute for a single tag, include it in the *style=* attribute:

```
<p style="color: blue">This is blue text.</p>
```

You can use the basic or extended color names, as described in Chapter 4, "Using Lists and Backgrounds," or you can use hexadecimal or RGB naming. Refer to the *colors.htm*, *extended.htm*, and *websafe.htm* files in the Reference folder of the downloadable companion content for full-color swatches of these groups of colors.

Remember from Chapter 4 that the *color* attribute refers to the foreground color (the color of the text). You can also set a background color for the text. This is different from the background color in the document itself. The *color* attribute refers only to the text within the tag in which it is applied. For example, you could use foreground and background color selections to create reverse text (set white text on a dark background). To do this, in the style sheet, use the *background-color* attribute, such as the following:

```
p {background-color: yellow}
```

Or, for an individual instance:

```
<p style="background-color: yellow">This text has a yellow background.</p>
```

In the following exercise, you will assign a font size to certain tags in the external style sheet. You will also set a background color and a text color for a class.

Specify a Font and Color

1. Open *default.css* in Notepad and then open *index.htm* in Internet Explorer from the files located in the *Documents\Microsoft Press\HTML5 Start Here\07Text\SelectingSize* folder.

2. In *default.css*, change the style rule for the *<p>* and *<li>* tags so they include a font size of *13px*:

   ```
   p, li {font-family: "Verdana", "Arial", "Helvetica", sans-serif; font-size:
   13px}
   ```

Note Don't forget to add the semicolon after *sans-serif* to separate the *font-family* rule from the *font-size* rule.

3. Change the style rule for the *copyright* class to make the text white:

```
.copyright {font-family: "Times New Roman", "Times", serif; color: white}
```

4. Change the style rule for the *copyright* class to make the background blue:

```
.copyright {font-family: "Times New Roman", "Times", serif; color: white;
background-color: blue}
```

Add a font size

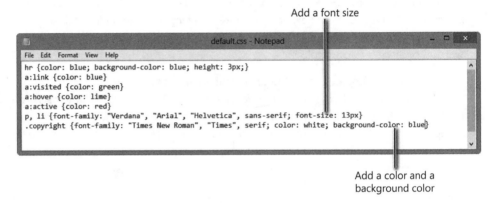

Add a color and a
background color

5. Save the file and then refresh Internet Explorer.

Notice that because the background color is the same color as the unvisited hyperlink color, the *Contact the Webmaster* hyperlink is no longer visible at the bottom of the page. (If you have already visited this hyperlink on your PC, the hyperlink might display as green instead of being invisible.) This occurs because the *a:link* style rule, which specifies the text should be blue, has a higher priority than the *<p>* tag in the style sheet, which specifies that text should be white. To force the hyperlink to be white, you must enter a style in an internal style sheet for the document (that is, a style sheet created in the *<head>* section of the page, as you learned in Chapter 6), or create an attribute for the individual instance's tag. Both have a higher priority than an external style sheet, so they will force the text to be white.

Hyperlink not visible

6. In *index.htm*, in the *<a>* tag for the *mailto* hyperlink at the bottom of the file, add a *style=* attribute that forces the hyperlink to be white:

```
<a href="mailto:webmaster@margiestravel.com" style="color: white">Contact the
Webmaster</a></p>
```

7. Save the file and then refresh Internet Explorer.

Copyright © Margie's Travel
No material may be reproduced without written permission
Contact the Webmaster

Applying Bold and Italics

You learned how to apply bold and italic formatting by using the *<b>* and *<i>* tags in Part I of this book. You can continue to use those tags to format individual words and phrases, but you can't use them in internal or external style sheets.

To include boldface in a style, use the *font-weight* attribute. For example, you might create a class called *boldface* in your style sheet:

```
.boldface {font-weight: bold}
```

You can apply boldface to a particular tag in a style sheet. For example, you can make all *<p>* paragraphs boldface:

```
p {font-weight: bold}
```

You can also apply boldface by using a *style=* attribute in an individual paragraph:

```
<p style="font-weight: bold">This text is bold.</p>
```

One of the advantages of using a style for bold formatting (instead of the *<b>* tag) is that you can control the intensity of the effect. You can specify *bolder*, *lighter*, or a numeric value from 100 (the lightest) to 900 (the darkest) to indicate the amount of bold formatting. However, the differences in the effects are noticeable only when using a font that supports multiple levels of boldface. Because most fonts have only two weights (normal and bold), not all the numeric values necessarily render differently. For most fonts, weights 100 through 500 render generically as normal text and weights 600 through 900 render as bold.

To apply italic formatting, use the *font-style* attribute. The font style can be normal (not italic), *italic*, or *oblique*. Oblique is also called "false italics" because it is a right-tilted version of normal (non-italic) text. Some fonts have a separate set of characters for italic, so there is a difference between oblique and italic; for fonts that do not, there is no difference. Most people prefer to use italic.

You can apply italic formatting in a style rule for paragraphs:

```
p {font-style: italic}
```

This rule would make all the *<p>* text within the document italicized. If you then wanted make a certain paragraph display without italic formatting, you might include a style tag in that paragraph's *<p>* tag:

```
<p style="font-style: normal">This paragraph is not italicized.</p>
```

In the following exercise, you will apply bold and italic styles to ordered and unordered lists.

Apply Bold and Italic with Styles

1. Open *default.css* in Notepad and then open *international.htm* in Internet Explorer from the files located in the *Documents\Microsoft Press\HTML5 Start Here\07Text\ApplyingBold* folder.

2. In *default.css*, add italic formatting to the definition of an unordered list:

   ```
   ul {font-style: italic}
   ```

3. Save the file and then refresh Internet Explorer.

4. In *default.css*, add bold formatting to the definition of an ordered list:

   ```
   ol {font-weight: bold}
   ```

5. Save the file and then refresh Internet Explorer.

   The entire list is now bold. The unordered lists are bold, too, because they are subordinate to the ordered list.

   1. **Call 1-800-555-1191 to register for your tour. Our expert tour advisors will let you know what you need to do to prepare for your trip.**
   2. **Four to six months before your trip:**
      - *Apply for a passport if you do not already have one.*
      - *Make sure you have the required immunizations for travel to your destination.*
   3. **One month before your trip:**
      - *Review your travel documents, including airline tickets, to make sure there are no errors*
      - *Make sure that you have a valid government-issued ID in addition to your passport, such as a driver's license*
      - *Check your wardrobe, and buy any additional travel clothes needed. Keep in mind that we may be travelling through multiple climates.*

6. Add a *font-weight:* style of *normal* to the style for unordered lists, so that the unordered list items will not inherit the bold weight from the ordered list:

   ```
   ul {font-style: italic; font-weight: normal}
   ```

7. Save the file and then refresh Internet Explorer.

   The unordered list items are no longer bold, but the ordered list items still are.

   Margie's Travel can take you to some of the world's most fascinating and exotic destinations. Here are some tips for making sure you are ready to travel beyond the United States:

   1. **Call 1-800-555-1191 to register for your tour. Our expert tour advisors will let you know what you need to do to prepare for your trip.**
   2. **Four to six months before your trip:**
      - *Apply for a passport if you do not already have one.*
      - *Make sure you have the required immunizations for travel to your destination.*
   3. **One month before your trip:**
      - *Review your travel documents, including airline tickets, to make sure there are no errors*
      - *Make sure that you have a valid government-issued ID in addition to your passport, such as a driver's license*
      - *Check your wardrobe, and buy any additional travel clothes needed. Keep in mind that we may be travelling through multiple climates.*

8. Close Notepad and Internet Explorer.

Applying Strikethrough and Underlining

Strikethrough formatting is typically used to denote text that has changed. For example, if you have marked down the price of an item, you might strike through the original price (see Figure 7-3).

List price: ~~$24.00~~ <u>Now only $9.99</u>

FIGURE 7-3 An example of strikethrough and underlined text.

Most web designers don't use underlining as a formatting technique because hyperlinks are underlined, and it is considered poor design to confuse your users with text that looks "clickable" but is not. In the example shown in Figure 7-3, you might think that the text *Now only $9.99* is a hyperlink, but it's not; it's just underlined.

If you simply want to underline or strike through a few words of text in one specific instance that probably won't recur elsewhere on your page (or site), it's easiest to use the *<ins>* tag for underlining or the *<del>* tag for strikethrough. These tag names come from the logical functions that underlining and strikethrough often serve in an edited document; insertions are commonly underlined and deletions are commonly struck through. Here's the code for the preceding example:

```
<p>List price: <del>$24.00</del> <ins>Now only $9.99</ins></p>
```

Note In early HTML versions, there was a *<strike>* or *<s>* tag for strikethrough and a *<u>* tag for underlining, but both were deprecated in HTML 4 and removed completely in HTML5. The *<ins>* and *<del>* tags will probably become deprecated at some point, but for now they are still in use.

To strike through or underline text by using a style (a more modern and "correct" method, although it requires a little more typing), use the *text-decoration* attribute. This attribute accepts several keywords:

- *underline*
- *overline* (line over the text)
- *line-through* (strikethrough)
- *blink* (flashing text)
- *none* (removes all inherited decoration)

Caution If at all possible, do not use blinking text. It is quite annoying. Visitors to your site will probably dislike it so much that they will leave your site and never return. It can also, in rare cases, cause some people with epilepsy to have a seizure.

You can use the *none* keyword to remove the underlining from text that would ordinarily be underlined automatically, such as a hyperlink. Be careful, though, because if you remove the underline from a hyperlink, many people will not realize they can click it. Here are some examples applied to individual paragraphs:

```
<p style="text-decoration: underline">This looks clickable, but isn't.</p>
<p style="text-decoration: line-through">This is struck-through.</p>
<p style="text-decoration: blink">Congratulations, you win!</p>
```

Here's an example of underlining applied within a style sheet to a class called *underlined*:

```
.underlined {text-decoration: underline}
```

In the following exercise, you will remove the underlining from a hyperlink and make some text strikethrough.

Apply Underlining and Strikethrough

1. Open *canyon.htm* in Notepad and also in Internet Explorer from the files located in the *Documents\Microsoft Press\HTML5 Start Here\07Text\ApplyingStrike* folder.

2. In the *<a>* tag for the *Contact the Webmaster* hyperlink at the bottom of the document, add a *text-decoration* attribute that removes the underline:

   ```
   <p><a href="mailto:webmaster@margiestravel.com?subject=Question/Comment"
   title="webmaster@margiestravel.com" style="text-decoration:none">Contact the
   Webmaster</a></p>
   ```

3. Save the file and then refresh Internet Explorer.

   The hyperlink is no longer underlined, but you can still point at it to see its ScreenTip, indicating it is still a live hyperlink.

4. In the price of the first tour (*$399*), use the *<del>* tag to strike through the price, and then insert *Now only $299* in boldface following it. (Use the *<b>* tag for the boldface.)

   ```
   <p><del>$399</del> <b>Now only $299</b> </p>
   ```

5. Repeat step 4 for the other two tour prices, reducing each price by $100.

6. Save the file and then refresh Internet Explorer.

Grand Canyon Indian Country West Rim Bus Tour

~~$299~~ **Now only $199**

After enjoying a morning snack at your hotel, you'll board a comfortable air-conditioned tour bus. The drive to the Grand Canyon will take you over the Hoover Dam Bypass Bridge and into the state of Arizona. Make sure you have your camera ready for pictures of the dam, Lake Mead, and the mighty Colorado River. Be on the lookout for Fortification Hill (built during World War II to protect the Dam) and the bighorn sheep that make this area their habitat.

7. Close Notepad and Internet Explorer.

Creating Inline Spans

Part of the problem with replacing the old style tags like *<b>*, *<i>*, and *<del>* with styles for individual items is that the *style=* attribute must be placed within an existing tag. For example, in the following sentence, how would you avoid using *<b>* to make only one word bold?

```
<p>I had a <b>great</b> time.</p>
```

The word *great* does not have any container tags surrounding it, so there's no place to put a *style=* attribute. The solution is to use an *inline span*. A span is simply a shell into which you can place any attributes you need. For example, the preceding example could be written as follows to use a style:

```
<p>I had a <span style="text-weight: bold">great</span> time.</p>
```

That's a lot of typing, but there's a good reason for it. By using a span, you can apply a class, and by applying a class, you can create consistency. For example, suppose you know that you want to make new vocabulary words stand out somehow, but you haven't yet decided whether you want to make them bold, italicized, or both. You can create a class called *vocabulary* and apply that class to each vocabulary word:

```
<span class="vocabulary">passport</span>
```

Then in your style sheet, you can define the class with the formatting you want. Suppose, for example, that you decide to make vocabulary words italicized. Simply create a style that defines *vocabulary* as italic:

```
.vocabulary {font-style: italic}
```

If you later change your mind, you need to make the change in only one place—the style sheet.

In the following exercise, you will format text by using inline spans.

Format Text with Inline Spans

1. Open *partners.htm* in Notepad and also in Internet Explorer from the files located in the *Documents\Microsoft Press\HTML5 Start Here\07Text\Creatingspan* folder.

2. Create a span around the company name in each of the list items, and then assign a class called *partner* to each one:

```
<ul>
<li><span class="partner">Silver Star Properties: </span>Luxury Condos and
Vacation Rentals in sunny Florida</li>
<li><span class="partner">Ocean Liner Vacations: </span>Caribbean and Mexican
Riviera cruises</li>
<li><span class="partner">Bright Lights Limited: </span>Deluxe accommodations
on the Las Vegas Strip</li>
<li><span class="partner">Peace Acres: </span>Family farm adventures in
America's heartland</li>
</ul>
```

Tip To save time, use the Clipboard to copy and paste the opening and closing *<span>* tags. They are identical for each entry.

3. In the *<head>* section of the document, create a two-sided *<style>* tag, and then in that tag, create a *partner* class that is bold, italic, and red:

```
<style>
.partner {font-style: normal; font-weight: bold; color: red}
</style>
```

Note In the previous example, the space following the colon in each property name is in-cluded within the span. The space could have gone outside of the span instead. If the class applied to the span specifies a very different font size than the font size used outside the span, the placement of the space inside versus the placement of the space outside could make a difference in how the text displays on the screen; in this exercise's example, it makes no difference.

4. Save the file and then refresh Internet Explorer.

5. Close Notepad and Internet Explorer.

> **Note** You could have placed the partner class in *default.css* instead. That would be a good idea if you thought this class would be reused on other pages that also use the same style sheet. In this case, however, the partner class is applicable only to this particular webpage.

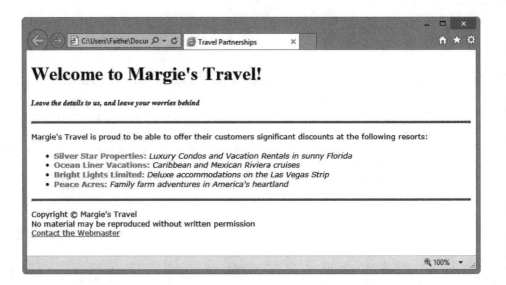

Adjusting Spacing between Letters

In many desktop-publishing applications, you can fine-tune the spacing between letters to subtly change the appearance of a paragraph. Thanks to styles, you can do the same thing in HTML.

There are two types of spacing you can control in HTML: word spacing and letter spacing. *Word spacing* controls the amount of space between each word and *letter spacing* controls the amount of space between each letter. The default is 0 for each; positive numbers increase the space and negative numbers decrease it. Usually, one or two pixels in either direction are plenty (see Figure 7-14).

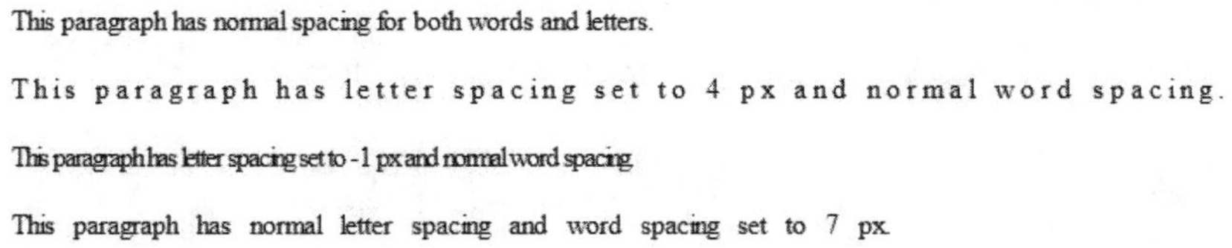

This paragraph has normal spacing for both words and letters.

This paragraph has letter spacing set to 4 px and normal word spacing.

This paragraph has letter spacing set to -1 px and normal word spacing.

This   paragraph   has   normal   letter   spacing   and   word   spacing   set   to   7   px.

FIGURE 7-4 Examples of different spacing options.

To apply word and/or letter spacing, add spacing to the *style=* attribute for a specific tag:

```
<p style="letter-spacing: 4px">This text has increased letter spacing.</p>
```

You can also add spacing to a style rule in the style sheet:

```
p {letter-spacing: 4px}
```

In the following exercise, you will increase the word and letter spacing for all paragraphs and headings in a document.

Change Word and Letter Spacing

1. Open *canyon.htm* in Notepad and also in Internet Explorer from the files located in the *Documents\Microsoft Press\HTML5 Start Here\07Text\ChangingSpacing* folder.

2. Examine the document in Internet Explorer. Note the overall look and the spacing between words and letters.

3. In the *<head>* section, create the following *<style>* section:

```
<style>
h1, h2, p {word-spacing: 1px; letter-spacing: 1px}
</style>
```

4. Save the file and then refresh Internet Explorer.

Notice the spacing difference. It's not very attractive, but it's different.

5. Edit the embedded style sheet to decrease the line spacing and word spacing to *0.5px*:

h1, h2, p {word-spacing: **0.5px**; letter-spacing: **0.5px**}

6. Save the file and then refresh Internet Explorer.

Now it looks more attractive and is more consistent with the rest of the pages for this website.

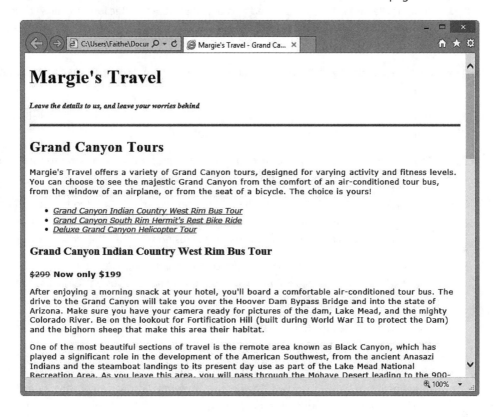

Key Points

- Font families are sets of fonts, listed in order of preference. Because not all web visitors have the same fonts installed on their computers, you should use the *font-family* attribute to help ensure that your website appears the way you want.

- Font size is typically measured in pixels (px) for onscreen display. To specify size, use the *font-size* attribute.

- You can define font color by using any color description method, including RGB, hexadecimal, and color names. Use the *color* attribute to define font color.

- To set the background color for text, use the *background-color* attribute. To set the background color for a paragraph, insert a *style=* attribute in the *<p>* tag.

- You can still use the *<b>* tag to apply bold formatting and the *<i>* tag to apply italic formatting. In style sheets, you can also apply bold formatting by using the *font-weight: bold* attribute and you can apply italic formatting by using the *font-style: italic* attribute.

- For individual instances of strikethrough formatting, use the *<del>* tag; for individual instances of underlining, use the *<ins>* tag. To apply this formatting by using styles, use *font-decoration: line-through* and *font-decoration: underline*.

- Inline spans create tags that serve as containers for attributes. Use the *<span>* tag to surround any amount of text to be marked in some way.

- Use the *word-spacing* attribute to define an amount of space between words. Use *letter-spacing* to define space between letters. The default amount is 0; specify a positive number to increase spacing or a negative number to decrease it.

Chapter 8

Formatting Paragraphs with CSS

In this chapter, you will:

- Indent paragraphs

- Apply a border to a paragraph

- Specify the horizontal alignment of a paragraph

- Specify vertical space within a paragraph

In Chapter 7, "Formatting Text with CSS," you learned how to use style rules to apply character formatting, including font style, size, and color. Now you can go a step further and apply those concepts to paragraph formatting.

Paragraph formatting refers to the layout of entire paragraphs, not the placement or spacing of individual characters. For example, a paragraph can be double-spaced, but an individual character cannot be double-spaced. You saw some style-based paragraph formatting in Chapter 4, "Using Lists and Backgrounds," when you applied bullet characters and numbering styles. Later, in Chapter 6, "Introduction to Style Sheets," you worked with several ordered and unordered list items. The same principles apply when formatting other types of paragraphs.

In this chapter, you'll learn how to control indentation and spacing around a paragraph and how to specify a paragraph's alignment. You'll also learn how to set the line height for a paragraph (that is, the space between lines of text) and how to place and format a border around a paragraph.

Important Before you can use the practice files provided for this chapter, you need to install them from the book's companion content page to their default locations. See "Code Samples" in the beginning of this book for more information.

Indenting Paragraphs

You can indent any paragraph-level element in HTML. Such elements include regular paragraphs, list items, definitions, quotations, and headings. *Indenting* is the process of offsetting text from its usual position, either to the right or to the left. You can apply three types of indentation in HTML:

- **First-line indent**   This indents only the first line of a paragraph. Use the *text-indent* attribute. For in-line styling of a single paragraph, specify this style:

  ```
  <p style="text-indent: 20px">
  ```

  In a style sheet, specify a rule similar to this:

  ```
  p {text-indent: 20px}
  ```

- **Padding**   This adds a specified amount of space between the border of an element and its contents (*inside* of the element). It applies equally to all lines of text in the paragraph. Use the *padding* attribute to create this space. For in-line styling of a single paragraph, specify this style:

  ```
  <p style="padding: 20px">
  ```

  In a style sheet, specify a rule like this:

  ```
  p {padding: 20px}
  ```

- **Margin**   This adds a specified amount of white space around an element, on the *outside* of the element. It applies equally to all lines of text in the paragraph. Use the *margin* attribute to create this space. For a single paragraph, specify this style:

  ```
  <p style="margin: 20px">
  ```

  In a style sheet, specify the following rule:

  ```
  p {margin: 20px}
  ```

The difference between applying the *padding* attribute and the *margin* attribute is most apparent when the paragraph has a visible border or when the paragraph's background contrasts with the surrounding area. You'll learn how to apply borders later in this chapter, but Figure 8-1 shows a quick comparison. Margins add space outside the border. In contrast, padding adds space between the text and the border.

Margins: space outside the border

> Margie's Travel offers a variety of Grand Canyon tours, designed for varying activity and fitness levels. You can choose to see the majestic Grand Canyon from the comfort of an air-conditioned tour bus, from the window of an airplane, or from the seat of a bicycle. The choice is yours!

Padding: space inside the border

FIGURE 8-1 Margins vs. padding.

By default *margin* and *padding* attributes apply to all four sides of an element, but you can add *-top*, *-right*, *-bottom*, or *-left* arguments to restrict the formatting to one or more specific sides:

```
p style="padding-left: 10px; padding-top: 5px; padding-bottom: 5px}
```

You can use either pixels (*px*) or percentage (%) as the unit of measure. For example, the following line indents the first line of a paragraph by 10 percent of its total width:

```
<p style="text-indent: 10%">
```

To apply the same formatting using a style sheet, specify the following rule:

```
p {text-indent: 10%}
```

In the following exercise, you will indent the first line of each paragraph in an article and add padding to the left and right sides of all paragraphs. Then you will create a CSS class that removes the first-line indent and applies that class style to some individual paragraphs.

Apply Paragraph Indentation and Padding

1. In Notepad and Internet Explorer, open the *mexico.htm* file located in the *Documents\Microsoft Press\HTML5 Start Here\08Paragraphs\CreatingIndents* folder.

2. In the *<style>* area, create a style for the *<p>* tag that inserts 20 pixels of padding at the left and indents the first line by 20 pixels:

   ```
   p {padding-left: 20px; text-indent: 20px}
   ```

3. Also in the *<style>* area, create a new class called *first*. Define it as having no first-line indent:

   ```
   .first {text-indent: 0px}
   ```

4. Apply the new class to the first *<p>* paragraph beneath each of the daily headings:

```
<h3>Day One: Tour of Chichén Itzá </h3>
<p class="first">Chichén Itzá, home of the mysterious temples and pyramids of
the Mayan<h1>Spraying...
. . .
<h3>Day Two: Xalapa</h3>
<p class="first">Xalapa or Jalapa is the capital city of the Mexican state of
Veracruz.
. . .
<h3>Day Three: Tajin </h3>
<p class="first">Tajin is located in Veracruz. Tajin is one of the most
outstanding
. . .
<h3>Day Four: Valle de Bravo </h3>
<p class="first">Valle de Bravo is a municipality in Mexico State located on
the shore of
. . .
<h3>Day Five: Cantona Archeological site </h3>
<p class="first">The Cantona archeological site, located west of Jalapa
(within Puebla)
```

5. Save the file and then refresh Internet Explorer. Each section now begins with an unindented paragraph, with subsequent paragraphs indented.

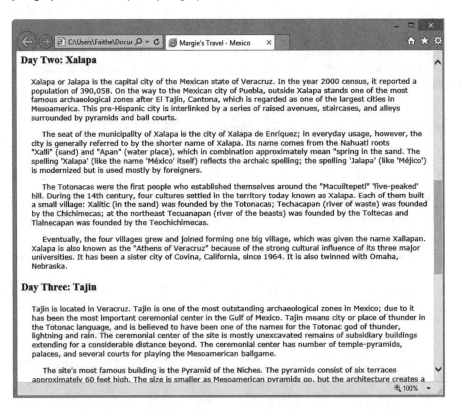

6. Scroll to the bottom of the page and view the copyright notice.

Copyright © Margie's Travel
No material may be reproduced without written permission

It is indented like other paragraphs, but you don't want it to be. This is an excellent example of an unintended consequence stemming from making a global change to a tag's style rules. There are several ways of removing the unwanted indentation: you could create a new class for the single line you don't want indented; you could create a span; or you could override that line's settings in its *<p>* tag. Because this situation occurs only once in the document, use the third option—change the *<p>* tag directly.

7. In the <p> tag for the copyright notice, add the following:

```
<p style="text-indent:0; padding:0">Copyright &copy; Margie's Travel<br>
```

8. Save the file and then refresh Internet Explorer.

The copyright notice now has no indentation or padding.

Copyright © Margie's Travel
No material may be reproduced without written permission

9. Close Notepad and Internet Explorer.

Applying a Border to a Paragraph

You can apply a border style rule to almost any two-sided tag. Border style rules are used most commonly with regular paragraphs, but they also work with headings, lists, and even spans. You can also apply a border to a division (*<div>*) tag to differentiate one area of the screen from another, as you will see in Chapter 11, "Creating Division-Based Layouts."

Specifying a Border Style

To select the line type for the border, use the *border-style* attribute along with one of the attributes listed in Table 8-1.

TABLE 8-1 Border style examples

Attribute	Example
solid	
dotted	
dashed	
double	
groove	
ridge	
inset	
outset	
none	

To apply a border style to an individual instance of a tag, use the following:

```
<p style="border-style: solid">
```

To apply the same formatting using a style sheet, specify the following rule:

```
p {border-style: solid}
```

Setting Border Padding

A border encloses the element very tightly by default. You will usually want to add a little more spacing. Create the spacing using the *padding* attribute. To apply padding using a style sheet, include a *padding* attribute:

```
p {border-style: solid; padding: 15px}
```

To apply the same formatting to an individual instance of a tag, include the *padding* attribute in the style at the individual tag level:

```
<p style="border-style: solid; padding: 15px">
```

Specifying Border Width and Color

By default, a border is black and 4 pixels wide. To change these attributes, use the *border-color* and *border-width* attributes. The color can be any basic or extended color name or any RGB or hexadecimal color number. (See the discussion of color choices in Chapter 4 if you need to review the color options in HTML.) For example, to decrease the border width and to color it blue using a style sheet, write a style rule:

```
p {border-style: solid; border-width: 2px; border-color: blue}
```

To apply the same formatting to an individual instance of a tag:

```
<p style="border-style: solid; border-width: 2px; border-color: blue">
```

> **Note** The default border style is *none*—and that doesn't change just because you specify a border width and color. Remember that when your border doesn't show up because you forgot to include the *border-style* attribute in addition to specifying the border's color and width.

Formatting Border Sides Individually

By default, border attributes apply to all four sides of the border unless you specify otherwise. To specify that a certain side of the border has special formatting, include the *-top, -right, -left,* or *-bottom* attribute between the word *border* and the property being set. For example, to set a color other than black for the top border using a style sheet:

```
p {border-style: solid; border-top-color: blue}
```

To apply the same formatting to an individual instance of a tag:

```
<p style="border-style: solid; border-top-color: blue">
```

You can use this technique not only with *border-color,* but with *style, padding,* and *width* attributes as well. For example, the following rule applies a dotted line and 15 pixels of padding to only the top and bottom of a paragraph:

```
<p style="border-top-style: dotted; border-bottom-style: dotted; padding-top: 15px;
padding-bottom: 15px">
```

Figure 8-2 shows the rendered paragraph.

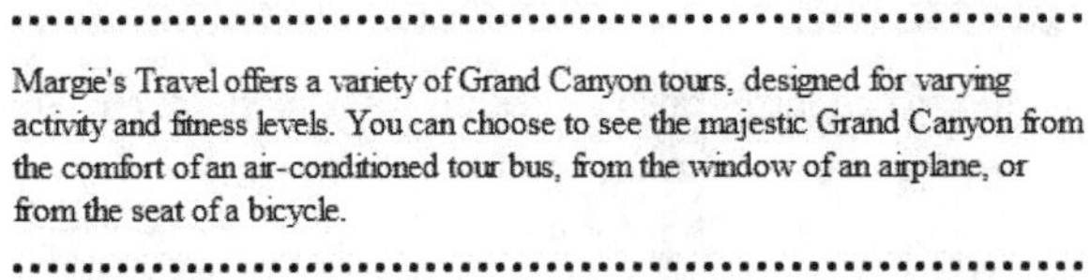

Margie's Travel offers a variety of Grand Canyon tours, designed for varying
activity and fitness levels. You can choose to see the majestic Grand Canyon from
the comfort of an air-conditioned tour bus, from the window of an airplane, or
from the seat of a bicycle.

FIGURE 8-2   This paragraph has a dotted border on the top and bottom only.

There's a shortcut for specifying arguments for each side of the border. Rather than writing each
one out individually, you can simply include four different settings for the argument. Specify them in
clockwise order, starting at the top: *top*, *right*, *bottom*, *left*. Using this method, the example you just
saw could be written like this:

```
<p style="border-style: dotted none dotted none; padding: 15px 0px 15px 0px">
```

Specifying fewer than four arguments applies the formatting differently. Specifying two arguments
sets the top and bottom border attributes, while specifying three arguments sets the top, bottom,
and left/right (same settings for both) border attributes.

Setting All Border Attributes at Once

A similar shortcut lets you specify border attributes for all four sides at once. Use the *border* attribute
and then specify all the settings together in the following order: *size*, *color*, *style*.

```
<p style="border: 2px green solid">
```

You can use the single *border* attribute when all sides are the same, but you cannot combine it with
individual border-formatting attributes. For example, the following would *not* work:

```
<p style="border: 2px green dotted none dotted none">
```

In the following exercise, you will add top and bottom borders to a paragraph.

Format Paragraph Borders

1. In Notepad and Internet Explorer, open the *mexico.htm* file located in the
   Documents\Microsoft Press\HTML5 Start Here\08Paragraphs\FormattingBorders folder.

2. Locate the following paragraph, near the beginning of the document:

```
<p>Ready to book this tour? Call 1-800-555-1191</p>
```

3. Add dotted top and bottom borders to the paragraph:

```
<p style="border-top-style: dotted; border-bottom-style: dotted">Ready to book
this tour? Call 1-800-555-1191</p>
```

4. Save the file and then refresh Internet Explorer.

The paragraph has a first-line indent (which we don't want) and the border is unattractively close to the top and bottom of the paragraph text.

Mexico Travel Diary

```
..................................................................................................
      Ready to book this tour? Call 1-800-555-1191
..................................................................................................
```

5. Add five pixels (5px) of padding to the top and bottom of the border and remove the first-line indent from the paragraph:

```
<p style="border-top-style: dotted; border-bottom-style: dotted; padding-
top: 5px; padding-bottom: 5px; text-indent: 0">Ready to book this tour? Call
1-800-555-1191</p>
```

6. Change the width of the border to 6px (six pixels) and set its color to green:

```
<p style="border-top-style: dotted; border-bottom-style: dotted; padding-top:
5px; padding-bottom: 5px; text-indent: 0; border-width: 6px; border-color:
green ">Ready to book this tour? Call 1-800-555-1191</p>
```

7. Save the file and then refresh Internet Explorer.

Mexico Travel Diary

```
• • • • • • • • • • • • • • • • • • • • • • • • • • • • • • • • • • • • • • • • • • • • • • • • •
      Ready to book this tour? Call 1-800-555-1191
• • • • • • • • • • • • • • • • • • • • • • • • • • • • • • • • • • • • • • • • • • • • • • • • •
```

8. Rewrite the border specification to be as concise as possible:

```
<p style="border: 6px green; border-style: dotted none dotted none; padding:
5px 0px 5px 20px; text-indent: 0">Ready to book this tour? Call 1-800-555-
1191</p>
```

Note Sharp-eyed students may have noticed in the above code that I included a 20px left-side padding value. Why? Because this document has an internal style sheet that specifies 20px of padding for *<p>* paragraphs, that same 20px had carried over when we wrote the code in step 6 because we did not specifically countermand it. However, in the rewrite in step 8, we specifically indicate an amount of left-side padding, which overrides the internal style sheet. To avoid having the left side padding changed, we must override it with the same value that is being overridden: *20px..*

9. Save the file and then refresh Internet Explorer. Even though the HTML code changed, the screen should look the same.

10. Close Notepad and Internet Explorer.

Specifying the Horizontal Alignment of a Paragraph

Alignment refers to the placement of a paragraph within its container. You can specify horizontal alignment in a style using the *text-align* attribute. You can apply alignment only to block-level elements, such as paragraphs, list items, headings, and so on. (A *block-level element* is one that occupies a complete paragraph or more.) The default alignment setting is *left*; the other choices are *center*, *right*, and *justify*, as shown in Figure 8-3.

This paragraph is left-aligned. The edges align neatly at the left, and the right edge is ragged. This paragraph is left-aligned. The edges align neatly at the left, and the right edge is ragged.

This paragraph is centered. The midpoints of each line are centered on the page, with ragged edges at left and right. This paragraph is centered. The midpoints of each line are centered on the page, with ragged edges at left and right.

This paragraph is right-aligned. The edges align neatly at the right, and the left edge is ragged. This paragraph is right-aligned. The edges align neatly at the right, and the left edge is ragged.

This paragraph is justified. The edges align neatly at both the left and right, and extra space is inserted between words to make that happen. This paragraph is justified. The edges align neatly at both the left and right, and extra space is inserted between words to make that happen.

FIGURE 8-3 Examples of horizontal alignment.

To make a single instance aligned differently from the norm (left), insert a *text-align* style in the opening tag:

```
<p style="text-align: justify">
```

To apply the same alignment to all instances of that tag, place it in the style sheet, either within the document (in the *<style>* area) or in a separate CSS file:

```
p {text-align: justify}
```

Notice that the *justify* option aligns all lines of the paragraph (except the last one) at both the right and left. The last line of a justified paragraph is always left-aligned. Justified text can sometimes result in awkwardly spaced lines, especially when the text column is fairly narrow (see Figure 8-4).

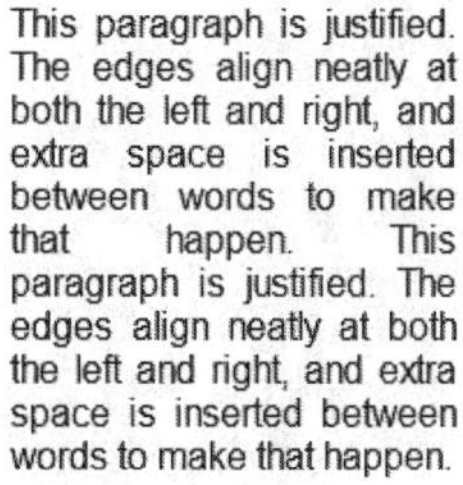

This paragraph is justified. The edges align neatly at both the left and right, and extra space is inserted between words to make that happen. This paragraph is justified. The edges align neatly at both the left and right, and extra space is inserted between words to make that happen.

FIGURE 8-4 When a narrow paragraph is justified, unattractive extra spaces between words might appear.

On a full-size webpage, justified paragraphs should not be a problem, because there is enough text to ensure even spacing. However, when you start working with table-based or division-based page layouts (such as those presented in Part III of this book) you might have some narrow columns of text like the one in the previous example. Avoid using justified alignment for text in narrow columns whenever possible.

In the following exercise, you will change the horizontal alignment of certain elements by editing the embedded style sheet.

Change Horizontal Alignment

1. In Notepad and Internet Explorer, open the *mexico.htm* file located in the *Documents\Microsoft Press\HTML5 Start Here\08Paragraphs\ChangingAlignment* folder.

2. In Notepad, in the *<style>* area, create the following style rule:

    ```
    h1, h2, h3, h4, h5 {text-align: center}
    ```

3. Save the file and then refresh Internet Explorer.

4. Change the style definition for the *<p>* tag to use justified alignment:

    ```
    p {padding-left: 20px; text-indent: 20px; text-indent: 20px; text-align: justify}
    ```

5. Save the file and then refresh Internet Explorer.

The text between the green dotted lines would also look better centered, but you don't want to create a style rule for the entire <p> tag for this. Instead you'll add the style to the individual tag for that paragraph.

6. Change the <p> tag's style for the paragraph with the greed dotted top and bottom border so the text is centered:

```
<p style="border: 6px green; border-style: dotted none dotted none; padding: 5px 0px 5px 20px; text-indent: 0; text-align: center">Ready to book this tour? Call 1-800-555-1191</p>
```

• •
Ready to book this tour? Call 1-800-555-1191
• •

7. Save the file and then refresh Internet Explorer.

8. Close Notepad and Internet Explorer.

Specifying Vertical Space within a Paragraph

The line height is the amount of space between each line. This is also referred to as *leading* (pronounced like the metal). You can use this setting to make paragraphs easier to read. You are not limited to just single-spacing or double-spacing like on a typewriter; you can specify any amount of space you like.

You can express line height either as a number or as a percentage. If you use a number, it's a fixed measurement (usually in pixels). If you later increase or decrease the font size, the line height will not change. If you use a percentage, the browser multiplies the line height percentage by the font size to derive a spacing amount. For example, you can specify 200 percent to make a paragraph double-spaced. If you later change the font size, the line height will be recalculated using the new font size. To specify the line height in a style sheet, set the *line-height* attribute, as follows:

```
p {line-height: 150%}
```

To specify the same formatting in an individual tag, use the following:

```
<p style="line-height: 150%">
```

In the following exercise, you will change the line height of certain elements by editing the embedded style sheet.

Change Vertical Spacing

1. In Notepad and Internet Explorer, open the *mexico.htm* file located in the *Documents\Microsoft Press\HTML5 Start Here\08Paragraphs\ChangingVertical* folder.

2. In the *<style>* area, modify the style rule for the *<p>* tag by setting the line height to *150%*:

    ```
    p {padding-left: 20px; text-indent: 20px; text-align:justify; line-height: 150%}
    ```

3. Create a style rule for *<h3>* headings that sets the line height to *125%*:

    ```
    h3 {line-height: 125%}
    ```

4. Save the file and then refresh Internet Explorer.

Margie's Travel

Leave the details to us, and leave your worries behind

Mexico Travel Diary

• •

Ready to book this tour? Call 1-800-555-1191

• •

Day One: Tour of Chichén Itzá

Chichén Itzá, home of the mysterious temples and pyramids of the Mayan people, is located within the jungles of Mexico and Guatemala. The ancient city, whose name means "in the mouth at the Itzáe's Well," was, in its time of grandeur (between 800 and 1200 A.D.), the center of political, religious, and military power in Yucatán, if not all of South-eastern Mesoamerica.

When Europe was still in the Dark Ages, the Maya had already created the only true writing system native to the Americas and were masters of mathematics. They invented the calendars we use today. Without metal tools or wheels, they were able to construct cities across a huge jungle landscape with an amazing degree of architectural perfection and variety. Their legacy in stone, which has survived in a spectacular fashion at places such as Palenque, Tikal, Tulum, Chichén Itzá, Copan, and Uxmal, lives on, as do the seven million descendants of the classic Mayan civilization. The Maya are probably the best known of the classical civilizations of Mesoamerica. They were also skilled farmers, clearing large sections of tropical rain forest and, where groundwater was scarce, building sizable underground reservoirs for the storage of rainwater. The Maya were equally skilled as weavers

🔍 100% ▾

5. Close Notepad and Internet Explorer.

Key Points

- You can indent the first line of paragraphs using the *text-indent* attribute.

- The *padding* attribute sets the amount of space between an element and its border; the *margin* attribute sets the amount of space around the outside of an element.

- The *border-style* attribute places a border around a paragraph. To specify the appearance of the border, use one of the following arguments: *solid*, *dotted*, *dashed*, *double*, *groove*, *ridge*, *inset*, *outset*, or *none*.

- To set the width of a border, use the *border-width* attribute followed by the width in pixels (*px*).

- To set the color of a border, use the *border-color* attribute followed by the color name or the RGB or hexadecimal notation for the color.

- To format each side of a border individually, specify four arguments, in clockwise order from the top: *top*, *right*, *bottom*, *left*. For example, *border-style: solid none solid bottom*.

- To specify the style, color, and size of a border in a single command, use the *border* attribute and specify the arguments in this order: *size, color, style*. For example, *border: 2px green dotted*.

- To set paragraph alignment, use the *text-align* attribute with one of these arguments: *left*, *center*, *right*, or *justify*.

- To set the line height, use the *line-height* attribute followed by the height expressed in pixels or as a percentage of the font height.

Chapter 9

Inserting Graphics

In this chapter, you will:

- Insert graphics

- Arrange elements on the page

- Control image size and padding

- Hyperlink from graphics

- Utilize thumbnail graphics

- Include alternate text for graphics

- Add figure captions

So far in this book, you have created text-only webpages. They're perfectly functional, but a bit dull. Webpages are more interesting and attractive when they include graphics.

> **Note** Graphic or image? The HTML5 specification uses the term *image*, but the term *graphic* is more popular in everyday usage. This book uses the two terms interchangeably.

In a word-processing program such as Microsoft Word, you embed graphics directly into the document. When you distribute a document to others, the graphics are included with the file. In HTML, however, each graphic displayed on a webpage is stored in a separate file and this file must reside on the web server or somewhere the web server can reach it.

In this chapter, you'll learn how to include images on a webpage and how to format and size the images. You will learn how to hyperlink from a graphic and how to create thumbnail images. You'll learn how to create alternate text that will appear if the graphic cannot load. Finally, you'll learn how to use the new HTML5 *<figure>* and *<figurecaption>* tags.

Important Before you can use the practice files provided for this chapter, you need to install them from the book's companion content page to their default locations. See "Code Samples" in the beginning of this book for more information.

Understanding Graphic Size and Resolution

A graphic image's *resolution* is the number of unique dots, or *pixels*, it contains. Resolution is expressed in width and height, always in that order. For example, an image that is 800 × 600 is 800 pixels wide and 600 pixels tall.

A graphic's *file size*—how many bytes the file will take up on disk—has a direct relationship to its resolution: the more pixels in a graphic, the larger the file. As a web designer, you must strike a balance between making the resolution of a graphic high enough to display optimally yet low enough to download quickly when users load your page.

There are two ways of controlling the size (in pixels) of a graphic on a webpage. One method is to use a graphics-editing program to resize it before using it on the webpage. This method results in the smallest file size possible, which will allow your page to load more quickly. It is also more work for you, though, and it prevents anyone visiting your page from downloading a high-quality copy of your graphic. (That could be a good or bad thing, depending on the purpose of your page.) The exercise entitled "Insert a Graphic," on page 147, uses a graphic that has already been resized in this manner.

The other way is to use attributes within the HTML code to specify the height and width at which the graphic is displayed. The web browser will scale the graphic down to the specified size when it displays the page. With this method, the file size is larger, so the page takes longer to load. (With the popularity of broadband access these days, that shouldn't make much of a difference for most users.) This method is also useful if you need to reuse a graphic at various sizes in multiple instances. For example, perhaps you use the same graphic as a small thumbnail image in one spot and as a large featured photo in another spot. You will practice using these sizing attributes in "Controlling Image Size and Padding," on page 150.

Note The most commonly accepted graphics formats on the web—and therefore the most reliable to use—are PNG, JPG, and GIF. Try to stick to those types when creating or downloading images for your site. The exercises in this chapter use a combination of PNG and JPG images. For large graphics, GIF is less desirable, generally, because it supports fewer colors; however, GIF does allow for simple animations embedded in a single graphic file. (That's beyond the scope of this book, but you might want to look into creating animated GIFs on your own.)

Inserting a Graphic

Inserting a graphic on a webpage is as simple as placing an *<img>* tag where you want the graphic to appear:

```
<img src="logo.png">
```

> **Note** HTML5 also supports a *<figure>* tag for inserting images that is discussed later in this chapter on page 158. However *<figure>* is not a replacement for the *<img>* tag; it's a container tag into which you place 1an *<img>* tag. You can then use the *<figurecaption>* tag to assign a caption to the figure; the caption stays with the image wherever it floats on the page.

As you saw in Chapter 5, "Creating Hyperlinks and Anchors," when a file resides in the same folder as the HTML document that references it, you can refer to that file using the file name only, without any additional path information. If you want to store your graphics in a subfolder of the folder containing the text files (to organize your files in a more tidy fashion), you must refer to the graphic using the subfolder name:

```
<img src="images/logo.png">
```

To refer to a file that is up one level in the folder structure, use two periods and a forward slash (../), such as the following:

```
<img src="../logo.png">
```

To refer to an image that is stored somewhere else—perhaps on your company's main web server or at a partner's server—use the complete absolute URL to the file, which might look something like this:

```
<img src="http://i2.microsoft.com/h/all/i/ms_masthead_8x6a_ltr.jpg">
```

By default, unless you place the image within a block-level tag such as a paragraph or heading, an image blocks off all the horizontal space across the rest of the page—even if the image itself takes up only a fraction of the available horizontal space (see Figure 9-1).

FIGURE 9-1 The image appears by itself by default.

To force an image to render on the left or right side of the screen and wrap surrounding text around the image, apply a *float* style rule that uses a *left* or *right* attribute:

```
<img src="logo.gif" style="float: left">
```

You could also create a style rule in the *<style>* area of the document or in a separate cascading style sheet that would make all images float unless otherwise specified:

```
img {float: left}
```

Figure 9-2 shows what the previous example looks like when you float the image to the left.

FIGURE 9-2 The image floats to the left of the text.

Figure 9-3 shows the image placed at the right of the page.

FIGURE 9-3 The image floats to the right of the text.

Notice that floating to the right moves the image all the way to the right end of the page, not simply to the right of the text. If you want to place the image in a precise location, see the section "Setting an Element's Position" in Chapter 11, "Creating Division-Based Layouts."

In the following exercise, you will insert a graphic located in a subfolder and set it to float to the left of the text.

Insert a Graphic

1. In Notepad and Internet Explorer, open the *index.htm* file located in the *Documents\Microsoft Press\HTML5 Start Here\09Graphics\InsertingImages* folder.

> **Important** If you copy the practice files for this exercise to some other location, you must also copy the *default.css* file and the images folder for the practice files to work properly.

2. Immediately after the opening *<body>* tag, add the following:

   ```
   <img src="images/stamp.png">
   ```

3. Save the file and then refresh Internet Explorer.

4. Modify the code to float the image to the left:

   ```
   <img src="images/stamp.png" style="float: left">
   ```

5. Save the file and then refresh Internet Explorer to check your work. Don't worry that the text is a little too close to the graphic; we'll fix that in a later exercise.

6. Close Notepad and Internet Explorer.

Clearing a Graphic

The image in the preceding exercise was carefully prepared to be the correct size to fit in the space where it was to be inserted. But what if the image is larger, like what's shown in Figure 9-4 (on the next page)?

In this example, there's a problem in that the horizontal rule doesn't "clear" the graphic-that is, the horizontal rule starts too soon, before the graphic is vertically completed. The horizontal line should start at the left margin, under the graphic. To make that happen, add a *clear* style to the horizontal rule's tag:

```
<hr style="clear: left">
```

You can also do this on the right, if a right-aligned graphic were causing such a problem:

```
<hr style="clear: right">
```

FIGURE 9-4 This large image interferes with the positioning of the text that follows it.

You can apply this style to any object, not just horizontal rules. For example, if there is a certain paragraph you want to clear the graphic, you could apply it to the <p> tag:

```
<p style="clear: left">
```

In the following exercise, you will move the top horizontal line—and everything following it below the graphic.

Set an Object to Clear a Graphic

1. In Notepad and Internet Explorer, open the *index.htm* file located in the *Documents\Microsoft Press\HTML5 Start Here\09Graphics\ClearingImages* folder.

Important If you copy the practice files for this exercise to some other location, you must also copy the *default.css* file and the images folder for the practice files to work properly.

2. Examine the document in Internet Explorer. Notice the placement of the text in relation to the graphic.

3. In Notepad, add a *clear* style rule to the *<hr>* tag near the top:

```
<hr style="clear: left">
```

4. Save the file and then refresh Internet Explorer.

    The horizontal line, and everything that follows it, displays below the graphic.

5. Close Notepad and Internet Explorer.

Of course, this isn't a look that you would want to keep, because the graphic is too big and there isn't enough white space between it and the horizontal rule. But in the next exercise, you will learn how to specify the graphic's size to fix that.

Controlling Image Size and Padding

Image size is expressed in pixels. If you want, you can specify only the width; the height will be resized proportionally. Or you can specify only the height; the width will be resized proportionally. But you can also specify both the width and the height. For example, suppose Figure 9-5 is your original image, which is 288 pixels high.

FIGURE 9-5 The graphic at its original proportions.

You could add a *height="150"* attribute to the *<img>* tag, without specifying a width, like this:

```
<img src="suitcase.png" height="150">
```

When you view the page, the image shrinks proportionally.

However, if you specify both height and width, the image will be distorted to fit the dimensions you specify, as shown in Figure 9-6:

```
<img src="suitcase.png" height="150" width="230">
```

FIGURE 9-6: The graphic with a height of 150 and a width of 230.

They look like two different suitcases, huh? That's a little trick you can use to change the appearance of some line drawings to fit your needs.

Like text, images can have margins and/or padding to separate them from surrounding elements. For example, in the example in the previous exercise, notice how close the text was to the graphic. It would be better if the text were moved slightly to the right.

As you learned in Chapter 8, "Formatting Paragraphs with CSS," the *padding* attribute controls the space around content, on the inside of the element, and the *margin* attribute controls the space surrounding the element. You can use either attribute for an image. When the image has a border, however, it is better to use the *margin* attribute.

To increase the space around the example, you can insert a right margin specification within the style rule:

```
<img src="images/stamp.png" style="float: left"; margin-right: 10px">
```

Notice that the margin measurement was added to the existing *style* attribute for the tag; it was not inserted as a separate attribute. A semi-colon separates the two style specs.

In the following exercise, you will set the size, padding, and margin for a graphic.

Size the Size, Padding, and Margin for a Graphic

1. In Notepad and Internet Explorer, open the *index.htm* file located in the *Documents\Microsoft Press\HTML5 Start Here\09Graphics\SizingPadding* folder.

2. In Notepad, edit the *<img>* tag for the graphic so that the image is exactly 75 pixels in height:

```
<img src="images/stamplarge.png" style="float: left" height="75">
```

3. Add a margin of eight pixels to the image:

```
<img src="images/stamplarge.png" style="float: left; margin: 8px" height="75">
```

4. Save the file and then refresh Internet Explorer.

5. Add another graphic immediately below the first one, with its floating style aligned right. Then refresh Internet Explorer to see the change.

```
<img src="images/stamplarge.png" style="float: left; margin: 8px" height="75">
<img src="images/bluestamp.png" style="float: right; margin: 8px" height="75">
```

6. Center the text between the two graphics:

```
<h1 style="text-align: center">Welcome to Margie's Travel!</h1>
<i><h5 style="text-align: center">Leave the details to us, and leave your
worries behind</h5></i>
```

7. Save the file and then refresh Internet Explorer.

8. Close Notepad and Internet Explorer.

Using a Graphic as a Hyperlink

In Chapter 5, you learned how to create text hyperlinks using the *<a>* tag. Recall that you place the URL in the opening *<a>* tag and then you place the hyperlink text between the *<a>* and *</a>* tags. You create a graphical hyperlink in much the same way, by placing an *<img>* tag in an *<a>* tag:

```
<a href="http://www.margiestravel.com" title="Home page">
<img src="images/stamplarge.png" style="float: left; margin: 8px" height="75">
</a>
```

The graphic displays as usual in the document, but when the user moves the mouse pointer over it, the pointer changes to a hand, indicating that the graphic is a hyperlink.

There's a slight problem with the previous code as it's written: by default, hyperlinked graphics have a border that is the same color as hyperlinked text, so you end up with a border like the one shown in Figure 9-7.

FIGURE 9-7 An image has a border around it when it's a hyperlink.

You can remove the border by adding *border: none* to the style rule for the graphic:

```
<a href="http://www.margiestravel.com" title="Home page">
<img src="images/stamplarge.png" style="float: left; margin: 8px; border: none"
height="75">
</a>
```

It's a common convention in web design to make the graphic in the upper-left corner of each page into a hyperlink to the website's home page and to display that hyperlinked graphic in the upper-left corner of every page in the site. In the following exercise, you will do just that by setting up the upper-left-corner graphic to hyperlink to the website's home page.

Create a Graphical Hyperlink

1. In Notepad and Internet Explorer, open the *index.htm* file located in the *Documents\Microsoft Press\HTML5 Start Here\09Graphics\CreatingHyperlinks* folder.

2. In Notepad, add an *<a>* tag that hyperlinks to *www.margiestravel.com* around the first *<img>* tag and specify a link title of *Home page*:

   ```
   <a href="http://www.margiestravel.com" title="Home page">
   <img src="images/stamplarge.png" style="float: left; margin: 8px" height="75">
   </a>
   ```

3. Save the file and then refresh Internet Explorer.

4. In Internet Explorer, move the mouse over the graphic to display the ScreenTip. Notice that the graphic has a border around it and a Home page ScreenTip displays. The graphic might not display a border in some browsers, such as Firefox.

5. Return to Notepad and remove the border by adding *border: none* to the style rule:

   ```
   <a href="http://www.margiestravel.com" title="Home page">
   <img src="images/stamplarge.png" style="float: left; margin: 8px; border:
   none" height="75">
   </a>
   ```

6. Save the file and then refresh Internet Explorer.

Pointer

7. Close Notepad and Internet Explorer.

Creating Thumbnails

High-resolution graphics can make a page load slowly, but avoiding high-resolution graphics altogether can limit your site's effectiveness in delivering content. A compromise is to include thumbnail images, which are low-resolution copies of the images that are linked to the larger, high-resolution versions.

> **Note** Some web-development programs create thumbnail images automatically when you set up a photo album page.

To create a thumbnail, you will need a small version of each graphic. You can create them by opening the original graphic in a program like Photoshop or Paint Shop Pro and then using that program to scale the picture to a lower resolution (for example, 100 to 150 pixels high). Then save the file under a different name. For example, if the original is *tree.jpg*, you might call the thumbnail *tree-small. jpg*. Then place the thumbnail images on the page and create hyperlinks to the larger files. Set each larger file to open in its own window by using the *target="_blank"* attribute:

```
<a href="tree.jpg" target="_blank"><img src="tree-small.jpg"></a>
```

In the following exercise, you will hyperlink thumbnails of several images to full-size versions that will open in a separate window.

Hyperlink Thumbnails of Images

1. In Notepad and Internet Explorer, open the *collage.htm* file located in the *Documents\Microsoft Press\HTML5 Start Here\09Graphics\CreatingThumbnails* folder.

2. In Notepad, enclose each image in a hyperlink that opens its full-size counterpart in a new window:

   ```
   <a href="images/acropolis.jpg" target="_blank"><img src="images/acropolis-small.jpg" style="margin: 8px></a>
   <a href="images/alps.jpg" target="_blank"><img src="images/alps-small.jpg" style="margin: 8px"></a>
   <a href="images/arc.jpg" target="_blank"><img src="images/arc-small.jpg" style="margin: 8px"></a>
   <a href="images/eiffel.jpg" target="_blank"><img src="images/eiffel-small.jpg" style="margin: 8px"></a>
   <a href="images/haussman.jpg" target="_blank"><img src="images/haussman-small.jpg" style="margin: 8px"></a>
   <a href="images/niagra.jpg" target="_blank"><img src="images/niagra-small.jpg" style="margin: 8px"></a>
   <a href="images/steamer.jpg" target="_blank"><img src="images/steamer-small.jpg" style="margin: 8px"></a>
   ```

3. Save the file and then refresh Internet Explorer. Test each graphic's hyperlink to make sure it works.

4. Notice that each graphic now has a thick border around it; as you learned previously in this chapter, that occurs when you make a graphic into a hyperlink (unless you specify otherwise).

5. Add the *border: none* style to each graphic so that it does not have the default hyperlink border around it:

```
<a href="images/acropolis.jpg" target="_blank"><img src="images/acropolis-
small.jpg" style="margin: 8px; border:none"></a>
<a href="images/alps.jpg" target="_blank"><img src="images/alps-small.jpg"
style="margin: 8px; border:none "></a>
<a href="images/arc.jpg" target="_blank"><img src="images/arc-small.jpg"
style="margin: 8px; border:none "></a>
<a href="images/eiffel.jpg" target="_blank"><img src="images/eiffel-small.jpg"
style="margin: 8px; border:none "></a>
<a href="images/haussman.jpg" target="_blank"><img src="images/haussman-small.
jpg" style="margin: 8px; border:none "></a>
<a href="images/niagra.jpg" target="_blank"><img src="images/niagra-small.jpg"
style="margin: 8px; border:none "></a>
<a href="images/steamer.jpg" target="_blank"><img src="images/steamer-small.
jpg" style="margin: 8px; border:none "></a>
```

6. Add a ScreenTip to each hyperlink by inserting a *title* attribute:

```
<a href="images/acropolis.jpg" target="_blank" title="The Acropolis,
Rome"><img src="images/acropolis-small.jpg" style="margin: 8px;
border:none"></a>
<a href="images/alps.jpg" target="_blank" title="The Swiss Alps"><img
src="images/alps-small.jpg" style="margin: 8px; border:none "></a>
<a href="images/arc.jpg" target="_blank" title="Arc De Triomphe, Paris"><img
src="images/arc-small.jpg" style="margin: 8px; border:none "></a>
<a href="images/eiffel.jpg" target="_blank" title="The Eiffel Tower,
Paris"><img src="images/eiffel-small.jpg" style="margin: 8px; border:none "></
a>
<a href="images/haussman.jpg" target="_blank" title="Haussman Tower,
Germany"><img src="images/haussman-small.jpg" style="margin: 8px; border:none
"></a>
<a href="images/niagra.jpg" target="_blank" title="Niagra Falls"><img
src="images/niagra-small.jpg" style="margin: 8px; border:none "></a>
<a href="images/steamer.jpg" target="_blank" title="Stockholm, Sweden"><img
src="images/steamer-small.jpg" style="margin: 8px; border:none "></a>
```

7. Save the file and then refresh Internet Explorer. Hover your mouse over each graphic to make sure the correct ScreenTip displays.

8. Close Notepad and Internet Explorer.

Including Alternate Text for Graphics

Placing an *alt* attribute (traditionally called an *alt tag*, although it isn't really a tag) in an *<img>* tag creates alternate text for the graphic. This alternate text is a pop-up box that contains a text explanation of the graphic, much like the title does for a hyperlink.

Alternate text is not just for decoration; it serves an important purpose for users who might not be able to view your graphics for some reason. This might include visually-impaired users who are accessing your page through the use of a screen-reading program or users browsing on phones or other handheld devices who try to reduce their usage fees by turning off the display of graphics.

Alternate text is simple to include; just place an *alt="text"* attribute in the *<img>* tag:

```
<img src="stamp.png" alt="Stamp logo">
```

In the following exercise, you will add alternate text to a picture.

Use Alt Tags

1. In Notepad and Internet Explorer, open the *index.htm* file located in the *Documents\Microsoft Press\HTML5 Start Here\09Graphics\UsingAlt* folder.

2. In Notepad, add an *alt* attribute to the *<img>* tag for the first image:

    ```
    <img src="images/stamplarge.png" style="float: left; margin: 8px; border:
    none" height="75" alt="stamp logo with plane and palm trees">
    ```

3. Add an *alt* attribute to the *<img>* tag for the second image:

    ```
    <img src="images/bluestamp.png" style="float: right; margin: 8px" height="75"
    alt="stamp logo with suitcase">
    ```

4. Save your work.

5. Close Notepad and Internet Explorer.

Note If you want to see first-hand how the *alt* attribute works, rename the image files in the image folder and then redisplay the page. The *alt* tag text displays onscreen.

Adding Figure Captions

HTML5 includes a new tag for marking figures: *<figure>*. It is not a replacement for *<img>*, but rather a container into which you place an *<img>* tag:

```
<figure>
<img src="images/diagram.gif">
</figure>
```

If the browser does not support HTML5, the *<figure>* tag is ignored.

The main advantage to using *<figure>* is that you can then use the *<figurecaption>* tag to associate a caption with the image. That caption will then stick with the image no matter where it floats in your layout. The following example shows how to use it:

```
<figure>
<img src="/images/diagram.gif">
<figurecaption>This diagram shows the life cycle of the product.</figcaption>
</figure>
```

Another advantage to using *<figure>* is that you can assign styles and other attributes to the *<figure>* element via an external or internal style sheet, just as you do for any other container tag.

You can also assign a single caption to a group of images, as shown in the following example:

```
<figure>
<img src="/images/stage1.jpg">
<img src="/images/stage2.jpg">
<img src="/images/stage3.jpg">
<figcaption>The three stages of the life cycle</figcaption>
</figure>
```

In the following exercise, you will add a single caption to a group of pictures by applying the *<figure>* and *<figcaption>* tags.

Add a Single Caption to a Group of Figures

1. In Notepad and Internet Explorer, open the *collage.htm* file located in the *Documents\Microsoft Press\HTML5 Start Here\09Graphics\CaptioningFigures* folder.

2. In Notepad, add an opening *<figure>* tag immediately above the first JPG photo's tag:

   ```
   <figure>
   <a href="images/acropolis.jpg" target="_blank" title="The Acropolis,
   Rome"><img src="images/acropolis-small.jpg" style="margin: 8px;
   border:none"></a>
   ```

3. Add a closing *</figure>* tag immediately below the last JPG image's tag:

   ```
   <a href="images/steamer.jpg" target="_blank" title="Stockholm, Sweden"><img
   src="images/steamer-small.jpg" style="margin: 8px; border:none "></a>
   </figure>
   ```

4. Add a *
* and a *<figurecaption>* tag immediately before the closing *</figure>* tag:

   ```
   <a href="images/steamer.jpg" target="_blank" title="Stockholm, Sweden"><img
   src="images/steamer-small.jpg" style="margin: 8px; border:none "></a>
   <br>
   <figurecaption>From top left: The Acropolis, The Swiss Alps, Arc De Triomphe,
   The Eiffel Tower, The Haussman Towwer, Niagra Falls, and Stockholm,
   Sweden</figurecaption>
   </figure>
   ```

5. In the document's *<head>* section, add the following style sheet:

```
<style>
figurecaption {font-size: 12px; font-style: italic}
</style>
```

6. Save the file and then refresh Internet Explorer.

7. Close Notepad and Internet Explorer.

Key Points

- When possible, use graphics files that are as close as possible in resolution to the size at which they will be displayed on the webpage. Use a photo-editing program to change the resolution.

- The most reliable graphics formats for web use are GIF, PNG, and JPG.

- Use the *<img>* tag to insert an image. The *src* attribute specifies the image file name.

- To refer to a graphic in a subfolder, precede the name with the subfolder name and a slash (/).

- To allow a graphic to float to the left or right of the text, use a *style="float: left"* or *style="float: right"* attribute within the *<img>* tag.

- To force text to be positioned below an image, add *style="clear: left"* or *style="clear: right"* to the opening tag of the text.

- To size an image proportionally, specify a height or width for it as an attribute in the *<img>* tag. To size an image and distort it if needed, specify both a height and a width.

- To make a graphic into a hyperlink, enclose it in an *<a>* tag.

- To use thumbnail images, create a smaller, low-resolution version of each image and then hyperlink it to the high-resolution version.

- As a contingency in the event that an image cannot be viewed, you can include a text explanation of the image in a pop-up box by inserting an *alt* attribute to specify alternate text.

- Enclose an image, or a group of images that should have a single collective caption, in a two-sided *<figure>* container. Then you can assign a caption with the *<figurecaption>* tag.

Page Layout and Navigation

Chapter 10

Creating Navigational Aids

In this chapter, you will:

- Plan your site's organization

- Create a text-based navigation bar

- Create a graphical navigation bar

- Redirect to another URL

- Create a custom error page

If you worked through the exercises in Parts I and II of this book, you have acquired most of the basic skills you need to create simple websites. Now it's a matter of putting all these skills together to make attractive and easy-to-use sites, and that's what you'll focus on in Part III.

One way to make your website easily accessible is to place a consistent navigation bar on each page. A *navigation bar* is a set of hyperlinks that users click to connect to the major pages of your website. These hyperlinks can be either text-based or graphical. You already saw how to create both kinds of hyperlinks in Chapter 5, "Creating Hyperlinks and Anchors," and Chapter 9, "Inserting Graphics," so creating a navigation bar is a logical next step. You'll learn how to plan your site's organization and then create a suitable navigation bar to match it.

This chapter also explains a couple of other useful techniques to help users navigate your site. You'll learn how to redirect users from one page to another and how to create a custom error page that appears when your site doesn't display a particular page correctly for whatever reason.

Important Before you can use the practice files provided for this chapter, you need to install them from the book's companion content page to their default locations. See "Code Samples" in the beginning of this book for more information.

Planning Your Site's Organization

Navigation bars can be easy to create, but they require some planning to be effective. Up to this point in the book, you've been creating single pages with a common theme for eventual inclusion in a website, but you probably have not yet given a lot of thought to how the pages fit together. So before creating a navigation bar, you want to consider the overall structural plan for the site.

A navigation bar should contain links to the most important sections of the website, plus a link to the Home page (see Figure 10-1).

FIGURE 10-1 A horizontal, text-based navigation bar.

The navigation bar should not contain hyperlinks to every page in the site unless the site is extremely small and simple. Although there is no specific rule about the number of items a navigation bar can contain, most people try for somewhere between four and seven for a horizontal bar like the one shown in Figure 10-1. With fewer than four, your site doesn't look very content-rich; with more than seven, the navigation bar becomes crowded and confusing. In addition, on low-resolution displays or in narrow browser windows, a horizontal navigation bar might wrap to a second (or even third) line or a vertical navigation bar might force the user to scroll down. This chapter discusses only horizontal bars, but you'll learn how to make vertical navigation bars in Chapter 12, "Creating Tables."

Note Some websites have navigation bars in which each hyperlink opens a menu of options when the user points to it or clicks it. You can't create those with plain HTML; those are constructed with JavaScript or another web-based programming language. You can find many online tutorials for making your own JavaScript menus, but it might be easier to use a software utility to generate them, such as uMenu, a free program you can download from *http://download.cnet.com*.

Before building your navigation bar, create a diagram that outlines the site's planned structure. It doesn't matter if you haven't created all the pages yet. You can be as fancy or as plain as you want with your chart. It can be scrawled on the back of a napkin or built using SmartArt (through a Microsoft Office application), Microsoft Visio, or some other charting tool. Choose file names for each planned page, so you can start referring to them in hyperlinks even if they don't exist yet.

The organization of the Margie's Travel site, which you've been creating pages for in this book's examples, might look something like what's shown in Figure 10-2.

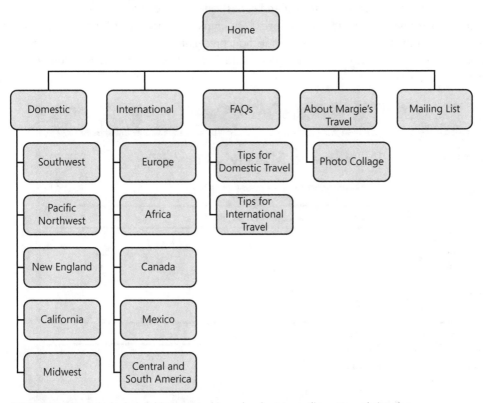

FIGURE 10-2 It might be helpful to create a hierarchy chart to outline your website plan.

Notice that the level directly below the Home page consists of five pages. The navigation bar will contain hyperlinks to each of these pages. Two of these, Domestic and International, are primarily "lobby pages" (that is, introductory pages) for larger sections of content; the lobby pages of those sections will link to each page within that section. This website is modest in scope initially, but there is plenty of room for future expansion. You could add dozens of additional pages, such as pages for each destination within the regional categories, and pages for each individual tour that the company will be escorting to each destination.

Notice also that not every page referenced from the navigation bar is a major section. For example, Mailing List has no pages subordinate to it at all. It is simply a page that is important for visitors to be able to access quickly from any page.

Creating a Text-Based Navigation Bar

A text-based navigation bar is the simplest and easiest, and it is also very user-friendly for all browsers and all users (including those with special needs). On simple webpages, text-based navigation bars are usually placed at the top of the page, in a single horizontal line (see Figure 10-3). Some web designers also place a copy at the bottom of each page so visitors don't have to scroll back up to the top of a page to access the links.

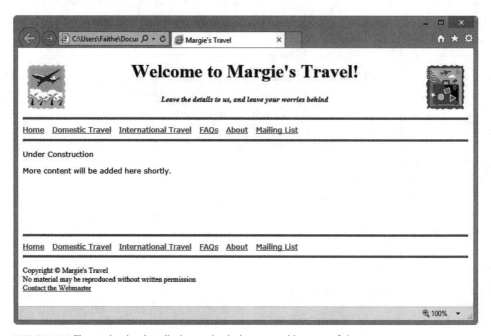

FIGURE 10-3 The navigation bar displays at both the top and bottom of the page.

Tip When you place a navigation bar at the bottom of a page, it is customarily a text-based bar rather than a graphical one.

HTML5 includes a *<nav>* tag, a two-sided container tag in which you can optionally place the code for a navigation bar. The *<nav>* tag is designed to help browsers and style sheets identify sets of links as a navigational element and then handle them appropriately. If the browser does not support the *<nav>* tag, it is ignored. You'll use the *<nav>* tag in this chapter because it's good practice to start including HTML5 tags in your code, but you won't be doing anything special with the *<nav>* tag's attributes. However, in sites you create yourself, you are free to define style attributes for the *<nav>* tag in internal or external style sheets; this can be a way to help ensure consistency among the navigation bars throughout all the pages in your website.

In the following exercise, you will add a text-based navigation bar to the top and bottom of a webpage.

Create a Text-Based Navigation Bar

1. In Notepad and Internet Explorer, open the *navbar.htm* file located in the *Documents\Microsoft Press\HTML5 Start Here\10Navigation\CreatingTextBar* folder.

2. Above the *Under Construction* paragraph, add a two-sided *<nav>* tag and then add two *<hr>* tags within it:

   ```
   <nav>
   <hr>
   <hr>
   </nav>
   ```

3. Between the two *<hr>* tags, add the following line:

   ```
   <p>Home Domestic Travel International Travel FAQs About Mailing List</p>
   ```

4. Save the file and then refresh Internet Explorer.

   The text of the intended navigation bar displays, but the items are not clearly separated.

   ```
   Home Domestic Travel International Travel FAQs About Mailing List
   ```

   HTML ignores multiple spaces, so you must instead use the nonbreaking space code (* *) when you want to insert extra spaces between words without creating a table or some other structural container.

5. Insert a nonbreaking space (and a normal space following it) between each section title:

   ```
   <p>Home   Domestic Travel   International Travel   FAQs  
   About   Mailing List</p>
   ```

6. Save the file and then refresh Internet Explorer.

   ```
   Home   Domestic Travel   International Travel   FAQs   About   Mailing List
   ```

   The horizontal spacing looks okay, but the navigation bar would look better if the blue lines were closer to it at the top and bottom.

7. Set the margin for the paragraph to zero:

   ```
   <p style="margin:0px">Home   Domestic Travel   International Travel
     FAQs   About   Mailing List</p>
   ```

8. Save the file and then refresh Internet Explorer.

The lines are closer to the text.

Home   Domestic Travel   International Travel   FAQs   About   Mailing List

9. Add hyperlinks to each of the six items in the navigation bar to the corresponding pages. Some of the pages being referenced do not exist yet, but that's okay.

Note Make sure the *@nbsp*; codes are outside of the *<a>* tag, so the spaces won't be underlined as part of the hyperlink.

```
<nav>
<hr>
<p style="margin:0px">
<a href="index.htm">Home</a>  
<a href="domestic.htm">Domestic Travel</a>  
<a href="international.htm">International Travel</a>   
<a href="faqs.htm">FAQs</a>   
<a href="about.htm">About</a>   
<a href="mailing.htm">Mailing List</a></p>
<hr>
</nav>
```

10. Save the file and then refresh Internet Explorer.

The navigation bar is complete. Point to each of the hyperlinks on it to check the links.

Home   Domestic Travel   International Travel   FAQs   About   Mailing List

11. In Notepad, select the code for the entire navigation bar, including the *<nav>* and *</nav>* tags, and then press **Ctrl+C** to copy it to the Clipboard.

12. Position the insertion point immediately above the copyright information and then press **Ctrl+V** to copy the navigation bar there.

13. Save the file and then refresh Internet Explorer.

Two navigation bars display, one above and one below the main content of the page.

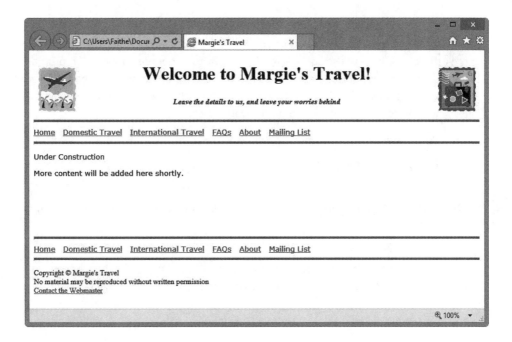

14. Close Notepad and Internet Explorer.

Creating a Graphical Navigation Bar

Text hyperlinks are clear and unambiguous but not all that attractive. You might prefer to create a navigation bar that uses buttons or other graphics instead of text links. You can create the graphics yourself in a graphics-editing program. If you do create your own, it's a good idea to follow these guidelines:

- Keep the size of each button small (150 pixels wide at the most).

- Make each button the same size and shape. The only variation should be in the text that they present.

- Save each button as a separate file in GIF or JPG format. GIF format has some advantages for buttons, such as the ability to use different shapes and transparency.

If you have no talent or inclination for art projects, search the web; there are thousands of sites with free graphical buttons that you can download. (Make sure the buttons you download are not copyrighted and are royalty-free, so the owner of them can't charge you a fee for using them.) Make several copies of a button you like and then use a text tool in a graphics-editing program to place different text on each copy. Here are a couple of links to free button sites to get you started:

- *http://www.aaa-buttons.com*

- *http://www.eosdev.com/eosdev_buttons.htm*

Most professional website designers do not create their own buttons, nor do they acquire them from others; they instead use *button-creation programs* to generate them. Such programs make it very easy to create groups of identical buttons with different text on each one. There are commercial programs and standalone programs that make buttons; there also are free web utilities. Here are two sites; you can find many more with a simple web search.

- Button Generator: *http://www.buttongenerator.com*

- Crystal Button: *http://www.crystalbutton.com*

Note The buttons provided for the exercises in this book were created with Button Generator.

You set up a graphical navigation bar just like a text-based navigation bar, but instead of hyperlinking from the text, you can hyperlink from the graphic by placing the *<img>* tag within the *<a>* tag:

```
<a href="product.htm"><img src="product_button.gif"></a>
```

In the following exercise, you will convert a text-based navigation bar to a graphics-based one.

Create a Graphical Navigation Bar

1. In Notepad and Internet Explorer, open the *navbar.htm* file located in the *Documents\Microsoft Press\HTML5 Start Here\10Navigation\CreatingGraphicBar* folder.

2. In Notepad, in the upper navigation bar, change the hyperlinks so that they reference the button graphics in the */images* folder rather than display text:

```
<nav>
<hr>
<p style="margin:0px">
<a href="index.htm"><img src="images/home.png" style="border: none"></a>
 
<a href="domestic.htm"><img src="images/domestic.png" style="border: none"></a>  
<a href="international.htm"><img src="images/international.png"
style="border:none"></a>    
<a href="faqs.htm"><img src="images/faqs.png" style="border:none"></a>    
<a href="about.htm"><img src="images/about.png" style="border:none"></a>
 
<a href="mailing.htm"><img src="images/mailing.png" style="border:none"></a></p>
<hr>
</nav>
```

> **Note** The preceding code also removes the spaces you previously placed between the links, because the spacing is now provided by the graphics themselves.

3. Save the file and then refresh Internet Explorer to view your work. If the buttons wrap to two lines, don't panic; the next exercise helps fix that.

4. Leave the files open in both Notepad and Internet Explorer for the next exercise.

> **Note** To make your page accessible, you will probably also want to include the *alt* attribute to each button, as you learned in Chapter 9. I have omitted it in these examples to keep the code as short and simple as possible.

After creating the graphical navigation bar in the previous exercise, you might have noticed a few design issues. For example, the buttons might wrap to multiple lines and the blue horizontal rules and blue hyperlinks don't display particularly well with the tan buttons. The navigation bar at the bottom of the page also looks bunched up at the left. In the following steps, you'll fix these problems.

1. In Notepad, delete the *About* button's code.

2. Save the file and then refresh Internet Explorer.

The buttons all fit on one line now. The *About* hyperlink remains in the text-based navigation bar at the bottom of the page, so that topic will still be accessible to your visitors; you've just demoted it in prominence by removing it from the top navigation bar.

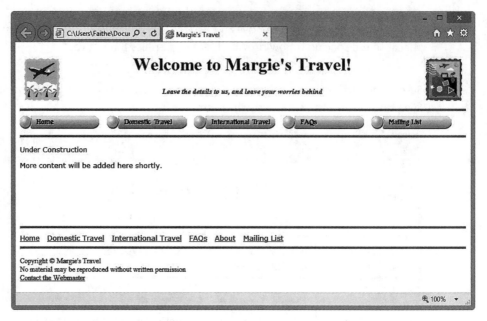

3. Change the style of the opening paragraph tag for the bottom navigation bar to include a *text-align* style:

```
<p style="margin:0px; text-align:center">
```

4. Open *default.css* in Notepad and change the color of the horizontal rules to brown:

```
hr {color: blue; background-color: brown; height: 3px;}
```

5. Delete the *a:hover* and *a:active* styles in *default.css*.

6. Change the *a:link* and *a:visited* colors to brown.

```
a:link {color: brown}
a:visited {color:brown}
```

7. Save and close *default.css*, and then refresh Internet Explorer to see the effect of the line color change.

8. Save your work and then refresh Internet Explorer again. The bottom navigation bar is now centered.

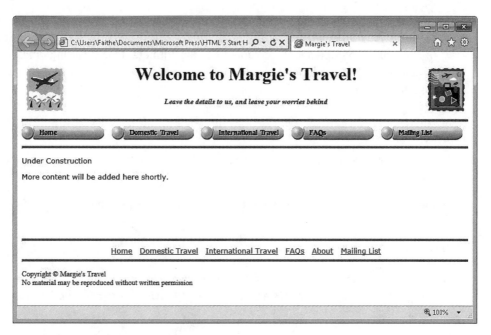

9. Close Notepad and Internet Explorer.

Redirecting to Another URL

After you have managed your own website for a while, you might decide you want to restructure its organization by renaming some pages, placing pages in folders, or hosting your site at a different location with a different URL. That is fine, but what about the people who bookmarked the original page? If you remove the old content entirely, they'll faced with an unfriendly *Page Not Found* message and they won't have any way of finding the page in its new location.

To help your past visitors find the new page, you can leave the old page in place and replace its text with a hyperlink that tells them where the new page is located. You already know how to create a hyperlink—that's simple. But you can take it one step further by setting up the old page to actually *redirect* to the new page. In other words, you can make the old page automatically display the new page.

It is customary for a redirection to include five seconds of delay, so users can cancel the redirect operation if desired. It is also customary to include a text hyperlink to the new page, in case the redirect operation fails for some reason (such as the browser not supporting it, although this is uncommon).

You implement a redirect operation by adding an attribute to a *<meta>* tag in the *<head>* section of the page (as you learned in Chapter 2, "Setting Up the Document Structure"). You must create a new *<meta>* tag for this operation; you cannot add the attributes to any existing *<meta>* tag that the document might have. For example, to redirect to the page *support.microsoft.com* after a five-second delay, use the following:

```
<meta http-equiv="refresh" content="5; url=http://support.microsoft.com">
```

Be sure to use a semicolon (not a comma) between the delay (the *content* attribute) and the *url* attribute.

In the following exercise, you will redirect one page to another page automatically after five seconds.

Redirect to Another URL

1. In Notepad and Internet Explorer, open the *oldpage.htm* file located in the *Documents\Microsoft Press\HTML5 Start Here\10Navigation\Redirecting* folder.

2. In the *<head>* section, add a new *<meta>* tag:

   ```
   <meta http-equiv="refresh" content="5; url=index.htm">
   ```

 Note Pay special attention to the syntax of the meta tag here. Notice that there is no closing quote after *5* and no opening quote before *index.htm*. That's because the content attribute's multiple properties are all enclosed within a single set of quotes. If your page won't redirect properly in step 4, check the placement of your quotation marks.

3. In the *<body>* section, make the text *click here* into a hyperlink to *index.htm*:

   ```
   <p>This page has been moved. <br>
   If your browser supports automatic redirection, the new page will appear in
   5 seconds. <br>
   If the new page does not appear, <a href="index.htm">click here</a>.</p>
   ```

4. Save the file and then refresh Internet Explorer.

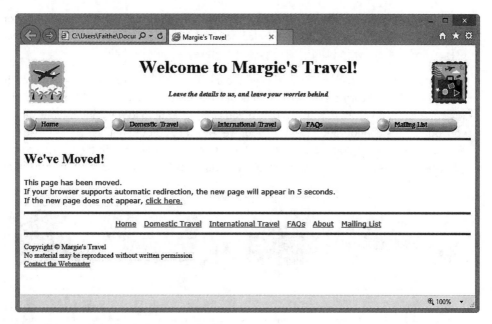

After five seconds, the index page displays.

5. Click the browser's Back button and then quickly click the *click here* hyperlink to test it.

6. Close Notepad and Internet Explorer.

Creating Custom Error Pages

When a site visitor requests a page that doesn't exist, the browser displays a *404 File Not Found* error message. It's not a very friendly-looking message (see Figure 10-4).

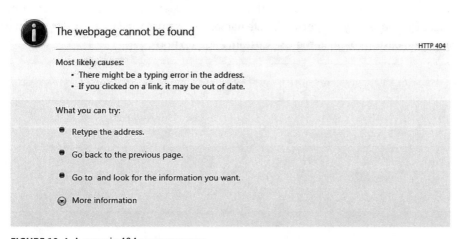

FIGURE 10-4 A generic 404 error message.

You can avoid users encountering such messages due to outdated links and information by keeping old pages up and redirecting, as you learned in the previous exercise. However, that won't help users who have the wrong URL due to typing mistakes—yours or theirs.

Most web-hosting companies enable you to create a custom error page—in place of the generic one—that automatically displays when someone has the domain name right but the page name wrong. A two-step process is involved: first you create and upload the page to your server, and then you log into the configuration tools for your web-hosting account and set your 404 error page preferences. The steps for doing that latter part are different, depending on the hosting company. Figure 10-5 shows a sample from GoDaddy.com, a popular web-hosting company, but yours might look very different.

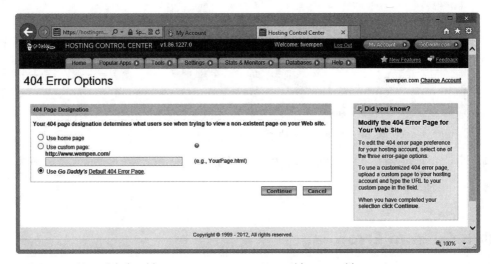

FIGURE 10-5 You might be able to set up your server to provide users with a custom error page or message.

Note You can name your error page anything you like; when you set up the 404 error page preferences for your site, you specify the file name. For example, in Figure 10-5, you could enter your own custom page in the Use Custom Page text box.

In the following exercise, you will use the redirect page you created in the previous exercise as the basis for a new page that will display whenever a user requests a page that does not exist.

Create a Custom 404 Error Page

1. In Notepad, reopen the *oldpage.htm* file from the previous exercise and then save it as *error.htm*. If you did not do the previous exercise, open the *oldpage.htm* file located in the *Documents\Microsoft Press\HTML5 Start Here\10Navigation\Creating404* folder.

2. Replace all the text between the two navigation bars with the following:

```
<h2>Oops!</h2>
<p>Something's not quite right here.</p>
<p>You may have typed the URL incorrectly, or there may be an error in the
link that brought you here. You will be redirected to our Home page in 5
seconds.</p>
<p>If you are not redirected automatically, <a href="index.htm">click here</
a>.</p>
```

3. Save your work and then open *error.htm* in Internet Explorer to make sure the redirection works.

4. Close Notepad and Internet Explorer.

Key Points

- A navigation bar contains a list of hyperlinks to the major pages on your site. It need not include every page in the site. The optimal number of links is between four and seven.

- In HTML5, you can use the *<nav>* tag as a container to indicate that a group of links constitutes a navigation element.

- Plan your site's organization before you create the navigation bar. Draw a diagram of all the pages and their connections to one another and then choose a file name for each page.

- Navigation bars are traditionally placed at the top or left side of a page. Placing a bar to the side requires the use of layout techniques discussed later in this book.

- Many web designers place a text version of their navigation bar at the bottom of each page for user convenience.

- A text-based navigation bar is simply a series of hyperlinks.

- A graphical navigation bar uses small graphics for the hyperlinks. You can create these graphics using a graphics program such as Photoshop or a utility designed specifically for creating web buttons.

- To redirect a page to a different URL, create a *<meta>* tag in the *<head>* section with the *http-equiv* attribute, like this:
  <meta http-equiv="refresh" content="5; url=http://support.microsoft.com">

- A 404 error means that the page cannot be found. You can create a custom 404 error message page that redirects to your Home page (or any other page) and then use the configuration tools for your web-hosting account to specify that your custom page be used.

Chapter 11

Creating Division-Based Layouts

In this chapter, you will:

- Understand HTML5 semantic tags

- Begin to think in divisions

- Create divisions

- Position divisions

- Format divisions

Until a few years ago, tables were a popular way of structuring a webpage. You'll learn about tables and their formatting in Chapter 12, "Creating Tables," and Chapter 13, "Formatting Tables," in case that's the route you want to go with your site's design. However, as Web designers move increasingly toward separating style and content, division-based layouts are becoming more appealing.

A *division-based layout* defines the area of a page with *<div>* tags, or some of the new HTML5 semantic tags such as *<article>* and *<aside>*, and then applies formatting to each area using styles. One big advantage of division-based layouts is that you can place the styles in an external style sheet and then make style changes to several pages at once simply by modifying the style sheet. For example, relocating the navigation bar from the left side of the page to the right on a dozen different pages is easy with a division-based layout that uses an external style sheet, but it's a huge chore with a table-based layout. Another advantage is that division-based layouts reduce the number of lines of code needed to produce a page. Division-based layouts are also much more accessibility-friendly than table-based layouts because they are more easily interpreted by screen-reading programs and other accessibility tools. In this chapter, you will learn how to create a separate area of a page (a *division*) in a document and how to control division and element positions on-screen. Then you'll learn how to format a division (which is mostly a matter of applying the same formatting styles that you've learned about in previous chapters) and how to overcome any problems introduced by the formatting.

Important Before you can use the practice files provided for this chapter, you need to install them from the book's companion content page to their default locations. See "Code Samples" in the beginning of this book for more information.

Understanding HTML5 Semantic Tags

HTML5 adds some *semantic tags* to define layouts in more intuitive ways than the generic *<div>* tag is capable of. A semantic tag is one in which the name of a tag reflects its purpose.

Here are the major semantic tags you should know:

- **<header>**   Defines the masthead or other header information on the page. Typically the header is repeated on every page of a site, although that is not required.

- **<footer>**   Defines the text at the bottom of a page, such as the copyright or contact information. Again, it is typically repeated on every page of the site.

- **<article>**   Defines a block of text that represents a single article, story, or message. An article can be distinguished from other text in that it can logically stand alone. For example, on a news site, each news story is an article.

- **<aside>**   Defines a block of text that is tangential to the main discussion, such as a note, tip, or caution. An aside can be distinguished from other text in that it could be pulled out and discarded without disrupting the main document in which it appears.

- **<section>**   Defines a generic content or application section. Examples of sections would be book chapters or the numbered sections of a thesis; a site's home page could be split into sections such as Introduction, News, and Contact Info. A section begins with a heading such as *<h1>* followed by other content. A general rule is to use *<section>* if the area being defined would be included in an outline of the document or page.

Note The *<section>* tag might sound similar to the *<div>* tag, but the HTML5 standard differentiates them, saying that *<section>* should not be used merely to define formatting. A section defines a particular type of meaningful content, not just a block of contiguous text that should be formatted the same way.

If you use semantic tags to structure your page and someone views it with a browser that doesn't support HTML5, the page might not look the way you want it to; the browser will ignore the tags it doesn't understand. That's why, for the time being, creating the page structure using *<div>* tags is the safest way to go. However, it's important that you learn the HTML5 semantic tags too, for future reference.

In this chapter, you'll learn to mark up a document both ways: with generic *<div>* tags that are readable in any browser and with the new HTML5 semantic tags.

Beginning to Think in Divisions

In an effective division-based layout, each part of the page you want to format separately should be a *division*. For now, don't think about whether the division will be a vertical or horizontal area on the page or how large or small it will be; just think about the content. For example, look at Figure 11-1. How many natural divisions do you see here?

FIGURE 11-1 Most pages can be naturally divided into divisions by content type.

If you were designing with *<div>* tags, you might divide the page like this: the masthead, the top navigation bar, the body text, the bottom navigation bar, and the copyright notice.

If you were designing with HTML5 semantic tags, you might divide it like this: *<header>* for the masthead, *<nav>* for the navigation bars, and *<footer>* for the copyright notice. Formatting each paragraph in the body with its own *<article>* tag might be overkill for this page, but in a page with more content, you might use *<article>*, *<aside>*, or *<section>* to divide it into manageable chunks.

Creating Divisions

To give a name to a division, use an *id* attribute:

```
<div id="masthead">
```

Each ID must be unique within the document, but multiple documents can use the same division names. Such reuse is good, in fact, because it lets you define the formatting of multiple documents with a single style sheet.

In the following exercise, you will create divisions within a page. Then in later exercises, you will position and format those divisions.

Create Divisions

1. In Notepad and Internet Explorer, open the *index.htm* file located in the *Documents\Microsoft Press\HTML5 Start Here\11Divisions\CreatingDivisions* folder.

2. Enclose the company name and tagline in a *<div>* tag and then name the tag *masthead*:

```
<div id="masthead">
<h1 style="text-align: center; margin: 3px">Margie's Travel</h1>
<i><h5 style="text-align: center; margin: 5px">Leave the details to us,
and leave your worries behind</h5></i>
</div>
```

3. Enclose the top navigation bar in a *<div>* tag and then name the tag *topnav*:

```
<div id="topnav">
<hr style="clear: left">
<p style="margin:0px">
<a href="index.htm"><img src="images/home.png" style="border:none"></a>  
<a href="domestic.htm"><img src="images/domestic.png" style="border:none">
</a>  
<a href="international.htm"><img src="images/international.png"
style="border:none"></a>   
<a href="faqs.htm"><img src="images/faqs.png" style="border:none"></a>   
<a href="mailing.htm"><img src="images/mailing.png" style="border:none"></a>
</p>
<hr>
</div>
```

 Note Make sure that you include the *<nav>* tags in the *topnav* division.

Note As you learned in Chapter 10, "Creating Navigational Aids," the *<nav>* tag is an HTML5 semantic tag that serves the same purpose as defining a *<div>* tag, but it is intended for a navigation bar. You'll use *<nav>* in the next exercise, where you apply HTML5 semantic tags.

4. Enclose the body paragraphs in a *<div>* tag and then name the tag *main*:

```
<div id="main">
<img src="images/eiffel.jpg" style="margin: 8px; float: right" height=300px>
<h2>Europe On Sale!</h2>
<p>For a limited time, all our European dream vacations are now up to 50% off
original prices! Enjoy exotic destinations you've always wanted to visit, such
as Buckingham Palace, The Eiffel Tower, The Louvre, and many others, and save
thousands! <a href="sale.htm">Click here to find out how much you can save!
</a></p>
<p>Nervous about travelling abroad? There's no need to be. All of our trips
are fully escorted, and include transportation by air, rail, or motorcoach,
lodging, meals, and admission fees. You won't have to worry about a thing,
as Margie's experienced and helpful tour guides lead you through the amazing
sights, sounds, and experiences of the countries and cultures of the world.
<a href="international-faqs.htm">Click here for some international travel
planning tips.</a></p>
<h2>Award-Winning Service</h2>
<p>Margie's Travel is proud to be the recipient of the Gold Star Award for
Travel Service, issued by Broadway Travel Reviews, Inc. This prestigious award
is given to only one tour provider in each region each year, for outstanding
tour services based on customer reviews. <a href="award.htm">Click here to learn
more about the award.</ha>
</div>
```

5. Enclose the bottom navigation bar in a *<div>* tag and then name the tag *bottomnav*:

```
<div id="bottomnav">
<hr style="clear: right">
<p style="margin:0px; text-align:center">
<a href="index.htm">Home</a>  
<a href="domestic.htm">Domestic Travel</a>  
<a href="international.htm">International Travel</a>  
<a href="faqs.htm">FAQs</a>   
<a href="about.htm">About</a>   
<a href="mailing.htm">Mailing List</a></p>
<hr>
</div>
```

6. Enclose the copyright notice in a *<div>* tag and then name the tag *copy*:

```
<div id="copy">
<p class="copyright">
Copyright &copy; Margie's Travel<br>
No material may be reproduced without written permission<br>
<a href="mailto:webmaster@margiestravel.com" style="color: white">
Contact the Webmaster</a></p>
</div>
```

7. Save the file and then refresh Internet Explorer.

> **Note** You have not made any changes that change the rendering or appearance of the page, so it looks the same as it did before. If it does not look the same as before, you have made a mistake.

8. Close Notepad and Internet Explorer.

Creating an HTML5 Semantic Layout

If you prefer to use the HTML5 semantic tags to create your layout, you choose the appropriate tags based on the *purpose* of the text. It's conceptually very much the same as using a *<div>* tag with an *id* attribute, but the tag itself provides the context. For example, instead of using the *<div id="masthead">* tag, you would use the *<header>* tag. It is also okay to have both in place simultaneously; a browser that can't use the HTML5 semantic tags can fall back upon the standard <div> tags. (Just make sure you style the equivalent tags in the same way, so there is no formatting confusion.)

In the following exercise, you will change a division-based document to one that uses semantic tags to define the layout.

Create an HTML5 Semantic Layout

1. In Notepad and Internet Explorer, open the *index2.htm* file located in the *Documents\ Microsoft Press\HTML5 Start Here\11Divisions\CreatingSemantic* folder.

2. Replace the *<div id="masthead">* tag with *<header>*, and change its closing *</div>* tag to *</header>*:

```
<body>
<header>
<h1 style="text-align: center; margin: 3px">Margie's Travel</h1>

<i><h5 style="text-align: center; margin: 5px">Leave the details to us, and
leave your worries behind</h5></i>
</header>
```

3. Replace the *<div id="topnav">* tag with *<nav>* and then change its closing *</div>* tag to *</nav>*:

```
<nav>
<hr style="clear: left">
<p style="margin:0px">
<a href="index.htm"><img src="images/home.png" style="border:none"></a>  
<a href="domestic.htm"><img src="images/domestic.png" style="border:none"></a>
 
<a href="international.htm"><img src="images/international.png"
style="border:none"></a>   
<a href="faqs.htm"><img src="images/faqs.png" style="border:none"></a>   
<a href="mailing.htm"><img src="images/mailing.png"
style="border:none"></a></p>
<hr>
</nav>
```

Note Because the bottom navigation bar should be formatted differently than the top one, we'll leave it formatted as a division. That way you can use the *<nav>* tag to define the formatting for only the top navigation bar.

4. Delete the *<div id="main">* tag and its closing *</div>* tag.

5. Enclose the *Europe On Sale!* heading and the two paragraphs that follow it in an *<article>* tag:

```
<article>
<h2>Europe On Sale!</h2>
<p>For a limited time, all our European dream vacations are now up to 50% off
original prices! Enjoy exotic destinations you've always wanted to visit,
such as Buckingham Palace, The Eiffel Tower, The Louvre, and many others, and
save thousands! <a href="sale.htm">Click here to find out how much you can
save!</a></p>
<p>Nervous about travelling abroad? There's no need to be. All of our trips
are fully escorted, and include transportation by air, rail, or motorcoach,
lodging, meals, and admission fees. You won't have to worry about a thing,
as Margie's experienced and helpful tour guides lead you through the amazing
sights, sounds, and experiences of the countries and cultures of the world.
<a href="international-faqs.htm">Click here for some international travel
planning tips.</a></p>
</article>
```

6. Enclose the *Award-Winning Service* heading and the paragraph that follows it in an *<article>* tag:

```
<article>
<h2>Award-Winning Service</h2>
<p>Margie's Travel is proud to be the recipient of the Gold Star Award for
Travel Service, issued by Broadway Travel Reviews, Inc. This prestigious award
is given to only one tour provider in each region each year, for outstanding
tour services based on customer reviews. <a href="award.htm">Click here to
learn more about the award.</a>
</article>
```

7. Beneath the second article, add this new section, which uses an *<aside>* tag:

```
<aside>
<p><b>Unfamiliar Terrain?</b> Run into a travel-related term here on our
site that you aren't familiar with? Look it up in our <a href="glossary.htm"
target="_blank">Glossary</a>.</p>
</aside>
```

Leave the bottom navigation bar's *<div>* tag as is.

8. Replace the *<div id="copy">* tag with *<footer>* and then change its closing *</div>* tag to *</footer>*:

```
<footer>
<p class="copyright">
Copyright &copy; Margie's Travel<br>
No material may be reproduced without written permission<br>
<a href="mailto:webmaster@margiestravel.com" style="color: white">
Contact the Webmaster</a></p>
</footer>
```

9. Save the file and then refresh Internet Explorer to check your work.

Note You have not made any changes that change the rendering or appearance of the page, so it looks the same as it did before. If it does not look the same as it did before, you have made a mistake.

10. Close Notepad and Internet Explorer.

Positioning Divisions

There are two ways of positioning a division (or equivalent semantic-tagged block): you can use the *float* style rule, as you did with pictures in Chapter 9, "Inserting Graphics," or you can use the *position* style rule. The following sections explain each method.

> **Note** In the rest of this chapter, for simplicity, I use the term *division* generically to mean both the *<div>* tag and the HTML5 semantic tags. In most cases, browsers handle the formatting and positioning the same way.

Floating a Division to the Right or Left

The easiest way to place one division beside another is to use the *float* style rule. For example, to make a navigation bar that floats to the left of the main body text, you can set the navigation bar's division to a certain width (perhaps 180 pixels or so), and then float it like this, with the line height increased to create a bit of extra space vertically between the buttons:

```
<div id="topnav" style="width: 180px; float: left; line-height: 250%">
```

If you were using the *<nav>* tag for the navigation bar, it would look like this (see Figure 11-2):

```
<nav style="width: 180px; float: left; line-height: 250%">
```

Vertical placement of navigation bar

FIGURE 11-2 A vertical navigation bar example.

Because the main advantage of using divisions is to promote consistency across documents, you would probably want to set up the style rule in an external style sheet rather than in the individual division tag or an internal style sheet.

In a style sheet, you precede the names of unique elements (such as divisions) with a pound sign (#), as shown in the following:

```
#topnav {width: 180px; float: left; line-height: 250%}
```

Alternatively, if you were using the *<nav>* tag for the navigation bar, the style rule in the style sheet would look like this:

```
nav {width: 180px; float: left; line-height: 250%}
```

Positioning a Division on the Page

If you need a division to be in a specific spot on the page, use the *position* style rule, which has three possible values:

- **position: absolute**   This value specifies a fixed position with respect to the parent element. Unless the element is within some other tag, the parent element is generally the <body> tag; in this case, the element would have a fixed position relative to the upper-left corner of the page.

- **position: relative**   This value specifies an offset from the element's natural position. Other elements on the page are not affected, even if the new position causes elements to overlap.

- **position: fixed**   This value specifies a fixed position within the browser window that doesn't change even when the display is scrolled up or down.

 Caution Absolute positioning is not very accessibility-friendly; it can cause problems for users who have special visual needs. For example, if the user requires exceptionally large fonts to see the page, using absolute positioning can hide some content from view.

You must use each of these values in conjunction with a *top*, *right*, *bottom*, and/or *left* style rule that specifies the location to which the *position* rule refers. For example, to position a division called *main* exactly 100 pixels from the top of the page and 200 pixels from the left side, create this style rule in the style sheet:

```
#main {position: absolute; top: 100px; left: 200px; line-height: 250%}
```

> **Note** When using semantic tags, you won't have one that defines the entire main body of the page content, so you might want to create a division for that purpose if you want to specify an exact position for all the body text on the page. As the previous example illustrates, it's okay to mix semantic tags with *<div>* tags in your work. The *<div>* tag is not deprecated in HTML5; it's still perfectly valid.

You can combine positioning with a *width* specification to position each division in a precise rectangular area on the screen. For example, to place the top navigation bar exactly 100 pixels from the top of the page and make it 180 pixels wide, use the following:

```
#topnav {position: absolute; top: 100px; width: 180px; line-height: 250%}
```

Or, if you are using the *<nav>* tag instead, use this:

```
nav {position: absolute; top: 100px; width: 180px; line-height: 250%}
```

The *position* style rule results in positioning that does not take into regard other elements on the page. This can get you in trouble because elements can potentially overlap unattractively, but it can also be used to intentionally create overlapping elements. For example, you can use this feature to overlay text on a photo.

In the following exercise, you will specify a size and position for several divisions by creating rules that refer to those divisions in an external style sheet.

Position Divisions

1. Open *index3.htm* in Internet Explorer and then open *default.css* in Notepad. The files for this exercise are located in the *Documents\Microsoft Press\HTML5 Start Here\11Divisions\ PositioningDivisions* folder.

   In Internet Explorer, note the position of the top navigation bar.

Horizontal navigation bar

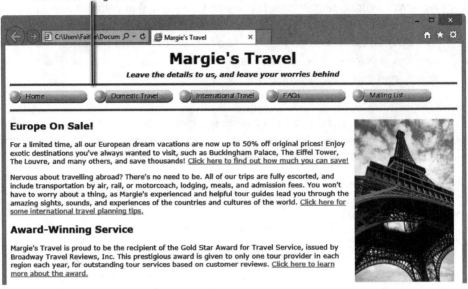

2. In Notepad, in the *default.css* file, add the following style rule:

   ```
   nav {float: left; width: 150px; padding-top: 15px; padding-right: 30px}
   ```

> **Note** You can add the style rule anywhere in *default.css*; adding it at the end of the file is fine.

3. Save the file and then refresh Internet Explorer.

   The navigation bar now displays at the left side of the page.

> **Note** Notice that there are a few problems with the layout. For one thing, when the navigation bar is laid out vertically, the horizontal rule below it looks awkward and there is not enough vertical space between the buttons. Another issue is that in some browsers, the Home button is not indented as much as the other buttons; that's because of the * * characters between the buttons.

This button is not indented as much as the others

Horizontal rules look out of place when
navigation bar is vertical

4. In Notepad, open *index3.htm*, remove the *<hr>* tags for the *<nav>* division, and then replace
   the * * characters in the *<nav>* division with *
* tags (for line breaks):

```
<nav>
<p style="margin:0px">
<a href="index.htm"><img src="images/home.png" style="border:none"></a> <br>
<a href="domestic.htm"><img src="images/domestic.png" style="border:none"></a> <br>
<a href="international.htm"><img src="images/international.png"
style="border:none"></a> <br>
<a href="faqs.htm"><img src="images/faqs.png" style="border:none"></a> <br>
<a href="mailing.htm"><img src="images/mailing.png" style="border:none"></a></p>
</nav>
```

5. Save your work and then refresh Internet Explorer to view your changes.

   The navigation bar looks better now, but there is still not enough vertical space between the
   buttons.

Navigation bar has been corrected

There are several ways to correct this problem. You could make each button its own paragraph, for example, or you could add an extra *
* tag after each button so that it not only line-breaks but also includes an extra line's worth of spacing. You could also add a *line-height* style attribute to the *<p>* tag that contains the buttons or add it to the nav division's style in css. That last option is what we'll do next.

6. In the *default.css* file, add a line-height attribute of *250%* to the nav tag's style definition:

```
nav {float: left; width: 150px; padding-top: 15px; line-height: 250%;
padding-right: 30px}
```

The nav, main, and article divisions
are all absolutely positioned

Notice that without the navigation bar at the top of the page, the masthead gets a little bit lost. Let's add a horizontal rule back in.

7. In *index3.htm*, add an *<hr>* tag immediately above the *</header>* tag:

```
<header>
<h1 style="text-align: center; margin: 3px">Margie's Travel</h1>
<i><h5 style="text-align: center; margin: 5px">Leave the details to us,
and leave your worries behind</h5></i>
<hr>
</header>
```

8. Save the file and then refresh Internet Explorer.

9. In Notepad, reopen *default.css* if necessary and then add a style rule that limits the width of the main division to 600 pixels:

```
#main {width: 600px}
```

10. Save the file, refresh Internet Explorer, and then close *index3.htm* in Notepad. The rest of the edits will be done in *default.css*.

11. In *default.css*, specify an absolute position for the top of the main division that is 82 pixels from the top and 180 pixels from the left:

```
#main {width: 600px; position: absolute; top: 82px; left: 180px}
```

12. Specify an absolute position for the top of the aside division so that it is 82 pixels from the top and 800 pixels from the left:

```
aside {width: 100px; position: absolute; top: 82px; left: 800px}
```

13. Save the file and then refresh Internet Explorer.

As shown in the figure, the footer and the bottom navigation bar are now bunched up at the top, behind the main section. This isn't acceptable, of course.

In *default.css*, add absolute positions for the footer and the bottom navigation bar that place them at 10px from the left and 10px and 75px from the bottom, respectively:

```
footer {position: fixed; bottom: 10px; left: 10px}
#bottomnav {width: 900px; position: fixed; bottom: 75px; left: 10px}
```

14. Save the file and then refresh Internet Explorer.

15. Drag the bottom of the browser window up and down to change the vertical size of the window. Notice how the bottom navigation bar moves in relation to the bottom of the window, but the rest of the page doesn't move.

16. Close Notepad and Internet Explorer.

Note The resulting page from this exercise is not something you would actually publish on a real website; it contains a hodge-podge of different techniques for positioning divisions, some of which might cause problems with each other if used on the same page, depending on the screen size. For example, placing elements relative to the browser window can interfere with absolute placement, and assuming a certain minimum screen width can cause problems for people viewing the page on low-resolution screens like smartphones. In the upcoming exercises, you'll go back to using example files that use simpler, less restrictive layouts.

Formatting Divisions

You format divisions as you would any other elements. You can use styles to specify the font family, font style, font weight, alignment, color, and everything else covered so far in this book.

You can change the background color of a division with the *background-color* style rule. For example, to add a khaki-colored background to the navigation bar, use the following:

```
nav {float: left; width: 175px; padding-top: 15px; line-height: 250%; background-color: tan}
```

When you do that, however, you might find some underlying problems that you need to correct. For example, when everything has a white background on the page, you don't notice spacing issues, but when one element is shaded, they become apparent. For example, in Figure 11-3, the tan color is too close to the main division.

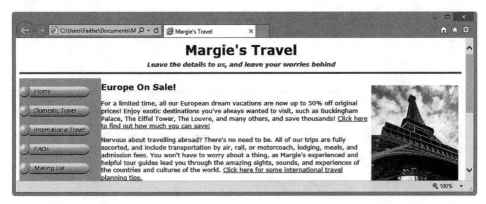

FIGURE 11-3 Adding a colored background to the nav division points out a spacing problem.

To correct that, you would need to adjust the size of the nav division and then add some padding to the main division at the left edge.

When applying a colored background to a navigation bar, you might also discover that the buttons do not have transparent edges; they need to be corrected using a graphics-editing program that supports transparency.

> **Note** When creating navigation buttons, if you need transparency, use the GIF or PNG format. JPEG format does not support transparency.

You can also add background images to divisions with the *background-image* style:

```
#header {background-image: url(images/leaf.jpg)}
```

In the following exercise, you will apply a colored background to one division and a background image to another; then you will fine-tune the settings to improve the appearance.

Format Divisions

1. Open *index4.htm* in Internet Explorer and then open *default.css* in Notepad. The files for this exercise are located in the *Documents\Microsoft Press\HTML5 Start Here\11Divisions\ FormattingDivisions* folder.

2. In the *default.css* style sheet, add the wheat background color to the bottom navigation bar by adding this line:

   ```
   #bottomnav {background-color: wheat}
   ```

   Note If you want to try other colors, check out the *Reference/extended.htm* file in the data files for this book.

3. Save the file and then refresh Internet Explorer.

   The bottom navigation bar is shaded.

   Home   Domestic Travel   International Travel   FAQs   About   Mailing List

4. In Notepad, open *index4.htm* and then remove the horizontal rules from the bottom navigation bar.

5. Save the file and then refresh Internet Explorer.

   Oops! Look what happened. Without the horizontal rules, the bottom navigation bar is now unattractively thin.

   Home   Domestic Travel   International Travel   FAQs   About   Mailing List

6. In *default.css*, add a height to the bottom navigation bar:

   ```
   #bottomnav {background-color: wheat; height: 22px}
   ```

7. Save the file and then refresh Internet Explorer.

   The bar is a little thicker now.

   Home   Domestic Travel   International Travel   FAQs   About   Mailing List

   Now give the site a new look by getting rid of the graphic and the horizontal line in the masthead, and then inserting a background image in the *header* division.

But first, let's change the way the header is set up. Some browsers don't interpret *<header>* correctly. The masthead is a fairly important page element to get right, so in the interest of compatibility, turn that *<header>* back into a division whose name is *header*.

8. In the *index4 file*, change the *<header>* tag to *<div id="header>* and then change the *</header>* tag to *</div>*. The header should look like this:

```
<div id="header">
<h1 style="text-align: center; margin: 3px">Margie's Travel</h1>
<i><h5 style="text-align: center; margin: 5px">Leave the details to us, and
leave your worries behind</h5></i>
</div><header>
```

9. Save the file.

10. In the *default.css* style sheet, add a style rule for the header division that applies an image as its background:

```
#header {background-image: url(images/pattern.jpg)}
```

11. Save the file and then refresh Internet Explorer.

Margie's Travel
Leave the details to us, and leave your worries behind

The new masthead looks interesting, but you need to add some padding so it doesn't look so crowded and you need to increase the font sizes a bit.

12. In *default.css*, modify the style rule for the header division to add 10 pixels of padding on all sides:

```
#header {background-image: url(images/pattern.jpg); padding: 10px}
```

13. In *index4.htm*, modify the styles for the *<h1>* and *<h5>* tags to use a fixed font size of *40px* and *16px*, respectively. We're doing this in the individual tags because we don't want this to affect all *<h1>* and *<h5>* headings:

```
<div id="header">
<h1 style="text-align: center; margin: 3px; font-size:40px">Margie's
Travel</h1>
<i><h5 style="text-align: center; margin: 5px; font-size:16px">Leave the
details to us, and leave your worries behind</h5></i>
</div>
```

14. Save the files and then refresh Internet Explorer to see the new masthead.

15. Close Notepad and Internet Explorer.

Key Points

- To create a division, surround a section of a page with a *<div>* tag.

- HTML5 uses semantic tags to define sections of a page. Some of the most common of these are *<header>*, *<footer>*, *<nav>*, *<article>*, *<aside>*, and *<section>*. Not all browsers support these tags yet. Internet Explorer 9.0 and higher does support these tags, as do the current versions of Google Chrome and Firefox.

- Each division tag has an *id* attribute that should be unique within that document. Multiple documents can have the same division names, though, and in fact, this is encouraged so that one external style sheet can format multiple documents.

- One way to position a division is with a *float* attribute. For example, to place a division at the left (for use as a navigation bar), use *float: left*.

- Another way to position a division is with a *position* attribute. The valid values are *absolute*, *relative*, and *fixed*. When you use the *position* attribute, you must also use a *top*, *bottom*, *left*, and/or *right* attribute to specify the numeric value for the position.

  - With absolute positioning, the element is positioned absolutely within its parent element, which is usually the *<body>* tag, so the element is positioned absolutely on the page.

  - With relative positioning, the element is positioned in relation to its default position.

  - With fixed positioning, the element is positioned in relation to the browser window.

- Divisions can be formatted by using the same character, paragraph, and page formatting styles you learned throughout the book, including *background-color* and *background-image*.

Chapter 12

Creating Tables

In this chapter, you will:

- Create a simple table

- Specify the size of a table

- Specify the width of a column

- Merge table cells

- Use tables for page layout

If you've used a word-processing program before, you're probably already familiar with the task of creating tables. A *table* is a grid of rows and columns, the intersections of which form *cells*. Each cell is a distinct area, into which you can place text, graphics, or even other tables.

HTML handles tables very well, and you can use them to organize and present complex data to your site visitors. For example, you could display your store's inventory in a table.

Tables can also be used as a page-layout tool. You can create a large table that occupies the entire page, and then place content into the cells to position that content on the page. For example, each of the sections (the masthead, the navigation bar, the body, and the footer) might reside in its own separate table cell.

> **Note** One Important drawback to using tables for layout is that they make a page less accessible. It is much more difficult for someone using a screen-reading program to access a tabular layout than a division-based one, for example. If accessibility is Important to you, you might want to use division-based layouts for your website.

In this chapter, you'll learn the basic HTML for creating tables, rows, and cells. You'll also learn how to specify cell sizes and merge cells to create larger areas. After you master these skills, you'll put them to work by creating a table-based page layout grid. Then, in the next chapter, you'll learn how to format tables.

Important Before you can use the practice files provided for this chapter, you need to install them from the book's companion content page to their default locations. See "Code Samples" in the beginning of this book for more information.

Creating a Simple Table

The *<table>* tag creates an HTML table. Within that tag, you include one or more *<tr>* tags, which define the table's rows, and within each *<tr>* tag, you define one or more *<td>* tags, which define the cells:

```
<table>
    <tr>
        <td>Cell 1</td>
        <td>Cell 2</td>
    </tr>
    <tr>
        <td>Cell 3</td>
        <td>Cell 4</td>
    </tr>
</table>
```

Displayed in a browser, this code creates a table that looks like what's shown in Figure 12-1.

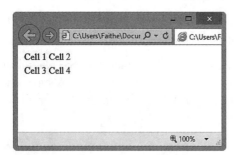

FIGURE 12-1 A simple table with no borders.

This table is not very interesting to look at in its default state. And because by default HTML tables have no borders or shading, you can barely even tell it's a table at all. The text simply appears where it's supposed to appear according to the table's specification. (That's a big hint about how you will use tables for layout later in the chapter.)

The number of columns within a table is equal to the largest number of *<td>* tags in any given row. Watch what happens when I add another *<td>* tag to the second row. I'm also going to add a *border="1"* attribute in the *<table>* tag to make the table borders visible so you can see what's going on more clearly (see Figure 12-2).

Note You'll learn more about that attribute in Chapter 13, "Formatting Tables."

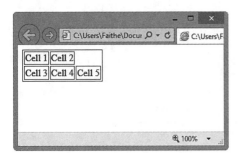

FIGURE 12-2 A table with two cells in the first row and three cells in the second row.

The additions are shown in bold text in the following code:

```
<table border="1">
   <tr>
      <td>Cell 1</td>
      <td>Cell 2</td>
   </tr>
   <tr>
      <td>Cell 3</td>
      <td>Cell 4</td>
      <td>Cell 5</td>
   </tr>
</table>
```

As shown in Figure 12-2, notice that because the rows do not have the same number of cells, the browser inserts a blank space in the row that doesn't include the extra cell. In the section "Spanning (Merging) Table Cells" on page 215, you will learn how to merge multiple cells into a single cell.

In the following exercise, you will create a simple table.

Create a Table

1. In Notepad and Internet Explorer, open the *products.htm* file located in the *Documents\Microsoft Press\HTML5 Start Here\12Tables\CreatingTable* folder.

2. In Notepad, immediately below the *<div id="main">* tag, create the table, leaving a few blank lines between the opening and closing tags:

    ```
    <table>
    </table>
    ```

3. Within the table, create three rows. Indenting the lines as shown in the following code is optional but recommended:

```
<table>
    <tr>
    </tr>
    <tr>
    </tr>
    <tr>
    </tr>
</table>
```

4. Within the first row, create four columns:

```
<table>
    <tr>
        <td> </td>
        <td> </td>
        <td> </td>
        <td> </td>
    </tr>
    <tr>
    </tr>
    <tr>
    </tr>
</table>
```

 Tip You might prefer to use *<th>* tags instead of *<td>* tags in rows that contain table headings. Using *<th>* for header row cells makes the table more accessible and some browsers automatically format table heading cells differently.

5. Type the text that will display in the first row of the table:

```
<table>
    <tr>
        <td>Tour</td>
        <td>Start Date</td>
        <td>Days</td>
        <td>Price</td>
    </tr>
    <tr>
    </tr>
    <tr>
    </tr>
</table>
```

Save the file and then refresh Internet Explorer.

Notice that the browser ignores the two empty rows.

6. In Notepad, type the information about two tours:

```
<table>
    <tr>
        <td>Tour</td>
        <td>Start Date</td>
        <td>Days</td>
        <td>Price</td>
    </tr>
    <tr>
        <td>Grand Canyon South Rim Adventure</td>
        <td>August 10</td>
        <td>5</td>
        <td>$599</td>
    </tr>
    <tr>

        <td>Phoenix, Sedona, and Albuquerque: The Best of the Southwest</td>
        <td>August 15</td>
        <td>8</td>
        <td>$799</td>
    </tr>
</table>
```

7. Save the file and then refresh Internet Explorer.

Notice that the columns have expanded to accommodate the longest entries.

8. Close Notepad and Internet Explorer.

Specifying the Size of a Table

By default, a table sizes itself to accommodate all of its cells, and each cell's height and width changes to accommodate the largest entry in that row or column. The table structure expands or contracts as needed when you add or remove cells or content within cells.

With these default settings, a table can end up looking rather cramped, especially if you don't use borders between cells (which you'll learn more about in Chapter 13). In the table from the previous exercise, for example, some extra space would be welcome.

One way to add extra spacing in this instance would be to set the overall size of the table to 100 percent. This forces the table to expand horizontally to fill the available space in the browser window. To do this, add a *width* attribute to the opening *<table>* tag:

```
<table width="100%">
```

Alternatively, you can place the width specification in a style:

```
<table style="width: 100%">
```

To apply the width specification to all tables, place it in a style sheet:

```
table {width: "100%"}
```

You don't need to specify 100 percent; you could also set the table's width to 50, 75, or any other percentage. You can do the same thing with table height, making it expand to fill the entire browser window vertically by using the following:

```
table (height: "100%")
```

The only drawback to specifying width and/or height by percentage is that you cannot be certain which size browser window the visitors to your site will be using. This example looks great in a moderate-sized window (see Figure 12-3).

FIGURE 12-3 In a moderately sized window, this table looks good.

But in a smaller window (see Figure 12-4), it becomes just as cramped as before and the text wraps to multiple lines.

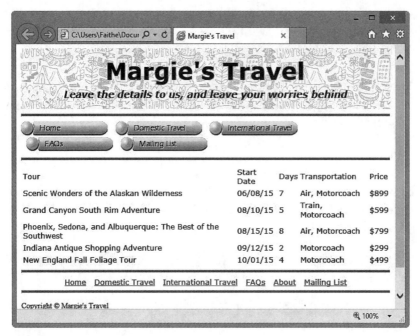

FIGURE 12-4 When the window size is smaller, the table is cramped.

And in a larger window, the extra space between the columns becomes exaggerated (see Figure 12-5).

FIGURE 12-5 When the window size is large, the table appears too spread out.

An alternative approach is to specify a number of pixels for the table's width. That way, the width the table requires in pixels does not change no matter what the size of the browser window.

For example, to lock the table to a width of 750 pixels, use the following:

```
<table width="750px">
```

When a browser renders a fixed-width table in a smaller browser window, a horizontal scroll bar appears in the window. When displayed in a larger window, extra horizontal space displays to the right of the table (assuming the table is left-aligned) rather than being distributed throughout the table.

Although it is less common, there might also be cases where it is useful to set a specific table height, either in percentage or pixels. You do this by using the same method, except you specify height instead. For example, in a tag, use this:

```
<table height="400px">
```

To specify height in a style rule, use this:

```
table (height: 400px}
```

In the following exercise, you will change a table's width using two different methods and then check its appearance in various browser window sizes.

Resize a Table

1. In Notepad and Internet Explorer, open the *products.htm* file located in the *Documents\ Microsoft Press\HTML5 Start Here\12Tables\SpecifyingSize* folder.

2. Modify the opening *<table>* tag to make the table exactly 700 pixels wide:

    ```
    <table width="700px">
    ```

3. Save the file and then refresh Internet Explorer. Experiment with different browser window sizes and note how the table looks at each size.

4. Edit the *<table>* tag to make the table fill the width of the browser window:

    ```
    <table width="100%">
    ```

5. Save the file and then refresh Internet Explorer. Experiment with different browser window sizes and note how the table looks at each size.

6. Remove the width attribute from the table tag:

    ```
    <table>
    ```

7. Create a style rule in the *<head>* section that sets the default width for all tables to 100 percent of the browser window width:

    ```
    <style>
    table {width: 100%}
    </style>
    ```

8. Save the file and then refresh Internet Explorer. It should not have changed from the last time you looked at it.

9. Add a *height* attribute to the *<table>* tag that sets the table height at exactly 250 pixels:

```
<table height="250px">
```

10. Save the file and then refresh Internet Explorer. Extra space has been distributed vertically throughout the table.

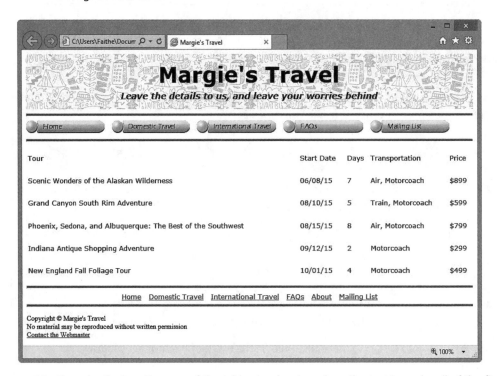

11. To make the heading row of the table stand out, enclose the text in each cell of the first row in *<b>* tags:

```
<tr>
        <td><b>Tour</b></td>
        <td><b>Start Date</b>/td>
        <td><b>Days</b></td>
        <td><b>Transportation</b></td>
        <td><b>Price</b></td>
</tr>
```

> **Note** If you use the *<th>* tag instead of *<td>* for the cells in heading rows, you don't have to manually make the content bold in those cells, because most browsers display *<th>* content in boldface. However, be aware that the *<th>* tag might also bring with it some unintended formatting consequences. For example, in Internet Explorer 10, *<th>* cells are centered horizontally.

12. Save the file and then refresh Internet Explorer to see the bold column headings.

13. Close Notepad and Internet Explorer.

Specifying the Width of a Column

Setting the overall table size is useful, but for more control, you might prefer to set the width of each column separately. To set the width of a column to a certain minimum amount, specify a width in the *<td>* tag for any cell within that column. You can use the same method you used for the *<table>* tag in the preceding section, as shown in the following:

```
<td width="200px">
```

To specify the width of a column by using a style, use this:

```
<td style="width: 200px">
```

The traditional place to set the column width is in the first row of the table, but that is not a requirement; you can set a width for any cell in any row. The column as a whole will be as wide as the widest cell in that column.

In the following code, specific values are set for the column widths:

```
<table border="1">
   <tr>
      <td width="100px"> </td>
      <td width="400px"> </td>
      <td width="100px"> </td>
   </tr>
   <tr>
      <td> </td>
      <td> </td>
      <td> </td>
   </tr>
</table>
```

This code creates a table that looks like that shown in Figure 12-6.

FIGURE 12-6 A blank table with specific widths for each column.

Tip The examples shown here use nonbreaking spaces (* *) as placeholders in empty cells. This is optional, but it makes an empty table display as it will when you place content in the cells, which can be important when you are checking your work in a browser window as you build your page.

If you enter some text in one of the cells that exceeds the column's width, Internet Explorer wraps the text into multiple lines, as needed (see Figure 12-7).

Hiking, Biking, and Swimming: Active Vacations		

FIGURE 12-7 Because the first column is fixed in width, text wraps to additional lines.

Note The text-wrapping behavior shown in the preceding example is not universal across all browsers. Some older versions of Internet Explorer, for example, will still expand the first column to fit all the text on one line, as does the current version of Google Chrome. This illustrates the importance of checking your work in multiple browsers.

If you widen the browser window, the text remains wrapped because the column width is fixed.

You can also specify column width in percentages, for different wrapping and resizing behavior at different browser window widths. Suppose in the previous example that you specified 20 percent, 60 percent, and 20 percent for each of the three columns, respectively:

```
<table border="1">
  <tr>
    <td width="20%"> </td>
    <td width="60%"> </td>
    <td width="20%"> </td>
  </tr>
```

```
   <tr>
      <td> </td>
      <td> </td>
      <td> </td>
   </tr>
</table>
```

You would start out with a very small table, because the table is only as large as it needs to be to hold its content (see Figure 12-8).

FIGURE 12-8 The table starts out small but will expand as you enter text into it.

However, when you add text to a cell, the table expands. Keep in mind that the table expands proportionally; the first column will always be 20 percent of the width of the entire table, the second column 60 percent, and so on. The width of the browser window determines how much that first column can expand while still maintaining the proportion. Figure 12-9 shows what the example table looks like in an 800 × 600 browser window, with sample text entered in the first cell, as in the previous example.

Train, Air, and
Motorcoach

FIGURE 12-9 The second and third columns adjust their sizes proportionally.

However, if you expand the browser window to, for example, 1024 × 768, the table cells stretch out to fill the available space, keeping their 20/60/20 percent proportions (see Figure 12-10).

Train, Air, and Motorcoach

FIGURE 12-10 The same table shown in Figure 12-9 but in a wider browser window.

As you might guess, things can get complicated when you start combining overall table widths with individual cell widths. If a table doesn't turn out the way you expected, try removing all width specifications from the *<table>* and *<td>* tags and all width-related style rules from the style sheet, and then start over.

In the following exercise, you will set specific widths for each column in a table.

Change Table Column Widths

1. In Notepad and Internet Explorer, open the *products.htm* file located in the *Documents\Microsoft Press\HTML5 Start Here\12Tables\SettingWidth* folder.

2. In Internet Explorer, examine the widths of the columns. Change the browser window to several different widths to see how the columns change.

3. In Notepad, set the width of the first column of the table to 400 pixels by using a *style* attribute:

```
<tr>
    <td style="width: 440px"><b>Tour</b></td>
    <td><b>Start Date</b></td>
    <td><b>Days</b></td>
    <td><b>Transportation</b></td>
    <td><b>Price</b></td>
</tr>
```

4. Set the width of the second column to 95 pixels:

```
<tr>
    <td style="width: 440px"><b>Tour</b></td>
    <td style="width: 95px"><b>Start Date</b></td>
    <td><b>Days</b></td>
    <td><b>Transportation</b></td>
    <td><b>Price</b></td>
</tr>
```

5. Set the width of the third column to 60 pixels and the fourth column to 150 pixels:

```
<tr>
    <td style="width: 440px"><b>Tour</b></td>
    <td style="width: 95px"><b>Start Date</b></td>
    <td style="width: 60px"><b>Days</b></td>
    <td style="width: 150px"><b>Transportation</b></td>
    <td><b>Price</b></td>
</tr>
```

 Note There is no need to set the width of the column farthest to the right at this point because its right edge is adjacent to blank space.

6. Save the file and then refresh Internet Explorer.

Experiment with various window widths in Internet Explorer to see how the table's column widths behave compared to step 1.

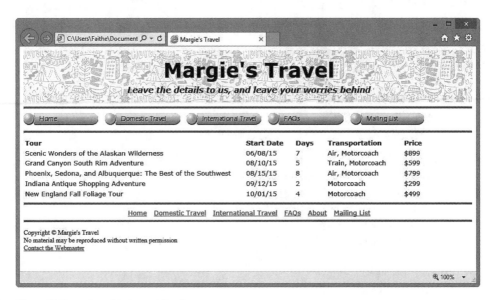

7. Close Notepad and Internet Explorer.

Spanning (Merging) Table Cells

As you have seen in the preceding sections, every cell in a given row must be the same height and every cell in a given column must be the same width. You can't make individual cells different heights or widths, but you can *span* (merge) two or more adjacent cells so that one cell spans multiple rows and/or columns. This technique is useful for centering text across several columns. It also comes in very handy when creating table-based page layouts, which you'll learn about on page 221.

To merge a cell into adjacent cells to its right, use the *colspan* attribute and specify the number of columns to be spanned:

```
<td colspan="3">
```

To merge a cell into adjacent cells below it, use the *rowspan* attribute and specify the number of rows to be spanned:

```
<td rowspan="2">
```

Using those two attributes, you can create sophisticated table layouts. For example, the following table has five columns and five rows, but some of the cells span multiple columns or rows:

```
<table border="1">
    <tr>
        <td colspan="2" rowspan="2">Survey Results</td>
        <td colspan="3">Age</td>
    </tr>
    <tr>
        <td>12 to 25</td>
        <td>26 to 40</td>
        <td>Over 40</td>
    </tr>
    <tr>
        <td rowspan="3">"What is your dream vacation destination?"</td>
        <td>Disneyworld</td>
        <td>25%</td>
        <td>50%</td>
        <td>25%</td>
    </tr>
    <tr>
        <td>Las Vegas</td>
        <td>25%</td>
        <td>50%</td>
        <td>25%</td>
    </tr>
    <tr>
        <td>Europe</td>
        <td>25%</td>
        <td>50%</td>
        <td>25%</td>
    </tr>
</table>
```

The preceding code creates the table shown in Figure 12-11.

Survey Results		Age		
		12 to 25	26 to 40	Over 40
"What is your dream vacation destination?"	Disney World	25%	50%	25%
	Las Vegas	25%	50%	25%
	Europe	25%	50%	25%

FIGURE 12-11 Several cells have been merged to create this look.

In the following exercise, you will create two simple column spans.

Change Table Column Widths

1. In Notepad and Internet Explorer, open the *products.htm* file located in the *Documents\Microsoft Press\HTML5 Start Here\12Tables\SpanningCells* folder.

 Important Make sure you use this copy and not the one you used in the previous exercise, because this copy has some extra text in it that you will need.

2. In Internet Explorer, view the *products.htm* file.

   Notice that the table title is not centered over the table and that the note at the bottom of the table is bunched up in the last column.

   Tour Listing

Tour	Start Date	Days	Transportation	Price
Scenic Wonders of the Alaskan Wilderness	06/08/15	7	Air, Motorcoach	$899
Grand Canyon South Rim Adventure	08/10/15	5	Train, Motorcoach	$599
Phoenix, Sedona, and Albuquerque: The Best of the Southwest	08/15/15	8	Air, Motorcoach	$799
Indiana Antique Shopping Adventure	09/12/15	2	Motorcoach	$299
New England Fall Foliage Tour	10/01/15	4	Motorcoach	$499
				Note: Prices shown do not include sales tax.

3. In Notepad, modify the table title to span all five columns and to be centered:

```
<tr><b>
    <td colspan="5" style="font-size: 1.2em; text-align: center">Tour
Listing</td>
    <td></td>
    <td></td>
    <td></td>
    <td></td>
</b></tr>
```

4. In the last row of the table, move the cell containing the note to the second position:

```
<tr>
     <td></td>
     <td>Note: Prices shown do not include sales tax.</td>
     <td></td>
     <td></td>
     <td></td>
</tr>
```

Note Step 4 is necessary because columns can be spanned only from left to right.

5. Format the note to span four columns:

```
<tr>
        <td></td>
        <td colspan="4">Note: Prices shown do not include sales tax.</td>
        <td></td>
        <td></td>
        <td></td>
</tr>
```

6. Save the file and then refresh Internet Explorer.

7. Close Notepad and Internet Explorer.

Using Tables for Page Layout

In addition to their value in laying out tabular data, tables are also useful in HTML for their page-structuring capabilities.

It is customary for a webpage to have a navigation bar at the top or on the left side. It is fairly easy to create a horizontal navigation bar with regular paragraphs, as you learned in Chapter 10, "Creating Navigational Aids," but to create a vertical navigation bar, you must somehow break the page into sections. One way to do that is by using divisions, as you learned in Chapter 11. Another way is to use a table.

When using a table for page layout, you might place your navigation hyperlinks in the column farthest to the left and then place the body of your content in the other columns. The table cells act as containers into which you can put anything: paragraphs, lists, headings, graphics, and so on.

Some web designers prefer to place everything in the table and use row and column spans to merge cells where needed. Others place only certain content in a table, letting the rest of the text float around it.

The skills you have learned so far in this chapter will serve you well when creating table-based layouts. You can specify the exact widths of the columns by pixels or their relative width in percentages, and you can create row or column spans as needed.

In the following exercise, you will convert a page with a horizontal navigation bar to one with a vertical bar by using a table.

Build a Table-Based Page Layout

1. In Notepad and Internet Explorer, open the *index.htm* file located in the *Documents\Microsoft Press\HTML5 Start Here\12Tables\BuildingLayout* folder.

2. View the *index* file in Internet Explorer. Note the navigation bar position.

3. Delete the *<hr>* tags before and after the top navigation bar.

4. Enclose the top navigation bar in a table cell by adding an opening *<table>*, *<tr>*, and *<td>* tag above it and then adding a closing *</td>* tag below it:

```
<table>
<tr>
<td>
<nav>
<p style="margin:0px">
<a href="index.htm"><img src="images/home.png" style="border: none"></a>
 
<a href="domestic.htm"><img src="images/domestic.png" style="border: none">
</a>  
<a href="international.htm"><img src="images/international.png"
style="border:none"></a>    
<a href="faqs.htm"><img src="images/faqs.png" style="border:none"></a>   
<a href="mailing.htm"><img src="images/mailing.png" style="border:none"></a>
</p>
</nav>
</td>
```

5. Enclose the main and aside divisions together in a single *<td>* tag and then end the row and the table after the aside division:

```
<td>
<div id="main">
<img src="images/eiffel.jpg" style="margin: 8px; float: right" height=300px>
<h2>Europe On Sale!</h2><td>


. . .


<aside>
<p><b>Unfamiliar Terrain?</b> Run into a travel-related term here on our
site that you aren't familiar with? Look it up in our <a href="glossary.htm"
target="_blank">Glossary</a>.</p>
</aside>
</td>
</tr>
</table>
```

6. Delete all the * * codes from the top navigation bar.

7. Delete the *<p>* and *</p>* tags that surround the top navigation bar and then enclose each of the buttons in the top navigation bar in its own separate *<p>* tag:

```
<table>
<tr>
<td>
<nav>
<p><a href="index.htm"><img src="images/home.png" style="border: none"></a></p>
<p><a href="domestic.htm"><img src="images/domestic.png" style="border:
none"></a></p>
<p><a href="international.htm"><img src="images/international.png"
style="border:none"></a></p>
<p><a href="faqs.htm"><img src="images/faqs.png" style="border:none"></a> </p>
<p><a href="mailing.htm"><img src="images/mailing.png" style="border:none">
</a></p>
</nav>
</td>
```

> **Note** In Chapter 9, you learned how to create extra vertical space between buttons by increasing the line spacing. The previous example takes an alternate approach by making each button a separate paragraph, allowing it to inherit the default spacing between paragraphs.

8. Save the file and then refresh Internet Explorer. It looks all right, except there needs to be more padding between the buttons and the body text and the buttons should top-align vertically rather than being vertically centered in their cells.

9. Format the first column to be exactly 170 pixels wide and to be vertically aligned at the top:

```
<table>
<tr>
<td style="width: 170px; vertical-align: top">
<nav>
```

Note I'm jumping ahead just a little with the previous example; you don't officially learn about aligning text in cells until Chapter 13. But the buttons look so much better top-aligned that I thought you might want to make them that way sooner rather than later. See Chapter 13 for more information about vertical and horizontal in-cell alignments.

10. Save the file and then refresh Internet Explorer.

The navigation buttons are now more attractively spaced and aligned with the top of the text in the main division.

11. Close Notepad and Internet Explorer.

Key Points

- To create a table, use the *<table>* tag. Enclose each row in a *<tr>* tag and enclose each cell in each row in a *<td>* tag.

- You can specify table size in either pixels or as a percentage of the page width. Use the *width* attribute like this: *<table width="400">*.

- You can also set width by using a style rule like this: *<table style="width: 400">*.

- You can specify the width of each cell, either in percentages or pixels, like this: *<td width="100">* or *<td style="width: 100">*.

- To merge (span) multiple cells, place the *colspan* or *rowspan* attribute in the cell at the top of or farthest to the left in the range to be spanned like this: *<td colspan="2">*.

- You can use tables as containers to facilitate page layout. You can place all or part of the body of a page in a table.

Formatting Tables

In this chapter, you will:

- Apply table borders

- Apply background and foreground fills

- Change cell padding, spacing, and alignment

Chapter 12, "Creating Tables," explained how to create tables structurally; now it's time to learn how to make them more attractive. By default, a table is just a plain container—no border, no shading, and no text formatting. It's up to you to add all those things if you want them.

Not every table needs elaborate formatting. If you are using a table as a container for a page layout, as demonstrated at the end of Chapter 12, you probably want the table to be as unobtrusive as possible. But even unobtrusive tables can benefit from some of the small improvements you'll learn about in this chapter, such as adjusting the amount of space between the border of a cell and its content. (That's called *padding*, as you might remember from Chapter 8, "Formatting Paragraphs with CSS.")

In this chapter, you'll learn how to apply borders to table cells and how to fill their backgrounds with color or images. You'll learn how to fine-tune cell spacing and padding, and how to make the contents of a cell align a certain way vertically and horizontally.

Important Before you can use the practice files provided for this chapter, you need to in-stall them from the book's companion content page to their default locations. See "Code Samples" in the beginning of this book for more information.

Applying Table Borders

Tables created using the default settings are pretty plain—in fact they're invisible—so it can be difficult to distinguish where one cell ends and the next cell begins. To help with this problem, you can place borders around cells, either globally or selectively. You might also choose to fill (shade) certain cells to help them stand out. For example, the spacing in the table shown in Figure 13-1 makes it difficult for a reader to follow a line across the page.

Tour Listing

Tour	Start Date	Days	Transportation	Price
Scenic Wonders of the Alaskan Wilderness	06/08/15	7	Air, Motorcoach	$899
Grand Canyon South Rim Adventure	08/10/15	5	Train, Motorcoach	$599
Phoenix, Sedona, and Albuquerque: The Best of the Southwest	08/15/15	8	Air, Motorcoach	$799
Indiana Antique Shopping Adventure	09/12/15	2	Motorcoach	$299
New England Fall Foliage Tour	10/01/15	4	Motorcoach	$499
Historic Boston	11/01/15	3	Motorcoach	$399
Museums and Monuments of Washington D.C.	11/06/15	4	Motorcoach	$499

FIGURE 13-1 Without borders, this table is difficult to read.

You could make it easier to read by applying borders like those shown in Figure 13-2.

Tour Listing

Tour	Start Date	Days	Transportation	Price
Scenic Wonders of the Alaskan Wilderness	06/08/15	7	Air, Motorcoach	$899
Grand Canyon South Rim Adventure	08/10/15	5	Train, Motorcoach	$599
Phoenix, Sedona, and Albuquerque: The Best of the Southwest	08/15/15	8	Air, Motorcoach	$799
Indiana Antique Shopping Adventure	09/12/15	2	Motorcoach	$299
New England Fall Foliage Tour	10/01/15	4	Motorcoach	$499
Historic Boston	11/01/15	3	Motorcoach	$399
Museums and Monuments of Washington D.C.	11/06/15	4	Motorcoach	$499

FIGURE 13-2 Adding borders to the cells makes it easier for the reader's eyes to follow across each row.

Tip If you don't like the double lines between each cell, set the cell spacing to 0. You'll learn how to do that in the "Changing Cell Padding, Spacing, and Alignment," section on page 237.

You can apply borders to a table either by adding attributes to the *<table>* tag or with styles, either applied to the individual table or placed in an internal or external cascading style sheet. This chapter shows both methods, but the style method is the more modern one, and it is also more reliable because it produces consistent results across all browsers.

Applying Borders by Using Attributes

By default, a table has no border. To add a one-pixel border around both the table as a whole and around each individual cell, you can add this attribute to the *<table>* tag:

```
<table border="1">
```

As shown in Figure 13-3, increasing the number increases the width of the outer border around the whole table, but not the inner borders. You might recall from Chapter 12 that the *border="1"* attribute is a quick way to see the borders of a table for the purposes of learning or debugging.

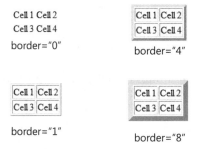

FIGURE 13-3 Border examples

If you want to play around with the above examples on your own, use the following code (changing the *border=* property to the desired value):

```
  <table border="8">
 <tr>
  <td>Cell 1</td>
  <td>Cell 2</td>
 </tr>
 <tr>
  <td>Cell 3</td>
  <td>Cell 4</td>
 </tr>
</table>
```

The *border* attribute applies a border to all sides of all cells. If you do not want the border on some of the sides, you can use the *frame* and/or *rules* attributes.

The *frame* attribute specifies which sides of the outer frame of the table will display the border. The valid values are:

- **above:** Top border only

- **below:** Bottom border only

- **border:** All four sides

- **box:** All four sides

- **hsides:** Top and bottom only (*hsides* stands for *horizontal sides*)

- **vsides:** Left and right only (*vsides* stands for *vertical sides*)

- **lhs:** Left side only (*lhs* stands for *left-hand side*)

- **rhs:** Right side only (*rhs* stands for *right-hand side*)

- **void:** No outer border

The *rules* attribute does the same thing for the inner lines of the table (the cell borders). The valid values are:

- **all:** All inner lines
- **cols:** Only vertical inner lines
- **groups:** Lines around defined groups, if any (such as column groups, which you'll learn about later in this chapter)
- **rows:** Only horizontal inner lines
- **none:** No inner lines

For example, if you want only vertical borders in your table, around both the table as a whole and around each of the cells, apply these attributes to the *<table>* tag:

```
<table border="1" frame="vsides" rules="cols">
```

Applying Borders by Using Styles

You can also apply borders by using cascading style sheets (CSS), which is the most flexible and consistent method. You should choose the CSS method in most cases, especially on sites that you expect to be active for many years to come, because the older methods of formatting tables may be deprecated in the future.

In Chapter 8, "Formatting Paragraphs with CSS," you learned about style-based borders for paragraphs. You use them the same way for the *<table>* and *<td>* tags. To review:

- The *border-width* attribute controls the thickness of the border. Specify a value in pixels.

- The *border-color* attribute controls the color of the border. Specify a color by name, hexadecimal number, or RGB value.

- The *border-style* attribute controls the line style. Choose among solid, dotted, dashed, double, groove, ridge, inset, outset, or none.

- To set all three attributes at once, use the *border* attribute and then place the settings after it in this order: *width, color, style*.

- To format the border sides individually, replace the *border* attribute with the *border-top*, *border-bottom*, *border-left*, or *border-right* attribute.

You can apply these attributes either to the entire table (by using the *<table>* tag or a style rule) or to individual cells (by using the *<td>* tags). You can apply them to individual instances within the opening tags themselves, you can create rules in the *<style>* area that govern all instances within a document, or you can create rules in the external style sheet that govern all documents that use it.

For example, the following code applies a black dotted border around the outside of a table and a silver grooved border around one specific cell (see Figure 13-4):

```
<table style="border-style: dotted; border-color: black">
    <tr>
        <td style="border-style: groove; border-color: silver">Cell 1</td>
        <td>Cell 2</td>
    </tr>
    <tr>
        <td>Cell 3</td>
        <td>Cell 4</td>
    </tr>
</table>
```

FIGURE 13-4 The first cell has a border; the other cells do not. The table itself has a dotted border.

To format all tables or all cells the same way, define the attributes in an embedded style sheet:

```
<style>
table {border-style: dotted; border-color: black}
td {border-style: groove; border-color: silver}
</style>
```

This code produces a result that looks as shown in Figure 13-5.

FIGURE 13-5 All cells are now formatted the same way.

As always, you can override the style rule with a *style* attribute placed specifically within an individual tag. For example, to make the first cell borderless, modify its *<td>* tag:

```
<table>
    <tr>
        <td style="border-style: none">Cell 1</td>
        <td>Cell 2</td>
    </tr>
    <tr>
        <td>Cell 3</td>
        <td>Cell 4</td>
    </tr>
</table>
```

This code produces a result that looks as shown in Figure 13-6.

FIGURE 13-6 Cell 1's formatting overrides the table-wide formatting specified by the style rule.

In the following exercise, you will add default table border settings to an external style sheet and then you will override those settings for an individual instance within a document.

Apply and Remove Table Borders

1. In Notepad, open the *default.css* file located in the *Documents\Microsoft Press\HTML5 Start Here\13FmtTables\ApplyingBorders* folder.

2. Add the following style rules to the *default.css* style sheet:

    ```
    table {border-style: outset; border-color: gray; border-width: 2px}
    td {border-style: solid; border-color: gray; border-width: 1px}
    ```

3. Save and close *default.css*, and then open *tours.htm* in Internet Explorer.

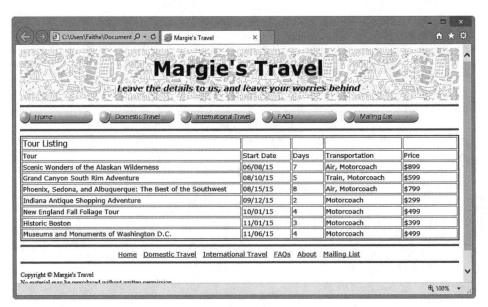

4. In Notepad, open *tours.htm* and then remove the outer border from all sides of the table.

    ```
    <table style="border-style: none">
    ```

5. Save the file and then refresh Internet Explorer.

Each cell has a border around it, but there is no overall border surrounding the table.

No outer border

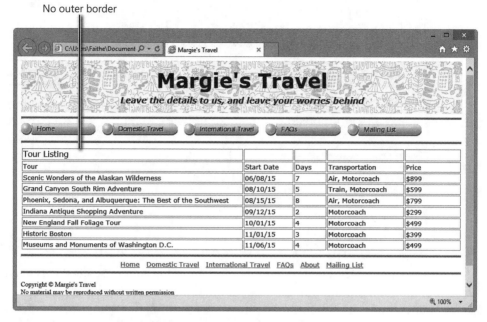

Remove the border from each cell in the top row. You have to do this for each cell individually, because you can't apply this particular style to the *<tr>* tag.

```
<table style="border-style: none">
<tr><b>
    <td style="font-size: 1.2em; border-style: none">Tour Listing</td>
    <td style="border-style: none"></td>
    <td style="border-style: none"></td>
    <td style="border-style: none"></td>
    <td style="border-style: none"></td>
</b></tr>
```

Note You can't apply border attributes to a *<tr>* tag because, technically, a row has no borders; it only has cells, which in turn have borders. Therefore, you must apply the border setting separately to each cell in the row.

6. Save the file and then refresh Internet Explorer.

The top cell now appears to be floating above the rest of the table, borderless.

Border removed from first row

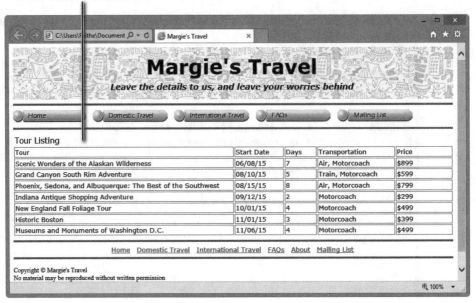

In the row containing the column headings, make the bottom border three pixels thick:

```
<tr><b>
        <td style="width: 440px; border-bottom-width: 3px">Tour</td>
        <td style="width: 95px; border-bottom-width: 3px">Start Date</td>
        <td style="width: 60px; border-bottom-width: 3px">Days</td>
        <td style="width: 150px; border-bottom-width: 3px">Transportation</td>
        <td style="border-bottom-width: 3px">Price</td>
</b></tr>
```

7. Save the file and then refresh Internet Explorer.

Thicker border below heading row

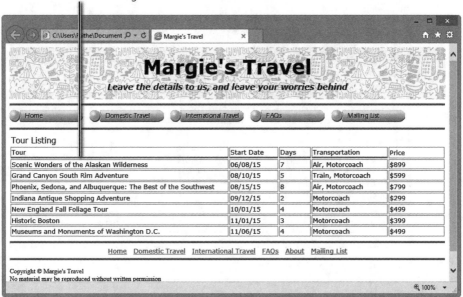

Remove the borders from all sides of the cells in the row containing the column headings. (Hint: type the attributes once, and then copy and paste.)

```
<tr><b>
<td style="width: 440px; border-bottom-width: 3px; border-top-style: none;
border-left-style: none; border-right-style: none">Tour</td>
<td style="width: 95px; border-bottom-width: 3px; border-top-style: none;
border-left-style: none; border-right-style: none">Start Date</td>
<td style="width: 60px; border-bottom-width: 3px; border-top-style: none;
border-left-style: none; border-right-style: none">Days</td>
<td style="width: 150px; border-bottom-width: 3px; border-top-style: none;
border-left-style: none; border-right-style: none">Transportation</td>
<td style="border-bottom-width: 3px; border-top-style: none; border-left-
style: none; border-right-style: none">Price</td>
</b></tr>
```

8. Save the file and then refresh Internet Explorer.

Top, left, and right borders
removed from this row

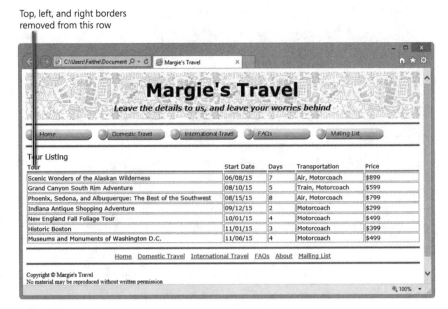

9. Close Notepad and Internet Explorer.

Applying Background and Foreground Fills

Each table, row, and cell is its own distinct area, and each can have its own background. For example, you might want to apply a different color background to a heading row to make it stand out, or change the color of every other line in a listing to help visitors track a line across the table, as shown in Figure 13-7.

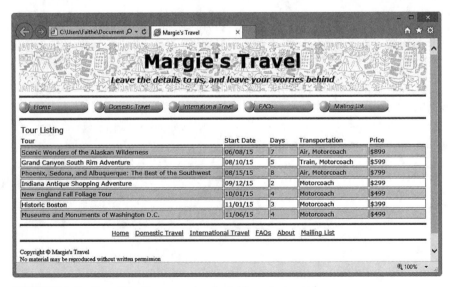

FIGURE 13-7 Shading alternate rows makes the table easier to read.

To apply a background color to a table, use the same *background-color* style rule that you use for documents. For example, to make a certain row orange:

```
<tr style="background-color: orange">
```

The table background can also be a picture, just like a document background. Apply the *background-image* attribute to any portion of a table. For example, to apply it to the entire table:

```
<table style="background-image: url(images/leaf.gif)>
```

If the image is smaller than the allotted space, it will be tiled, just as when you apply an image to a page background.

Note If you apply both a background color and a background image to the same cell(s), the more specific application takes precedence. For example, if you apply a background color to the table as a whole, and then apply a different color to an individual cell, the different color will appear in that cell.

The foreground of an element is its text, as you learned in Chapter 4, "Using Lists and Backgrounds." You can set the color of any table element like this:

```
<table style="color: blue">
```

In the following exercise, you will apply background and foreground colors to a table and use an image as a background.

Format a Table's Foreground and Background

1. In both Notepad and Internet Explorer, open the *tours.htm* file located in the *Documents\Microsoft Press\HTML5 Start Here\13FmtTables\ApplyingBackground* folder.

2. Add a style to the third row of the table (*Scenic Wonders of the Alaskan Wilderness*) that sets the background color to wheat:

```
<tr style="background-color: wheat">
        <td>Scenic Wonders of the Alaskan Wilderness</td>
        <td>06/08/15</td>
        <td>7</td>
        <td>Air, Motorcoach
        <td>$899</td>
</tr>
```

3. Copy the edited *<tr>* tag from the third table row and then insert it into every other row (the fifth, seventh, and ninth rows):

```
<tr style="background-color: wheat">
        <td>Phoenix, Sedona, and Albuquerque: The Best of the Southwest</td>
        <td>08/15/15</td>
        <td>8</td>
        <td>Air, Motorcoach
        <td>$799</td>
</tr>


<tr style="background-color:wheat">
        <td>New England Fall Foliage Tour</td>
        <td>10/01/15</td>
        <td>4</td>
        <td>Motorcoach
        <td>$499</td>
</tr>


<tr style="background-color:wheat">
        <td>Museums and Monuments of Washington D.C.</td>
        <td>11/06/15</td>
        <td>4</td>
        <td>Motorcoach
        <td>$499</td>
</tr>
```

4. Save the file and then refresh Internet Explorer.

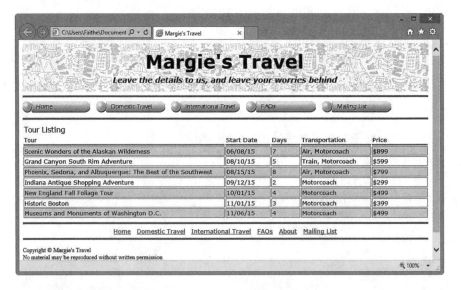

5. In Notepad, in the row containing the column headings, add a style rule that sets the background to the *marble.jpg* file (located in the images folder) and sets the foreground (text) color to white:

```
<tr style="background-image: url(images/marble.jpg); color: white">
<td style="width: 440px; border-bottom-width: 3px; border-top-style: none;
border-left-style: none; border-right-style: none"><b>Tour</b></td>
<td style="width: 95px; border-bottom-width: 3px; border-top-style: none;
border-left-style: none; border-right-style: none"><b>Start Date</b></td>
<td style="width: 60px; border-bottom-width: 3px; border-top-style: none;
border-left-style: none; border-right-style: none"><b>Days</b></td>
<td style="width: 150px; border-bottom-width: 3px; border-top-style: none;
border-left-style: none; border-right-style: none"><b>Transportation</b></td>
<td style="border-bottom-width: 3px; border-top-style: none; border-left-
style: none; border-right-style: none"><b>Price</b></td>
</tr>
```

6. Save the file and then refresh Internet Explorer.

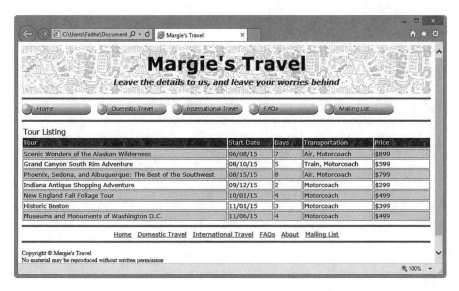

7. Close Notepad and Internet Explorer.

Changing Cell Padding, Spacing, and Alignment

Cell padding, cell spacing, and cell alignment are three different ways you can control how cell content displays on a page. You learned about these features in previous chapters, but let's briefly review them.

- *Padding* refers to the amount of space between an element's content and its outer edge. For a table cell, padding refers to space between the cell border and the text or graphic within it (see Figure 13-8).

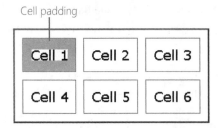

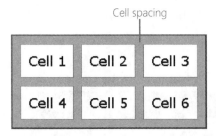

FIGURE 13-8 Cell padding is the space between the text and the cell's border.

- *Spacing* refers to the amount of space between the outside of an element and the adjacent element. For a table cell, spacing refers to the space between the border of one cell and the border of the adjacent cell (see Figure 13-9).

FIGURE 13-9 Cell spacing is the space between the border of one cell and the border of the adjacent cell.

- *Alignment* (see Figure 13-10) refers to the placement of the content within its allotted area, either vertically or horizontally. For normal paragraphs (not in a table), alignment refers only to horizontal placement between the margins. For a table cell, however, there are separate settings for vertical and horizontal alignment.

FIGURE 13-10 Examples of cell alignment.

Setting Cell Padding

To set the padding for the entire table, use the *cellpadding* attribute in the *<table>* tag. (The *cellpadding* attribute does not work with individual row and cell tags.)

```
<table cellpadding="4px">
```

To set the padding for an individual cell, use the *padding* attribute in a style, as you did in Chapter 8 for a paragraph:

```
<td style="padding: 4px">
```

To set padding in a style sheet:

```
td {padding: 4px}
```

> **Note** As with borders, you can't apply padding to a row, because, technically, a row has no cells to be padded. The *<tr>* tag is just a container for cells; only *<td>* tagged cells (or an entire table) can have padding.

Setting Cell Spacing

The default table border looks like a double line, but this effect is just a combination of the border around the table as a whole and the border around each cell. The double effect is created by the spacing between the cells.

To make the borders a single solid line between one cell and another, set the cell spacing to zero (see Figure 13-11):

```
<table cellpadding="10px" cellspacing="0px">
```

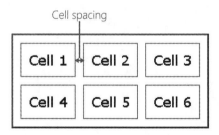

FIGURE 13-11 Cell spacing is the amount of space between two cells.

Setting Horizontal and Vertical Alignment

A cell's content has two alignments: vertical (top, middle, or bottom) and horizontal (left, center, right, or justify). You can set these with attributes or with styles. To set alignment with attributes, use the *align* attribute to specify the horizontal alignment and use the *valign* attribute to specify the vertical alignment:

```
<td align="center" valign="middle">
```

You can also set alignment with a style by using *text-align* to specify the horizontal alignment and *vertical-align* to specify the vertical alignment:

```
<td style="text-align: center; vertical-align: middle">
```

These can be applied to the entire table, to individual rows, or to individual cells. (Yes, alignment works with rows, unlike spacing and padding.)

In the following exercise, you will adjust the padding, spacing, and alignment of a table.

Change a Table's Padding, Spacing, and Alignment

1. In both Notepad and Internet Explorer, open the *tours.htm* file located in the *Documents\Microsoft Press\HTML5 Start Here\13FmtTables\ChangingPadding* folder.

2. Set the padding for the entire table to *4px*:

    ```
    <table style="border-style: none; cellpadding="4px">
    ```

3. Set the cell spacing for the entire table to *0px*:

    ```
    <table style="border-style: none" cellpadding="4px" cellspacing="0px">
    ```

4. Save the file and then refresh Internet Explorer.

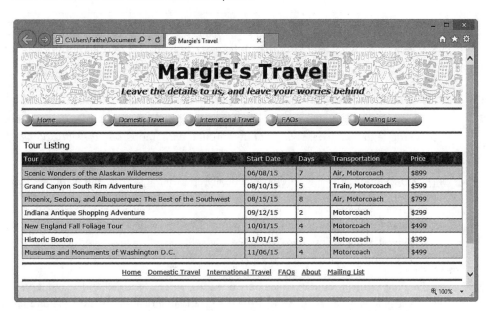

Note Notice that wherever two bordered cells touch, the border appears double thick. You can change that by removing the border from one side of each of those cells. For example, you can remove the right and bottom border on a cell like this:

```
<td style="border-right-style: none; border-bottom-style: none">
```

Alternatively, you can simply increase the table's outer border thickness so that it matches the thickness of the inner borders.

5. Close Notepad and Internet Explorer.

Key Points

- To apply a simple default border to a table, include the *border="1"* attribute in the table's opening tag. A value greater than 1 increases the table border but not the cell borders.

- The *frame* attribute specifies which sides of the table frame display the border; the *rules* attribute specifies which sides of the cell borders display the border.

- For maximum flexibility, specify borders by using style sheets. Border style attributes in tables are the same as border style attributes around paragraphs: *border-width*, *border-color*, and *border-style*.

- To format one side of a border individually, specify the side in your attribute: *border-top-width*, *border-bottom-style*, and so on.

- You can apply a background color by using the *style="background-color: color"* attribute for the whole table or for an individual row or cell. To set the text color (foreground color), use the *color* attribute.

- Padding is the amount of space between the border of the cell and its contents. Set it by using the *cellpadding* attribute in the *<table>* tag. For an individual cell, set the padding by using a style, like this: *<td style="padding: 4px">*.

- Spacing is the amount of space between the outside of an element and an adjacent element. Set it by using the *cellspacing* attribute in the *<table>* tag.

- Alignment is the placement of the content within the cell. For vertical alignment, use the *valign* attribute; for horizontal alignment, use *align*. To align using a style, use *text-align* for horizontal or *vertical-align* for vertical.

Creating User Forms

In this chapter, you will:

- Create a basic form

- Create check boxes and option buttons

- Create menu lists

Gathering feedback from your website's visitors can be a valuable way of assessing your site's success, and it can help you build a customer or subscriber database. For example, a business could collect the addresses of people who are interested in receiving product samples, email newsletters, or notifications of special offers.

To receive feedback, you can set up an email hyperlink, as you did in Chapter 5, "Creating Hyperlinks and Anchors," but an email message is not structured, and respondents are given no guidance as to the type of information you want to collect. When you need specific information, such as complete mailing addresses, it is helpful to provide visitors with a form to complete. You can use HTML to create user input forms that can send their results to you in an email message, or you can store the data in a file on your server.

In this chapter, you will learn how to create several types of user input forms. You'll set them up to deliver their results to you in an email message because that's the simplest method—and the most convenient for a low-traffic website. You'll learn how to create forms with text boxes, option buttons, check boxes, and drop-down lists. You'll also learn about some of the new HTML5 form controls, such as date boxes. At the end of this chapter, you'll find some information and web resources that can help you create even more advanced forms by using Common Gateway Interface (CGI) scripting and third-party utilities and services.

Important Before you can use the practice files provided for this chapter, you need to install them from the book's companion content page to their default locations. See "Code Samples" in the beginning of this book for more information.

Caution Many web design professionals strongly recommend against using email to deliver web form results. Not only is email not secure, but web forms do not interface very well with some email programs and some older browsers (such as Internet Explorer 3.0). If a visitor's email program or browser does not support web form submittal, the form won't work, but the visitor won't know until he clicks the Submit button, at which point the form will simply be cleared or a blank message window will open. The dilemma, though, is that nearly all of the other alternatives to email submission require either programming knowledge or going through an external service. In this chapter, you'll test your forms by using email, but use caution when relying on them for your real-world sites. Be sure to read the section "Understanding CGI and Other Advanced Tools" at the end of this chapter for alternatives.

Creating a Basic Form

You can place a form anywhere in the body of an HTML document. Some people like to use a table to organize form elements; others create form fields within ordinary paragraphs. A form is enclosed in a two-sided *<form>* tag:

```
<form method="post">
...
</form>
```

The *method* attribute specifies what will happen when the form is submitted. Almost all forms use the *method="post"* attribute, meaning that the data users enter into the form will be collected and either delivered (by email) or sent to the server, where server-side code can retrieve it and perform tasks such as storing it (in a database).

Within the opening *<form>* tag, you specify an *action* attribute. This is typically either an email address to which to send information or the URL of a script that will run when the user submits the form. For an email delivery, the *action* attribute might look like this:

```
<form action="mailto:margie@margiestravel.com" enctype="text/plain">
```

Note The *enctype* attribute specifies how the results will be encoded. An encoding type of *text/plain* is required when sending result by using email; otherwise, the results might be unreadable.

To send the form contents to a CGI script, include the URL for the appropriate CGI script stored on your server:

```
<form action="http://www.margiestravel.com/cgi-bin/feedback.pl">
```

You place the various tags that create form controls between the opening and closing *<form>* tags. Form controls available include text boxes, buttons, check boxes, lists, and/or command buttons. A *command button* is a button that executes a function, such as submitting the form or resetting it.

Creating a Text Box

The most basic type of control is a *text box*. Users can enter data such as names, addresses, phone numbers, and comments into text boxes. There are two types of text boxes: regular text boxes (single line) and text areas (multi-line). In Figure 14-1, the top four fields are single-line text boxes, while the Comments box is a multi-line text area.

First Name: [   ]   Last Name: [   ]

City: [   ]   State: [   ]

Comments:

[   ]

FIGURE 14-1 This form contains both single-line and multi-line text boxes.

You create a regular text box using a single-sided *<input>* tag with a *type="text"* attribute:

```
<input type="text">
```

Each control within a form must have a unique name, expressed with the *name* attribute. For example, to name a particular text box *phone*:

```
<input type="text" name="phone">
```

You can specify a width for the text box with the *size* attribute. The default width is 20 pixels.

```
<input type="text" name="phone" size="30">
```

You can also specify a maximum length for the text string that users enter into the text box. This is different from the size of the text box. If the specified maximum length is greater than the text box width, the text scrolls horizontally as the user types. When users reach the specified maximum number of characters, the text box does not accept any more input. Use the *maxlength* attribute:

```
<input type="text" name="phone" size="30" maxlength="100">
```

In HTML5, you can require users to fill out a field before they submit the form (this applies only to HTML5-compliant browsers). To mark a field as required, add the *required* attribute to its tag:

```
<input type="text" name="phone" size="30" maxlength="100" required>
```

Special Field Types for Email and Web Addresses

Two new *input* field types in HTML5 support email addresses and web addresses. Use the attribute *type="email"* instead of *type="text"* to define a field designed to collect email addresses. If a browser doesn't support HTML5, the field defaults to a text type, so you don't risk anything by using it.

```
<input type="email" name="email-address">
```

The same is true of web addresses (also known as uniform resource locators or URLs). There is a special *type* attribute in HTML5 for them:

```
<input type="URL" name="website">
```

In most browsers, you won't notice any difference, but there are a few exceptions. One exception is in the Apple iPhone browser; a special version of the on-screen keyboard pops up when the user selects an email or web field. This special keyboard provides dedicated keys for the most common symbols used for typing email addresses and URLs. Other browsers, especially in other smartphone operating systems, might implement special treatment for these field types, too.

Creating a Text Area

You create a multi-line text area by using a two-sided *<textarea>* tag containing a *rows* attribute that specifies the number of lines of text that the box should accommodate:

```
<textarea name="comments" rows="5"></textarea>
```

You can also include a *columns* attribute that specifies how many characters (each character represents a single column) wide the text area will be. The default is 40 characters.

```
<textarea name="comments" rows="5" cols="60"></textarea>
```

The *columns* attribute affects only the size of the box, not the maximum number of characters that can be entered. You can use the *maxlength* attribute to limit the number of characters a user can enter.

Creating a Submit or Clear Button

You will need to include a Submit button on the form so visitors can send the information to you. *Submit* refers to the button's function, not the wording that appears on the button face. The default button text is *Submit*, but you can use a *value* attribute to display different text on the button. For example, to make the word *Submit* appear on the button face, set up the *value* attribute:

```
<input type="submit" value="Send">
```

You can also include a Reset button on the form, which allows the user to clear all the fields (see Figure 14-2). Again, use the *value* attribute to change the text on the button:

```
<input type="reset" value="Clear">
```

FIGURE 14-2 Submit and Clear buttons.

Many web designers find it useful to place form fields in tables to make it easier to align the fields. For example, as shown in Figure 14-3, you could place field labels in one column and the actual fields themselves in another. You'll see this type of design in the next exercise.

First Name:	
Last Name:	
City:	
State:	
Comments:	

Submit   Clear

FIGURE 14-3 You can use a table to make the fields and labels align neatly.

Adding Default or Placeholder Text

By default, text boxes and text areas are blank when the form loads. You can optionally place either default or placeholder text in them.

- **Default text** is regular text that is submitted with the form results as if the user had actually typed it in.

- **Placeholder text** is "phantom" text that appears as a prompt within the text box but disappears when the user types something else there. If the user chooses to leave that text box blank, nothing is submitted.

Most browsers support the use of default text, even if they do not support HTML5. For a text box, add a *value* attribute to the tag that specifies the default text:

```
<input type="text" name="country" value="United States of America">
```

For a text area, you should place default text between the opening and closing *<textarea>* tags:

```
<textarea name="comments" rows="5">Great job! Keep up the good work.</textarea>
```

Placeholder text displays only in HTML5-compliant browsers. To use placeholder text, add the *placeholder* attribute:

```
<input type="text" name="country" placeholder="Enter your country here">
```

In the following exercise, you will create a simple form with text boxes and text areas in a table.

Create a Simple Form with Text Boxes

1. In Notepad and Internet Explorer, open the *signup.htm* file located in the *Documents\Microsoft Press\HTML5 Start Here\14Forms\CreatingForm* folder.

2. Immediately following the opening *<table>* tag, create an opening *<form>* tag that sends results to your own email address. Substitute your address for *youremail*:

```
<table>
<form method="post" enctype="text/plain"
action="mailto:youremail?subject=Comment">
```

3. In the empty *<td>* tag following *Name:*, create a single-line text box:

```
<colgroup align="right" valign="top">
<tr>
    <td>Name:</td>
    <td><input type="text" name="name"></td>
</tr>
```

4. In the empty *<td>* tag following *E-mail address:*, create a single-line text box with a type of *email* and a maximum length of *100* characters:

```
<tr>
    <td>E-mail address:</td>
    <td><input type="email" name="email" maxlength="100"></td>
</tr>
```

5. Add a placeholder for the email field of *Enter your email address*:

```
<tr>
    <td>E-mail address:</td>
    <td><input type="email" name="email" size="30" maxlength="100"
    placeholder="Enter your email address"></td>
```

6. In the empty *<td>* tag following *Comments:*, create a six-line text area with a width of 50 characters:

```
<tr>
   <td>Comments:</td>
   <td><textarea name="comments" rows="6" cols="50"></textarea></td>
</tr>
```

7. Add a *placeholder* attribute for the *comments* field of *Enter comments here*:

```
<tr>
   <td>Comments:</td>
   <td><textarea name="comments" rows="6" cols="50" placeholder="Enter
   comments here"></textarea></td>
</tr>
```

8. Save the file and then refresh Internet Explorer to check your work.

9. Immediately before the closing *</colgroup>* tag, add another row at the bottom of the table. Leave the first cell empty, and in the second cell, place a *Submit* button and a *Reset* button, separated by a nonbreaking space:

```
<tr>
   <td></td>
   <td><input type="submit" value="Submit"> 
   <input type="reset" value="Clear"></td>
</tr>
```

10. Save the file and then refresh Internet Explorer. Depending on the version of Internet Explorer you are using, the placeholder text might or might not appear.

11. In Internet Explorer, type some text into each field on the form (it doesn't matter what you type) and then click the Submit button.

12. Depending on what browser and version you are using, one of two things will happen at this point: either a warning will display alerting you to the fact the message is about to be sent (click Yes to allow it) or your email program will open up a new email message with the appropriate fields filled in from the form (click Send to send it).

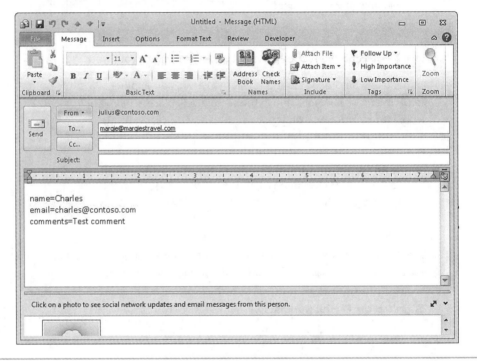

 Note The speed at which mail servers deliver messages can vary. The results might arrive almost immediately or take an hour or more.

13. Close Notepad and Internet Explorer.

Creating Check Boxes and Option Buttons

When the valid responses to a particular prompt will always be one of a few simple options, such as sex or employment status, you will get more consistent and easier-to-evaluate results by using *check boxes* and *option buttons* rather than text boxes.

> **Note** There are security benefits to using check boxes and option buttons as well. Text box controls on forms can sometimes be used by hackers to get into the associated database. Using controls other than text boxes can help minimize that risk.

For example, suppose you are asking site visitors a yes/no question such as, "Are you interested in receiving our catalog by mail?" If you provide a text box, people might answer the question in any number of ways: *y, n, Y, N, yes, no, Yes, No, YES, NO, maybe, Sure, No Thanks*, and so on. Tabulating such results would be tedious because a human would need to evaluate each one. But by providing a check box, you remove any doubt: a check mark means yes; the lack of a check mark means no.

You use *check boxes* for single binary (yes/no) questions. A form might contain multiple check boxes, but each one is a separate decision for the person filling out the form (see Figure 14-4).

Which destinations are you interested in?

☑ Europe

☑ South America

☑ United States

FIGURE 14-4 Check boxes allow users to make multiple independent selections.

To create a check box, use the *type="checkbox"* attribute with the *<input>* tag:

```
<input type="checkbox" name="europe">
```

By default, the results of the form will show a value of *On* when the check box has been selected. For the check box shown in Figure 14-4, the results would display like this:

europe=on

You can change that default by specifying a *value* attribute. For example, you could report the word *Yes* for the check box:

```
<input type="checkbox" name="europe" value="Yes">
```

By default, check boxes display unselected; users must click each check box to select it. In some cases, however, it might be advantageous to have a check box preselected. For example, to encourage people to sign up for your newsletter, you could select the Newsletter check box by default, so that users must click it to clear it. To do this, add the *checked="checked"* attribute:

```
<input type="checkbox" name="europe" value="Yes" checked="checked">
```

Use *option buttons* (also called *radio buttons*) to present a group of mutually-exclusive options. When you select an option button, all the other option buttons in the group are cleared (see Figure 14-5).

When do you expect to travel next?

- Within 30 days
- 30 to 90 days
- 90 to 120 days
- More than 120 days
- Not sure

FIGURE 14-5 Option buttons enable users to select only one of a group of related choices.

To create a group of option buttons, choose a name for the group. You will specify the same name in the *name* attribute for each individual button. Use the *value* attribute (which will be different for each button in the set) to specify the value that will be reported for the group in the form results.

For example, suppose you want users to choose among three membership categories: Gold, Silver, and Bronze. Because you make the most money on a Gold membership, you want to make it the default choice:

```
<p><input type="radio" name="category" value="gold" checked="checked"> Gold<br>
<input type="radio" name="category" value="silver"> Silver<br>
<input type="radio" name="category" value="bronze"> Bronze</p>
```

As shown in Figure 14-6, each button is followed by text describing that option (Gold, Silver, Bronze). The words *Gold*, *Silver*, and *Bronze* are just ordinary text within the paragraph, as shown in the previous code.

- Gold
- Silver
- Bronze

FIGURE 14-6 In this option button set, Gold is the default choice.

Note The space before the text is inserted by default to prevent the option buttons from running into the text. You don't need to add any space yourself.

When the form results are returned, this button group will report its name and the selected value:

category=gold

In the following exercise, you will enhance a form by adding a group of option buttons and a check box.

Add Option Buttons and a Check Box to a Form

1. In Notepad and Internet Explorer, open the *signup.htm* file located in the *Documents\Microsoft Press\HTML5 Start Here\14Forms\CreatingButtons* folder.

2. Immediately above the row containing the Submit and Clear buttons, add a new row that allows the user to choose their age range:

```
<tr>
   <td>How old is the oldest person in your travel group?</td>
   <td>
   <input type="radio" name="level" value="under40">Under 40<br>
   <input type="radio" name="level" value="40to55">40 to 55<br>
   <input type="radio" name="level" value="55to70">55 to 70<br>
   <input type="radio" name="level" value="over70">Over 70<br>
   </td>
</tr>
```

3. Save the file and then refresh Internet Explorer.

4. Immediately after the row you just created, create a new row that contains a checkbox to the left of *Yes, I would like to receive offers from other travel-related companies.* Set its name to *partner* and then set its default value to *checked*:

```
<tr>
   <td></td>
   <td><input type="checkbox" name="partner" value="Yes"
checked="checked">Yes, I would like to receive offers from other travel-
related companies.</td>
   </tr>
```

5. Change the *mailto* address in the opening *<form>* tag to your own email address.

6. Save the file and then refresh Internet Explorer.

Sign Up for E-Mail Specials

Name:

E-mail address:

Comments:

How old is the oldest person in your travel group?

- ⚪ Under 40
- ⚪ 40 to 55
- ⚪ 55 to 70
- ⚪ Over 70

☑ Yes, I would like to receive offers from other travel-related companies.

[Submit] [Clear]

7. Fill out the form (use any text you like, and select any of the option buttons) and then click Submit to send it to yourself.

8. Close Notepad and Internet Explorer.

Creating Menu Lists

Check boxes are good for yes/no questions, and option buttons are appropriate when there are a few options to choose from, but what if you have a dozen or more choices? Option buttons for that many choices can take up a lot of space onscreen and can overwhelm a web visitor.

For situations involving many options, consider a *list*, also called a *menu*. A list can contain as many options as needed, yet it takes up very little space on the form (see Figure 14-7).

FIGURE 14-7 A menu list when closed (left) and when opened (right).

To create a list, start with a two-sided *<select>* tag. Within it, place each option in its own *<option>* tag. Place the text that you want to appear on the list between the opening and closing *<option>* tags. For example, to create the list shown in Figure 14-7, use the following code.

```
<p>Color: <select name="colors" size="1">
<option>Red</option>
<option>Blue</option>
```

```
<option>Green</option>
<option>Yellow</option>
<option>Pink</option>
<option>Brown</option>
<option>Black</option>
<option>Teal</option>
<option>Beige</option>
</select></p>
```

> **Note** By default, the form results will report the text of the selected option. If you want
> to make the form report something different, include it in a *value* attribute in the option's
> opening tag.

A list can be any height you like. In the preceding code, the *size* attribute is set to 1, which creates a drop-down list. If you set the *size* attribute to a larger value, the element renders as a list box instead. If there are more items in the list than will fit in the viewing space, a scroll bar displays automatically at the right side of the box. For example, you might change the opening *<select>* tag in the preceding code to this:

```
<p>Color: <select name="colors" size="5">
```

The result would be a list like the one shown in Figure 14-8.

FIGURE 14-8 A menu list with a size greater than 1 appears as a scrolling list box.

If the list's choices fall into categories, you might want to divide them into sections (see Figure 14-9).

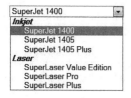

FIGURE 14-9 A multi-level list divides choices into categories.

To format a list as shown in Figure 14-9, surround the groups of options with an *<optiongroup>* tag. Include a *label* attribute that specifies the heading text for each option group. Here's the code for the preceding example:

```
<select name="printers" size="1">
    <optgroup label="Inkjet">
        <option>SuperJet 1400</option>
        <option>SuperJet 1405</option>
        <option>SuperJet 1405 Plus</option>
    </optgroup>
    <optgroup label="Laser">
        <option>SuperLaser Value Edition</option>
        <option>SuperLaser Pro</option>
        <option>SuperLaser Plus</option>
    </optgroup>
</select>
```

In the following exercise, you will add a drop-down menu list to a form.

Create a Drop-Down Menu List on a Form

1. In Notepad and Internet Explorer, open the *signup.htm* file located in the *Documents\ Microsoft Press\HTML5 Start Here\14Forms\CreatingMenus* folder. Make sure you use the version provided for this exercise; do not use a previous version.

2. In Notepad, replace the *<input>* tag for the text box that follows *State:* with an empty *<select>* tag:

```
<tr>
    <td>State:</td>
    <td><select name="state">

    </select>
    </td>
</tr>
<tr>
```

 Note Because it would be time-consuming to type *<option>* tags for all 50 states, I have created them for you.

3. In a separate Notepad window, open the *states* text file, which can be located in the data files for this exercise.

4. Press **Ctrl+A** to select the entire content of the file and then press **Ctrl+C** to copy it to the Clipboard.

5. In the *signup* file, click between the opening and closing *<select>* tags. Press **Ctrl+V** to paste the options for each state into the file.

6. Save the file and then refresh Internet Explorer. Click the down arrow to the right of the *State* box to ensure the drop-down list displays.

7. Enclose the 50 states in an *<optgroup>* tag with a label of *States*:

```
<optgroup label="States">
  <option>Alabama</option>
...
  <option>Wyoming</option>
</optgroup>
```

8. After the closing tag of the *States* option group, add a *Territories* option group that contains entries for *American Samoa, Guam, Northern Mariana Islands, Puerto Rico,* and the *U.S. Virgin Islands*:

```
...
  <option>Wyoming</option>
```

```
    </optgroup>
    <optgroup label="Territories">
        <option>American Samoa</option>
        <option>Guam</option>
        <option>Northern Mariana Islands</option>
        <option>Puerto Rico</option>
        <option>U.S. Virgin Islands</option>
    </optgroup>
</select>
```

9. Save the file and then refresh Internet Explorer. Scroll to the bottom of the *State* drop-down list to see the changes.

10. Close Notepad and Internet Explorer.

Additional Input Types in HTML5

HTML5 provides several other field types that can add that extra bit of polish to your forms. If the user's browser does not support them, it renders and treats them as text fields, so you can use them freely without worrying about backward compatibility.

Spin boxes (see Figure 14-10) are used to increment numeric values.

FIGURE 14-10 A spin box is a text box that includes increment buttons on the right side.

The spin box shown in Figure 14-10 was created by using the following code:

```
<input type="number" name="copies" min="0"max="100" step="1" value="1">
```

The *min* and *max* attributes control the minimum and maximum values, respectively. The *step* attribute specifies how much the value increments or decrements when you click the up or down arrow buttons. The *value* attribute specifies the default value.

A *slider* (see Figure 14-11) is a sliding bar that you can drag from side to side. Its type is *range* and its attributes are nearly identical to those for a spin box.

Interest level:

Not interested ——————⬤———————— Very interested

FIGURE 14-11 A slider is a bar you can drag to choose a setting within a range.

```
<input type="range" name="copies" min="1"max="4" step="1" value="1">
```

Note Internet Explorer 9 does not support spin boxes or sliders, but Internet Explorer 10 does, as do Google Chrome and most other HTML5-compliant browsers.

Understanding CGI and Other Advanced Tools

As you have learned in this chapter, directing form results to an email address is a quick, no-hassle way of collecting information, provided the visitor's web browser and email program support it. As the volume of messages increases, however, organizing all the information you receive can become a challenge. You need to copy the information from the form results into a database or you need to at least print out a copy of the email messages. When you start receiving hundreds of form submissions a day, that responsibility can become overwhelming.

As an alternative, you can rely on a server-based script or application to handle the form results. A Common Gateway Interface (CGI) script written in a programming language such as Perl is one common, low-cost possibility. You reference the script in your *<form>* tag's *action* attribute. The server on which you host your site must allow CGI scripts (some do not, for security reasons.)

Important One drawback of using CGI scripts is their lack of security. Unless you put security measures in place, the collected data resides in a file on the server, which is a potential security risk. For this reason, you shouldn't use a CGI script to collect sensitive information such as credit card or Social Security numbers unless you also implement security measures that prevent the data from being compromised. Most commercial sites use a secure server for that; you can partner with a company that offers secure form processing, including credit card processing, for a monthly fee.

There are hundreds of websites that offer free CGI scripts that you can modify in a text editor (such as Notepad) to meet your needs. To do this, you must know a little something about programming, which is beyond the scope of this book. However, if you are interested in learning about Perl and CGI scripting or you are looking for a service that will host your CGI script, see one of these websites:

- Comprehensive Perl Archive Network: *www.cpan.org*

- Matt's Script Archive: *www.scriptarchive.com*

- The CGI Resource Index: *cgi.resourceindex.com*

- BigNoseBird.Com: *www.bignosebird.com*

As your website becomes more sophisticated, you also might want to include a public bulletin board area where people can post and read comments, or a guest book where people can leave public comments. You cannot create one of those by using only HTML, but you can integrate add-on components into your site that will do the job. There are many free and low-cost sources of programming code for a message board, both in CGI (see the previously mentioned sites) and in other languages. For example, check out the phpBB open-source bulletin board package at *www.phpbb.com*. (In order to use that package, your server must support PHP.) There are also many servicessuch as ProBoards (*www.proboards.com*) that will host your bulletin board on their servers,. You place a link to the message board hosting site on your webpage; to your visitors, it seems like the message board is part of your site.

Key Points

- To create a form, use a two-sided *<form>* tag. Within it, place one or more *<input>* tags that define the form fields.

- In the opening *<form>* tag, place a *method="post"* attribute and an *action* attribute that describes how the form should be processed. The most common attribute is *action="mailto:address"* where *address* is a valid email address. If you are collecting form results by using email, include an *enctype="text/plain"* attribute.

- To create a text box, use *<input type="text" name="fieldname">*, where *fieldname* is the unique name you assign to the text box. Optional additional attributes include *size* and *maxlength*.

- For web and email collection, you can optionally use the *URL* and *email* input types, respectively. These work only in HTML5-compliant browsers.

- To create a multi-line text box (a text area), use a two-sided *<textarea>* tag with a *name* attribute and a number of rows and columns. For example:

```
<textarea name="comments" rows="5" columns="40"></textarea>
```

- To create a Submit button, use an *<input>* tag with a *type="submit"* attribute. To change the button text, use the *value* attribute. For example, *<input type="submit" value="Send">*. Use *type="reset"* to create a Reset button that clears the form.

- A check box is a one-sided, standalone element. Use an *<input>* tag with a *type="checkbox"* attribute.

- An option button operates in a group with other option buttons; only one in a group can be selected at a time. Use a one-sided *<input>* tag with a *type="radio"* attribute. For each option, use a common *name* attribute and a unique attribute.

- To create a list, use a two-sided *<select>* tag, and within it, include two-sided *<option>* tags for each list item.

- Use a *size="1"* attribute with the *<select>* tag to create a drop-down list, or specify a higher number to create a list box with a scroll bar.

- To create category headings on a list, use a two-sided *<optgroup>* tag with a label for the text that should appear. For example, *<optgroup label="Inkjet">*.

- HTML5 offers several other input types for special cases, such as spin boxes (*type="number"*), sliders (*type="range"*), and date pickers (*type="date"*).

- To process form input on a server, use a Common Gateway Interface (CGI) script or a third-party program.

Incorporating Sound and Video

In this chapter, you will:

- Understand the purpose and scope of the *<audio>* and *<video>* tags in HTML5

- Choose multimedia formats and codecs

- Use the *<video>* tag

- Use the *<audio>* tag

Playing video and audio on the web is a bit more difficult than other web-related tasks. This stems from the multitude of formats that are available from competing vendors and open source groups. These formats have varying degrees of support in the popular modern web browsers; often they have no support at all in older browsers. Together, these factors make it difficult to deliver audio and video that's consistently playable for all of your visitors.

The addition of the *<video>* and *<audio>* tags in HTML5 makes the process of delivering and playing video and audio more straightforward. Playing multimedia will get easier over time as newer browsers support the tags and people upgrade their older browsers. However, for the foreseeable future, it will still be necessary to encode your multimedia files into multiple formats.

Important Before you can use the practice files provided for this chapter, you need to install them from the book's companion content page to their default locations. See "Code Samples" in the beginning of this book for more information.

Understanding Audio and Video in HTML5

Traditionally, developers and designers have most commonly set up pages to play video and audio on the web using Adobe Flash. Sites such as YouTube (*http://www.youtube.com*) embed video inside of a Flash file. This requires that the end user has the Flash player installed.

The HTML5 specification introduces an alternative to that: a standard tag, *<video>*, which enables the playing of video content. However, the *<video>* tag still requires a video file and also requires end users to have an appropriate player installed on their computers.

Prior to HTML 5, the traditional delivery method for audio clips was to use the *<object>* or *<embed>* tag to embed a clip on a page. HTML5 provides the *<audio>* tag to do this instead.

As of this writing, not all browsers support the *<audio>* and *<video>* tags. Adding to the complexity is the need to support multiple formats for video, depending on what your visitor's browser can play.

This chapter shows you how to take advantage of the *<audio>* and *<video>* tags and helps to sort out the difficulties surrounding video compatibility.

Before going further you should understand that at the time of this writing support for these two new tags is limited to the following browsers:

- Internet Explorer 9+
- Firefox 3.5+
- Safari 3+
- Chrome 3+

- Opera 10.5+
- iPhone 1+
- Android 2+

Browsers that don't support these tags ignore them, but if you want to deliver your audio or video to a full range of browsers—new and old—you'll need to be able to do it without the use of these tags. This chapter shows both the old and new methods.

HTML Multimedia Basics

Before getting into the details of creating multimedia-rich webpages, you should have a basic understanding of how HTML5—and previous versions of HTML—present audio and video clips.

The most common method of placing multimedia content on a webpage is to *embed* an audio or video clip in the page so that it plays within the page itself when the visitor clicks a button. For this to work, visitors to your site must be using a web browser that supports the type of sound or video file you're providing or they must download and install a plug-in (a helper program) to add support for that file to their browser. If everyone in your audience uses Internet Explorer version 5.5 or higher, you can use the *<object>* tag for this; otherwise you should use the *<embed>* tag. Or, if your audience uses an HTML5-compliant browser, you can use the new *<audio>* and *<video>* tags.

As an alternative, you can *link* to an audio or video clip so that it plays in an external application (such as Microsoft Windows Media Player) when the visitor clicks its hyperlink. For this to work, the visitor must have an external application that supports the type of sound or video file you're providing, or they must download and install a separate program. This technique works the same in all browsers, though, which is a plus. Use the *<a>* tag for the link, just like with any other hyperlink. For example:

```
<a href="mysong.mp3">Playing my song!</a>
```

This chapter focuses mainly on the embedding type of multimedia presentation.

Multimedia Formats and Containers

When people talk about video files, they're usually talking about files with an .avi, .mp4, .ogg, .flv, or .mkv extension. These extensions are simply indicators of the container format for the video file itself; they don't indicate the format in which the video was encoded. When the video includes an audio track, the container file includes both the video and audio components.

Common container formats include Ogg (.ogv), Flash Video (.flv or .f4v), the aforementioned Audio Video Interleave (.avi), MPEG-4 Part 14 (.mp4), Matroska (.mkv), and many others. There is also a new format called WebM, which is an open-source video container format that will likely grow in popularity due in part to its support by Google. WebM is meant to be used exclusively with the VP8 video codec and the Vorbis audio codec (more on codecs in the next section).

Codecs: Decoding the Video and Audio

When a producer (the person or organization making the audio or video available) encodes multimedia, they choose the format in which to encode the file. The person who views that video or listens to the audio must have the appropriate decoding software installed on their computer to play the file. This decoding software is called a *codec*.

The word *codec* is shorthand for compressor/decompressor (or coder/decoder, depending on whom you ask). The codec refers to the style in which the video or audio file was encoded or formatted. To decode a video or audio file means that the computer uses an algorithm to decipher the encoded video or audio into a human-consumable form.

Now throw in the web browser. The browser, such as Internet Explorer, either needs to have built-in support for a format or needs to have a plug-in available to recognize that it can play the audio or video file. Luckily, all of the common formats and codecs today are either supported natively or are readily available in some form of plug-in installer for the popular web browsers. As newer browsers that support HTML5 appear, the use of specific third-party plug-ins—at least for video and audio—will (hopefully) become a thing of the past.

Just as there are numerous container formats, there are also several common video encoding formats. Some of the most popular ones include H.264, VP8, DivX, Theora, and several others. If you plan to do much video work on the web, you'll likely need to account for several different formats and containers to reach the widest possible audience.

As with video, playing audio through a computer or hand-held mobile devices (such as smart-phones) requires a codec to read the file and play it back. Two popular formats are MPEG-4 Audio Layer 3, which you might recognize as MP3, and AAC, which is frequently used by Apple. Vorbis is another audio format, frequently used in an Ogg container.

Which Format to Choose?

If all of this sounds complex, it is. Not only is it tough to choose among the multiple formats, but whatever your choice, there's no guarantee that your visitors will be able to play that format anyway.

So how do you choose which format to use? The answer is that you don't choose one format; you make the clip available in multiple formats. The tag in your webpage page's code lists all the alternate versions you are providing and in the order you want the browser to attempt to use them. When the browser renders your page, it selects the first one in that list that it is able to use and ignores the others.

Table 15-1 shows the three most common container file formats, not including Flash. The text in the Container column refers not only to the container type but to the file extension used for the containers.

TABLE 15-1 Common Video Formats for the Web

Container	Browser support	Video Codec	Audio Codec
Ogg	Firefox, Opera	Theora	Vorbis
mp4	Internet Explorer, Safari	H.264	AAC
WebM	Firefox 3.5+, Opera	VP80	Vorbis

An easy way of converting your video to these three formats is to use a utility such as the open source VLC Media Player (*www.videolan.org/vlc/index.html*). You can also use your own favorite video format conversion utility, if you have one. Later in this chapter I'll show you how to use VLC Media Player to convert a clip.

Encoding Video

Now that you have a high-level view of video and audio playback on the web, you might be wondering how you encode your favorite vacation videos into three formats (four if you count Flash). The clips provided for the exercises in this chapter are ready-to-go, but you will need to prepare your own video clips on your own.

Just as playback is complex, so too is encoding. People frequently employ a combination of software to encode and convert videos between formats. Fortunately, there is good free and open-source software for doing so.

In the following exercise, you will use VLC Media Player to encode a video clip in two different container formats, in preparation for making them available on a webpage. If you don't want to go to the trouble of doing this, it's okay to skip it; I will provide you with the already-converted files in a later exercise.

In this exercise, you will encode a video clip in .ogv and .webm formats.

Encode a Video Clip with VLC Media Player

1. Download and install VLC Media Player from *www.videolan.org/vlc/index.html*. The video clip to use for this exercise is located in the *Documents\Microsoft Press\HTML5 Start Here\15Multimedia\EncodingVideo* folder.

2. In VLC Media Player, on the Media menu, click Open File. Navigate to the location containing the data file for this exercise (*Agility.mod*), select it, and then click Open.

3. The clip starts playing immediately in VLC Media Player. If you don't want to watch the entire video right now, click the Pause button in the playback controls.

4. On the Media menu, click Convert/Save. The Open Media dialog box displays.

5. Click the Add button. The Select One or Multiple Files dialog box displays.

6. Click Agility.mod and then click Open. That file now displays in the File Selection section of the Open Media dialog box.

7. Click the down arrow to the right of the Convert/Save button and then click Convert.

8. Click the Browse button. The Save File dialog box displays.

9. Navigate to the folder where you want to save the file (for example, the folder for this exercise's files). Click in the File name box, type **Agility.mp4**, and then click Save.

10. In the Settings section, click the Profile drop-down list and then click Video – Theora + Vorbis (OGG).

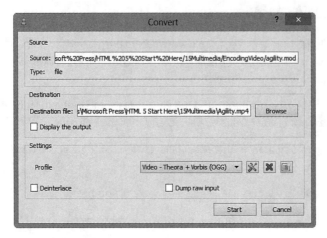

11. Click Start and then wait for the clip to be converted. The progress bar below the preview window shows the progress.

12. Repeat the process for the following format:

    Create Agility.webm using the Video – VP80 + Vorbis (Webm) profile

13. Close VLC Media Player.

 Note The VLC Media Player also encodes in MP4 format, but as I was writing this chapter, I found that some versions of Internet Explorer did not want to play the resulting file. Therefore, to create the MP4 clip for this chapter, I ended up using another free program, Handbrake.

Embedding Video Clips

Now that you have your video clips in order, you are ready to place them on a webpage. This section shows how to use the *<video>* tag to place video on a page as well as how to fall back to Flash video if necessary.

Introducing the *<video>* Tag

At a basic level, the *<video>* tag looks like this:

```
<video src="myvideo.mp4"></video>
```

There are several attributes and different ways to use the *<video>* tag that make it more configurable for your needs and the needs of your audience. Several attributes are helpful, including:

- autoplay
- controls
- height
- loop
- preload
- width

Not surprisingly, you use the *width* and *height* attributes to set the width and the height of the video display area on the page:

```
<video src="myvideo.mp4" width="320" height="240"></video>
```

The *controls* attribute determines whether a default set of playback controls should be visible within the browser. This can be helpful and I recommend using it. In fact, if you don't use the controls attribute, the visitor has no way to replay the video without reloading the entire page. How annoying! Here's an example of the *controls* attribute:

```
<video src="myvideo.mp4" controls></video>
```

The *preload* attribute tells the browser to begin downloading the video immediately when the element is encountered. If the video is the central theme of the page, and it's likely that all (or most) visitors will want to watch the video, then it's a good idea to use the preload option. However, if the video element is a small part of the page and visitors aren't likely to watch it, then preloading the video is just a waste of bandwidth. Here's the preload attribute in action:

```
<video src="myvideo.mp4" preload></video>
```

The *loop* attribute tells the browser to restart the video immediately when it's finished playing:

```
<video src="myvideo.mp4" loop></video>
```

Finally, the *autoplay* attribute makes the video automatically play when the page is loaded. For most purposes this is generally a bad idea from a usability and accessibility standpoint. Most users will want control over the video; they'll play it when their attention is focused and they're ready to consume the video element. And even with the *autoplay* attribute enabled, your visitors might have that option disabled in their browsers. For that reason, along with the usability problem, I recommend not using the *autoplay* attribute with one notable exception: if you don't include the controls attribute, then you need to include *autoplay*; otherwise, the video won't play and visitors will have no way to start it. Here's an example of the *autoplay* attribute:

```
<video src="myvideo.mp4" autoplay></video>
```

Putting it together, a real-world video element looks like this:

```
<video src="myvideo.mp4" width="320" height="240" controls></video>
```

The *<video>* tag enables more than one source (via the source element) which you can capitalize on by including links to multiple versions of a video. You can also add a *type* attribute to tell the browser a bit more about the video file to which you're linking. For example, a *<video>* tag that includes an .ogg container, an .mp4 container, and a .webm container would look like this:

```
<video width="320" height="240" controls>
    <source src="myvideo.mp4" type="video/mp4">
    <source src="myvideo.ogg" type="video/ogg">
    <source src="myvideo.webm" type="video/webm">
</video>
```

With those options you now have Internet Explorer and Safari covered (thanks to the mp4 container); Firefox and Chrome covered (thanks to the Ogg container); and other browsers covered, too (thanks to the WebM container).

The *<embed>* Tag: Your Fallback Plan

But what happens when someone visits your site with an older browser that doesn't support HTML5, so it can't use your *<video>* tag? Older browsers will simply ignore the *<video>* tag, so its mere presence won't cause errors. However, you still need to find a way for those visitors to view the video.

You'll find that most Internet Explorer users also have Flash installed. With that in mind, you can also include a Flash version of the video on your page. You can include an extra element with the help of the *<embed>* tag. Flash can play H.264 encoded video with AAC audio; therefore, you don't need to convert your video to yet another format. You can simply refer it to the existing .mp4 container version of your video. Here's an example:

```
<video width="320" height="240" controls>
    <source src="myvideo.mp4" type="video/mp4">
    <source src="myvideo.ogg" type="video/ogg">
    <source src="myvideo.webm" type="video/webm">
<embed src="myvideo.mp4" type="application/x-shockwave-flash" width="320"
height="240" allowscriptaccess="always" allowfullscreen="true">
</video>
```

Note that you place the *<embed>* tag within the *<video>* tag. You do that because if any of the sources that appear before it are able to execute, the browser will ignore the *<embed>* tag. Only if the *<video>* tag itself is unrecognized will the *<embed>* tag take effect.

Place a Video Clip on a Webpage

Now that you've got a handle on the theory, it's time to put it into practice with an exercise.

In the following exercise, you will add a video to an HTML page as an embedded clip with the *<video>* tag and provide an alternative copy as a downloadable link with the *<a>* tag. You will also practice embedding the clip with the *<embed>* tag.

Add a Video Clip to a Webpage

1. In Notepad and in Internet Explorer, open the *blog.htm* file located in the *Documents\Microsoft Press\HTML5 Start Here\15Multimedia\AddingVideo* folder.

2. Modify the *<video>* tag to specify a width, a height, autoplay, and controls:

   ```
   <video width="320" height="240" autoplay controls>
   ```

3. On the line below the *<video>* tag, add the following sources:

   ```
   <video width="320" height="240" autoplay controls>
   <source src="videos\agility.webm">
   <source src="videos\agility.ogv">
   <source src="videos\agility.mp4">
   </video>
   ```

4. Refresh Internet Explorer to view the clip on the page. If you see a warning message that Internet Explorer restricted the content, click Allow Blocked Content to continue. The clip begins playing. Because it is Internet Explorer, it is actually playing the MP4 version of the clip, but you don't know that; the clip selection is invisible to the user.

5. Open the page in a different browser.

   To do that, you can right-click the *blog.htm* file, click Open With, and then select the desired browser. Or you can copy the address from the Address bar in Internet Explorer and then paste it into the Address bar in the other browser.

   The page loads in the other browser. You might notice some minor differences in the way the page is formatted and the video clip displays. For example, the controls might look different.

   Next, we'll add a Flash version for users who don't have access to an HTML5-compliant browser.

6. Return to Notepad. Immediately before the closing *</video>* tag, add an *<embed>* tag to play the clip via Flash, along with a note explaining what is required to play the Flash version.

Note The AVI version provided in the sample files for this chapter has a watermark on it because it was created with a trial version of Aimersoft Video Converter. Despite the watermark, the file still plays just fine for the purposes of this demonstration.

```
<video width="320" height="240" autoplay controls>
<source src="videos/agility.webm">
<source src="videos/agility.ogv">
<source src="videos/agility.mp4">

<embed src="videos/agility.mp4" type="application/x-shockwave-flash"
width="320" height="240" allowscriptaccess="always" allowfullscreen="true">
<p>Click here to download a high-resolution version of the clip in AVI
format.</p>
</video>
```

7. Make the words *Click here* into a hyperlink that points to the *agility.avi* file:

```
<p><a href="videos/agility.avi">Click here</a> to download a high-resolution
version of the clip in AVI format.</p>
```

8. Save your work in Notepad and then try out the file in several different browsers.

9. Close Notepad and Internet Explorer.

> **Note** The Flash version won't run unless the browser doesn't support the *<video>* tag. If
> you don't have such a browser and you want to see what the Flash version is like, rename
> *blog.htm* to some other name and then delete the *<video>* and *<source>* tags from the file,
> leaving only the *<embed>* tag. Then view the page in various browsers to see how they
> implement Flash. A drawback to the Flash version is that it lacks user controls.

Incorporating Audio on a Webpage

The good news is that by working your way through the video information in this chapter, you've
already learned nearly all the background that you need to play audio on a webpage. The bad news is
that the same format and encoding problems that plague video on the web also apply to audio, except
that the audio problems are a bit worse. This section examines the *<audio>* tag and its alternatives.

Playing Audio with the <audio> Tag

You might be thinking that playing audio on a webpage would be easier than video, but for the most
part, it's not. You still need to provide for different browsers and encode your audio into different
formats. In addition, for the most part, your visitors will still need special plug-ins to play audio. With
that said, the *<audio>* tag is new to HTML5 and, assuming that the browser manufacturers can come
to some type of agreement, playing audio on the web should become easier a few years in the future.

Like the *<video>* tag, the *<audio>* tag supports multiple sources. With no common format, you'll
need to encode the audio multiple times to try to get the audio out to the widest possible audience. Also like the *<video>* tag, the *<audio>* tag supports attributes such as *controls, autoplay, loop,*
and *preload*. Therefore, the syntax for the *<audio>* tag is essentially the same as the syntax for the
<video> tag.

> **Tip** There are numerous applications that convert audio between formats. As with the
> video conversions, I used VLC to do most of the audio conversion to create the sample files
> for this chapter. VLC is available at *http://www.videolan.org/vlc/.*

If you provide MP3 support and Ogg Vorbis support for audio files on a page, you'll hit most of the browsers that people viewing your page are likely to be using. You'll find support for at least one of these two formats in Firefox, Chrome, Safari, Opera, and Internet Explorer. Again, as with video, you should also embed your audio stream into a Flash object so older versions of Internet Explorer can use it, and you might also choose to provide a downloadable copy as a last resort, like we did with the .avi file in the previous exercise.

Here's an example that shows the *<audio>* tag with two files, which are called with the help of the *<source>* element that you saw earlier in the video section of this chapter:

```
<audio controls>
    <source src="myaudio.mp3"></source>
    <source src="myaudio.ogg"></source>
</audio>
```

Playing Audio in Older Browsers

As with video, playing audio in older browsers requires the *<embed>* tag. When used with audio, you'll typically use two attributes, *src* and *autostart*; *src* configures the source of the audio and *autostart* controls whether the audio clip should play automatically upon page load. Adding the *<embed>* tag to the previous example results in this HTML:

```
<audio controls>
<source src="myaudio.mp3">
<source src="myaudio.ogg">
<embed src="myaudio.mp3">
</audio>
```

By default, content included with *<embed>* will be automatically played. If you don't want this, then add the *autostart="false"* attribute tag, like so:

```
<embed src="myaudio.mp3" autostart="false">
```

> **Note** Even when using *<embed>* to include audio, the visitor must still have software capable of playing the type of file being provided.

One other attribute commonly used with *<embed>* is the *loop* attribute. The *loop* attribute, when set to *true* or *infinite*, restarts the audio clip when it completes. It can also be set to *false* to indicate that the audio clip should play only once. However, the default is to play the audio clip only once; therefore, omitting the *loop* attribute is the same as setting it to *false*.

Now you get to practice placing an audio clip. In the following exercise, you'll add an audio file to an HTML5 page.

Add an Audio Clip to a Webpage

1. In Notepad and in Internet Explorer, open the *index.htm* file located in the *Documents\Microsoft Press\HTML5 Start Here\15Multimedia\AddingAudio* folder.

2. Immediately above the *<div id="bottomnav">* tag, add the tags for the audio clip:

    ```
    <audio autoplay>
    <source src="audio/margie.mp3">
    <source src="audio/margie.ogg">
    </audio>
    ```

3. Before the closing *</audio>* tag, add an *<embed>* tag that will play the clip in a non–HTML5-compliant browser:

    ```
    <audio autoplay>
    <source src="audio/margie.mp3">
    <source src="audio/margie.ogg">
    <embed src="audio/margie.mp3">
    </audio>
    ```

4. Open Internet Explorer 9 or later and then view the page.

    The audio should start playing automatically. You might need to click Allow Blocked Content if Internet Explorer prevents the audio from playing automatically.

5. Close Notepad and Internet Explorer.

Key Points

- Incorporating sound and video is accomplished by providing video and audio files in multiple formats to ensure that your visitors can view the multimedia no matter what browser they're using.

- It's important to understand the different containers and codecs available for video and audio and how those are supported across your visitor's browsers.

- HTML5 introduces the *<video>* and *<audio>* tags, which enable multimedia to be included in webpages.

- Older browsers don't support the *<audio>* and *<video>* tags, so it's important to provide video in legacy formats such as Flash to enable visitors who use these browser to view the content as well.

- Use *<embed>* to include audio and video content in a format that non-HTML5-compliant browsers can interpret.

HTML and Microsoft Expression Web

In this chapter, you will:

- Use the Expression Web interface

- Create a new website

- Create a new page using a CSS template

- Insert text and graphics

- Apply text and page formatting

- Insert hyperlinks

Throughout this book, you've been building your HTML knowledge by working directly with the code in Notepad. That's the best way to understand what is really going on in a webpage.

However, after you achieve basic HTML proficiency, you might decide that using a web-development application such as Microsoft Expression Web makes sense for your situation. Web development software can dramatically cut down on the amount of typing that you need to do and provides you with the ability to both edit and preview your pages within a single application.

In this chapter, you will learn the basics of Microsoft Expression Web, which is one possible application that you might choose for HTML editing. Expression Web is a simple graphical web-design application, sold in retail stores and online. You'll learn how to create a basic website using Expression Web, how to create a page that uses a CSS-based layout, and how to place and format text and graphics on the pages of your website.

This chapter uses Expression Web 4 for its examples. You can get a free trial of Expression Web 4 at *http://www.microsoft.com/download/details.aspx?id=7764*. Expression Web 4 provides only limited support for HTML5, but you can manually type in any HTML5 tags as needed. After experimenting in this chapter with Expression Web, you might want to go further with the program, or you might want to try out some other web development applications such as Dreamweaver or Visual Studio.

Important Before you can use the practice files provided for this chapter, you need to install them from the book's companion content to their default locations. See the section "Code Samples" in the beginning of this book for more information.

Exploring the Expression Web Interface

You can purchase Expression Web either as a standalone product or as a part of the Microsoft Expression Studio suite, along with several other development tools. After installing Expression Web on your PC, you can run it from the Start screen (or you can run it from the Start menu if you are using a in Windows version prior to Windows 8), the same as any other application.

When you open Expression Web, you'll see a five-pane interface (see Figure 16-1). The large pane in the center is where you will create your webpages; the four smaller panes along the sides provide access to tools and lists. The figures in this chapter show Expression Web running under Windows 8, where the interface is mostly black and gray; if you are using an earlier Windows version, the colors might be different.

Folder List pane shows the
pages in the active Web site

Toolbox contains tags you
can drag into the document

Properties pane enables you to
add attributes and properties to code

Styles pane enables you
to create and manage CSS

FIGURE 16-1 The Expression Web interface consists of five panes.

In the following exercise, you will open a webpage in Expression Web and view it in several ways.

View a Webpage in Expression Web

1. From the Start screen (Windows 8) or Start menu (earlier Windows versions), click Microsoft Expression Web.

2. Click File | Open.

3. Navigate to the folder containing the files for this lesson. Double-click the *ViewingPage* folder and then double-click the *index.htm* file.

   The files to use for this exercise are located in the *Documents\Microsoft Press\HTML5 Start Here\16Expression\ViewingPage* folder.

   The file displays in Expression Web.

4. At the bottom of the editing page, click the Code tab.

   The page displays as HTML code.

   When in Code View, you see the actual HTML tags as if you were working in Notepad; however, Expression Web understands the syntax of HTML elements, so it colors content, tags, and attributes differently, in order to simplify reading the code.

Click here for Code view

5. Click the Design tab at the bottom of the window.

The code disappears and the page now displays in what-you-see-is-what-you-get (WYSIWYG) mode, which is similar to previewing it in a web browser window.

If the pane is not as wide as the page, content might wrap differently when previewed here

6. Click the Split tab.

This view provides the best of both worlds. The top half of the screen shows the Code View and the bottom half shows the Design View.

```
index.htm ×
<body> <div#header> <h1>
 9 <div id="header">
10 <h1 style="text-align: center; margin: 3px; font-size: 40px">Margie's Trav
11 <i><h5 style="text-align: center; margin: 5px; font-size: 16px">Leave the
12 </div>
13 <table>
14 <tr>
15 <td style="width: 170px; vertical-align: top">
16 <nav>
17 <p><a href="index.htm"><img src="images/home.png" style="border: none"></a
18 <p><a href="domestic.htm"><img src="images/domestic.png" style="border: no
19 <p><a href="international.htm"><img src="images/international.png" style="
20 <p><a href="faqs.htm"><img src="images/faqs.png" style="border:none"></a>
21 <p><a href="mailing.htm"><img src="images/mailing.png" style="border:none"
22 </nav>
23 </td>
```

Design   Split   Code
```

Click here for
Design view

Click here for
Split view

**7.** In the lower (Design) pane, change *worries* to **troubles.** The word also changes in the upper pane.

**8.** In the Code pane, change *troubles* back to **worries.** The word also changes in the lower pane.

**9.** In the Code pane, in the bar across the top, click *<div id="header">*.

The Design pane shows the entire header division highlighted.
```

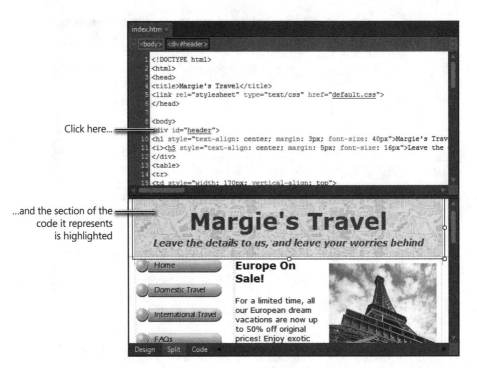

Click here...

...and the section of the
code it represents
is highlighted

10. In the Design pane, click in the first body paragraph (the one beginning with *For a limited time...*).

A border displays around the text, with a small *p* tab at the top, indicating that it is a paragraph that uses the *<p>* tag.

Tab shows the tag
assigned to the paragraph

11. Close the file (File | Close).

You do not have to save changes because you did not make any. (Well, you made one change, but then you changed it back again.)

12. Leave Expression Web open for the next exercise.

Creating Websites and Webpages

In Expression Web lingo, a website is a folder that contains all the files you need for a set of interconnected Webpages. That folder might reside locally on your own hard disk or remotely on a server. In most cases, you will want to develop the site locally and then upload it to the server when it is ready to be published. (It is called a website even if it is not technically on the web yet.)

To work with websites, use the Site menu in Expression Web. From there you can create a new site or open an existing one. You can also import content from other sites, and manage the publishing settings for a site.

After you have your site established, you can then create new pages or import existing pages into your site.

In the following exercise, you will start a new website and add a new blank page to it.

Start a New Website

1. In Expression Web, click Site | New Site.

The New dialog box displays.

2. Click Empty Site.

This creates a site without any pages in it; you'll add the pages later.

3. In the Location box, delete the *mysite* portion at the end of the current path and type **\travel** in its place.

Note You can optionally change the entire path to a different location if you have somewhere else that you prefer to store the examples for this book.

4. In the Name box, type **Travel**.

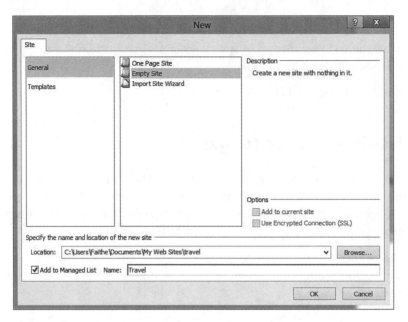

5. Click OK.

Expression Web creates the site, including a new folder in the chosen location. The folder displays in the Folder List pane in the upper-left corner of the Expression Web window.

At this point you have a new site, but it has no pages in it yet. Next you'll add a page.

6. Click File | New | HTML.

A new webpage document displays. As you can see in the Code pane, Expression Web fills in all the basic tags for you automatically. However, notice that the document type is not HTML5, but an earlier type: XHTML Transitional. To use Expression Web for HTML5-compliant code, you must change the document type, as you will learn next.

7. Click the X on the Untitled_1.html tab to close the unsaved new page. If prompted, do not save your changes.

8. Click File | New | Page.

The New dialog box displays.

9. Click the Page Editor Options hyperlink.

The Page Editor Options dialog box displays.

10. Open the Document Type Declaration drop-down list and then click HTML5.

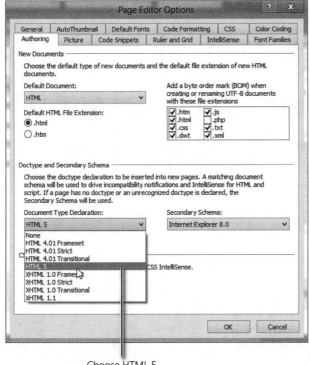

Choose HTML 5

11. In the Default HTML File Extension section, click .htm.

You can use either .htm or .html for your file extensions, but because the rest of this book has used .htm, you might want to continue that convention here.

12. Click OK to close the Page Editor Options dialog box.

13. In the New dialog box, ensure that HTML is selected on the General list and then click OK.

Once again, Expression Web creates a new page, but this time with HTML5 as its type.

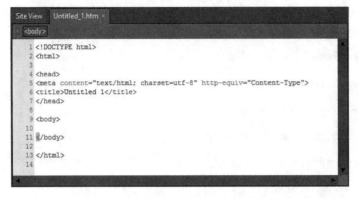

14. Click File | Save.

The Save As dialog box displays.

15. In the File Name box, type **blank**.

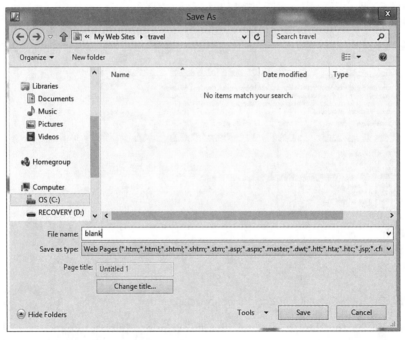

16. Click the Change Title button to open the Set Page Title dialog box. Type **Margie's Travel** and then click OK.

The new page title displays in the Page Title area.

17. Click Save to save the page.

18. Click the X on the blank.htm tab. If prompted to save changes, click Yes.

Expression Web saves and closes the page. The page now displays in the Folders List pane (in the upper-left corner of the Expression Web window).

19. Leave the website open for the next exercise.

Create a Page by Using a CSS Template

When creating a new page, you can start with a blank layout (as you just saw) or you can choose one of the templates that come with Expression Web. These templates use CSS layouts, like those that you learned how to create manually in Chapter 11.

In the following exercise, you will create a webpage using one of the CSS templates that ship with Expression Web.

Create a Website Using a CSS Template

1. In Expression Web, click File | New | Page.

The New dialog box displays.

2. Click CSS Layouts.

3. Click the layout titled Header, nav, 1 column, footer.

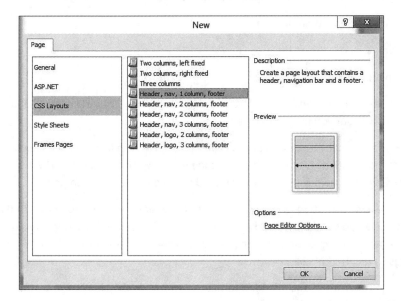

4. Click OK.

Expression Web creates your new page. Two separate tabs display at the top of the editing pane: one for the new untitled HTML document and one for the untitled external cascading style sheet.

 Note Even though you previously set the Page Editor Options to use the HTML5 document type, the layout does not use HTML5; it uses XHTML 1.0 Transitional. That's because the template that Expression Web uses is pre-created with that document type.

5. In the Code pane, edit the document type tag so it shows the following:

```
<!DOCTYPE html>
<head>
```

6. Click File | Save.

The Save As dialog box displays.

7. In the File name box, type **index**.

8. Click Save.

A separate Save As dialog box displays for the CSS file.

9. In the File name box, type **default**.

10. Click Save.

Notice the following:

- In the Code pane, the *<link>* tag references *default.css*. Expression Web linked and applied the style sheet without you having to do any manual coding.

- In the Folder List pane, the index and default files appear. The icon for the index.html file displays as a house, indicating it is the home page for the website. Expression Web shows it that way because of its name; index is the standard name given to the main page.

- In the Styles pane (bottom-right corner), the *#Masthead* style is selected because that's the currently selected division. The red circle next to it indicates that it's a uniquely named division, as does the number sign (#) sign preceding its name. Other types of document sections and tags have different colors of circles.

11. Click File | Properties. In the Page Properties dialog box, in the Title box, type **Margie's Travel**.

12. Click OK.

Notice that in the Code pane, the title displays as follows:

```
<title>Margie&#39;s Travel</title>
```

Tip The method you just used of setting the page title is an alternative to specifying a page title when you save your work, as you did in the previous exercise. Notice that the apostrophe is represented as a *'* code—again, automatically.

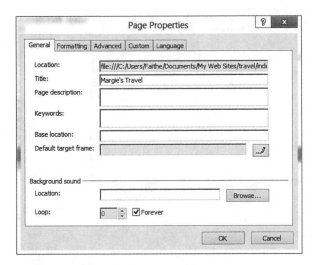

Note Notice that there are four divisions in the document and that each division is represented both in the code and in the Design pane.

13. In the Design pane, click in the upper-most box.

A div#masthead tab displays above it. Look in the Code pane and notice that the insertion point there is in the *<div id="masthead">* tag area.

14. Type **Margie's Travel**.

The text displays in both the Design pane and the Code pane.

Tip The border around the division in the Design pane is on-screen only; it will not display when the page is viewed in a web browser.

15. Leave the page and the website open in Expression Web for the next exercise.

Insert Graphics

When you insert a graphic image on a page, Expression Web automatically creates the <a> tag needed to reference it and makes sure that the graphic's location is appropriately referenced. That can be a big time-saver compared to manual coding when you have a lot of graphics.

Import an Images Folder

As in the examples in earlier chapters, you will probably want to create a special folder (such as "images") within your main website folder to store the images you're using for the site. One easy way to do this is to copy an existing images folder into the website in Expression Web. You'll learn how to do that in the following exercise.

In the following exercise, you will copy the Images folder from the data files for this lesson into the website that you have created in Expression Web.

Import an Images folder

This exercise starts in File Explorer (Windows Explorer), but Expression Web should also be open, with the website still open from the previous exercise.

1. In File Explorer (Windows Explorer), navigate to the *16Expression* folder for this lesson.

2. Select the Images folder and press **Ctrl+C** to copy it.

3. Switch to Expression Web and click in the Folder List pane.

4. Press **Ctrl+V** to paste the folder.

   The folder and all its images are now accessible from the Folder List pane.

5. Click the + (plus character) next to the folder.

   The folder expands to list all the graphics available.

6. Leave the page and the website open in Expression Web for the next exercise.

Place Images on a Page

After you have added images to a website, you can easily drag them into the Webpage layout wherever you want them. In the following exercise, you will insert graphics on a webpage.

Insert Graphics

1. In Expression Web, drag the home.png button from the Folder List pane into the #topnav division in the Design pane (the second division from the top).

   An Accessibility Properties dialog box displays.

2. In the Alternate Text box, type **Home navigation button**.

3. Click OK.

4. Press the space bar once to add a blank space after the button.

5. Repeat steps 1–4 for the following buttons, in the order shown, placing each new button to the right of the previous one. You can assign alternate text as appropriate for the button's name. Depending on the width of the Expression Web window, the buttons might wrap to a second row.

- domestic.png
- international.png
- faqs.png
- about.png
- mailing.png

6. Leave the page and the website open in Expression Web for the next exercise.

Drag each button from here...

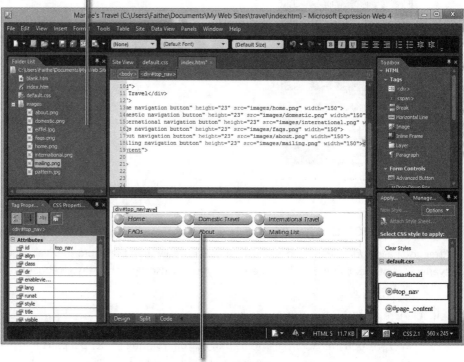

...to here

Add a Background Image to a Division

You can also add graphics as background images to divisions, as you learned in Chapter 6, "Introduction to Style Sheets." To do so, select the division and then work in the Properties pane (lower-left corner) to define the CSS style for that division.

In the following exercise, you will apply a background image to a division.

Add a Background Image to a Division

1. In Expression Web, click in the Masthead division in the Design pane. (That's the division where the text Margie's Travel currently displays.)

2. In the Properties pane (lower-left), click the CSS Properties tab if it is not already selected.

3. Scroll down through the properties and find the Background category. If it is not already expanded, click the + (plus character) to expand it.

4. Click the background-image property.

   A Build button (...) displays to its right.

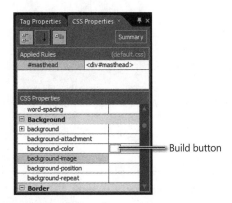

Build button

5. Click the Build button.

   A Select File dialog box displays.

6. Browse to the exercise files for this lesson, open the Images folder, select the pattern.jpg file, and then click Open.

   The image displays as the background for the Masthead division.

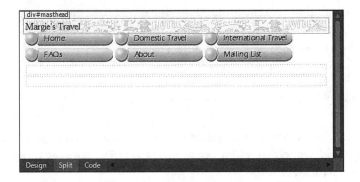

Note The Masthead division is not very tall, and that's okay for now. We'll fix that later.

7. Above the Code pane, click the default.css tab to switch to viewing the associated CSS file. Notice that:

- The tab displays as default.css*. The asterisk means that there are unsaved changes to the file.

- The code that places the background image in the Masthead division is in the CSS file, not in the HTML document itself. Division-level formatting is placed in the external style sheet by default, if an external style sheet is in use.

```
Site View   default.css* ×   index.htm*
 1  /* CSS layout */
 2  #masthead {
 3      background-image: url('images/pattern.jpg');
 4  }
 5  #top_nav {
 6  }
 7  #page_content {
 8  }
 9  #footer {
10  }
```

8. Leave the page and the website open in Expression Web for the next exercise.

Formatting Text

As you know from earlier chapters, there are many ways to format text. Here's a quick review:

You can use direct formatting, in which an individual block of text receives certain formatting. For example, you might make a word bold in a paragraph by using the *<b>* tag, as follows:

```
This is a <b>great</b>party.
```

You can create a span and then apply formatting to the text within the span:

```
<p>This is a <span style="font-size: 13px">great</span> party.
```

You can place a style in the opening tag for a certain paragraph or other block of text. For example, you might specify a certain color for a paragraph's text:

```
<p style="color: green">This is a great party.</p>
```

You can create a style that refers to the tag used for that text block. For example, you could create a style for the *<p>* tag that formats all list items a certain way. This style can be placed in either an internal or external style sheet:

```
p {font-family: "Verdana", "Arial", sans-serif; font-size: 13px}
```

You can define formatting for a new class in a style sheet:

```
.tangent {font-family: "Verdana", "Arial", sans-serif; font-size: 13px}
```

And then you can assign the class to certain tags within the document:

```
<p class="tangent">This is a great party.</p>
```

When you apply formatting in Expression Web, the application chooses an appropriate formatting method based on its internal rules. These rules take into consideration the type of formatting being applied and the size of the block to which it is being applied. If you don't like the method that Expression Web selects, you can edit the code manually.

In the following exercise, you will apply text formatting in several ways, resulting in several types of tags and attributes being created in the code.

Format Text

1. In Expression Web, click the index.htm tab.

2. In the Page Content division, in the Design pane, type the following:

   For a limited time, all our European dream vacations are up to 50% off original prices! Enjoy exotic destinations you've always wanted to visit, such as Buckingham Palace, the Eiffel Tower, The Louvre, and many others, and save thousands!

3. In the Code pane, enclose the paragraph you just typed in *<p>* and *</p>* tags:

   <p>For a limited time, all our European dream vacations are up to 50% off original prices! Enjoy exotic destinations you've always wanted to visit, such as Buckingham Palace, the Eiffel Tower, The Louvre, and many others, and save thousands!**</p>**

> **Note** When you type *<p>* in the Code pane, Expression Web automatically adds a *</p>* tag following it. Cut this *</p>* tag (Ctrl+X is one way) and then paste it (Ctrl+V) at the end of the paragraph.

4. Select the words *50% off* and then click B (the bold button) on the toolbar or press Ctrl+B.

The selected text is enclosed in a *<strong></strong>* tag pair.

```
<p>For a limited time, all our European dream vacations are up to <strong>50%
off</strong> original prices! Enjoy exotic destinations you've always wanted
to visit, such as Buckingham Palace, the Eiffel Tower, The Louvre, and many
others, and save thousands!</p>
```

5. In the Styles pane (lower-right), on the Manage Styles tab, click #page_content to select that division.

6. In the Properties pane (lower-left), click the CSS Properties tab.

7. Under the Font heading, click in the box to the right of the font-family property. A drop-down arrow displays. Click that arrow to open a menu and then choose the item named Arial, Helvetica, sans-serif.

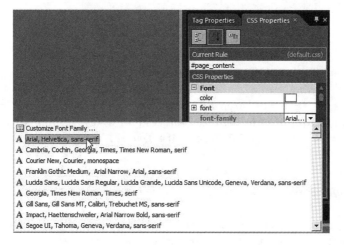

8. Click the default.css tab at the top of the Code pane to view the CSS.

Notice that a style rule has been created for the *#page_content* division:

```
#page_content {
    font-family: Arial, Helvetica, sans-serif;
}
```

9. Press **Ctrl+Z** to undo the last action.

Expression Web removes the style rule for that division.

10. Click Back to return to the index.htm tab.

11. In the Styles pane (bottom-right), click New Style.

    The New Style dialog box displays.

12. Open the Selector drop-down list and then click p.

13. Open the Define In drop-down list and then click Existing Style Sheet.

14. In the URL box, type **default.css** or select it from the drop-down list.

Note This places the new style in default.css rather than in an internal style sheet, which is the default.

15. On the Category list, make sure Font is selected.

16. Open the Font-Family drop-down list and then click Arial, Helvetica, sans-serif.

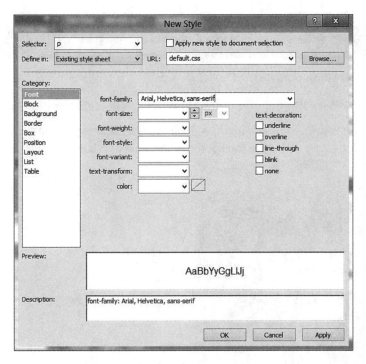

17. Click OK to close the dialog box and create the new style.

18. Click the default.css tab and confirm that the new style rule for paragraphs displays there, as shown in the following:

```
p {
font-family: Arial, Helvetica, sans-serif;
}
```

Note The *p* style displays in the Styles pane (lower right) with a blue circle next to it. The blue circle indicates that it is a style applied to one of the standard HTML tags.

19. In the Styles pane, right-click the p style, and then click Modify Style.

The Modify Style dialog box displays. It is just like the New Style dialog box you saw earlier.

20. In the Font-Size text box, type **13**.

21. Click OK to apply the change and then click the index.htm tab to see the results of the change.

22. In the #Masthead division, select *Margie's Travel*.

23. On the toolbar, open the Font drop-down list and select the Arial, Helvetica, sans-serif item.

24. Click the Font Size drop-down list and select xx-large.

25. Click the down arrow adjacent to the Font Color to open its drop-down list.

If the Expression Web window is not wide enough to see that button on the toolbar, click the down arrow at the right end of the toolbar to see the additional buttons, and then click it from there.

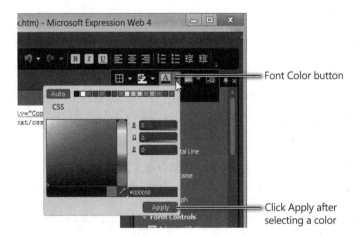

26. Click the dark-red square on the top line, setting the color to 128, 0, 0. Then click Apply.

Look in the Code pane. You'll see that a new class has been created, called *auto-style1*, and applied to that text:

```
<div id="masthead" class="auto-style1">
```

```
Margie&#39;s Travel</div>
```

Look in the *<head>* section of the code. Notice that a *<style>* tag has been inserted, creating an internal CSS style sheet for the document:

```
<style type="text/css">
.auto-style1 {
    font-family: Arial, Helvetica, sans-serif;
    font-size: xx-large;
    color: #800000;
}
</style>
```

> **Tip** If you want to avoid using an internal style sheet, you can select the style and then cut and paste it over to the *default.css* style sheet. Some web designers prefer to keep all styles in one place so they don't need to be concerned about where a particular style is stored.

27. Press **Ctrl+S** to save *index.htm*.

A Save Embedded Files dialog box displays, prompting you to also save the associated style sheet.

28. Click OK to save both files.

29. Leave the page and the website open in Expression Web for the next exercise.

Formatting a Division

As you just saw, one way to format text is to apply certain formatting to the division that contains the text. You can also format divisions in other ways, such as specifying certain positions, margins, or padding for them. Making changes such as these is easy in Expression Web; you can resize and reposition a division by simply dragging elements in the Design pane.

In the following exercise, you will apply text formatting in several ways, resulting in several types of tags and attributes being created in the code.

Format a Division

1. In Expression Web, at the bottom of the editing pane, click Design to display the page in Design view only (not split).

2. Click in the #Masthead division to select it. (That's the division with the navigation buttons in it.)

3. Position the mouse pointer over the bottom of the Masthead division.

   White square selection handles appear around the division.

4. Drag the center bottom selection handle downward to increase the height of the Masthead to 70 pixels in total (a ScreenTip displays as you drag, showing the current measurement).

Drag the bottom border

5. In the Properties pane (bottom-left), make sure #*Masthead* is selected at the top.

6. Under the Box category, click in the padding-top property.

7. Open the drop-down list for the property and click Pick Length.

The Length dialog box displays.

8. In the Length dialog box, type **3** and then click OK. Expression Web adds 3 pixels of padding to the top of the *masthead* division.

9. Repeat steps 6–8 for the padding-left property and add 12 pixels of padding to the left side.

10. View the *default.css* file in the Code pane to see what Expression Web added to the style definition for the division.

```
#masthead {
    background-image: url('images/leaf-green.jpg');
    padding-top: 3px;
    padding-left: 12px;
}
```

11. Click the index tab and then press **Ctrl+S** to save *index.htm*.

A Save Embedded Files dialog box displays, prompting you to also save the associated style sheet.

12. Click OK to save both files.

13. Leave the page and the website open in Expression Web for the next exercise.

Inserting Hyperlinks

Expression Web provides an easier way of inserting hyperlinks than typing them manually. You can use the Insert | Hyperlink command or you can press Ctrl+K to open the Insert Hyperlink dialog box; then type the specifications for the hyperlink you want. Alternatively, you can right-click a button or a block of selected text and then choose Hyperlink, which opens the same dialog box.

In the dialog box, you can choose from any of these hyperlink types:

■ **Existing File or Webpage** This is the standard type of hyperlink that inserts a reference to another page or file. You would use this for the navigation buttons on a site, for example.

■ **Place in This Document** This type of hyperlink is for an anchor point within the current document.

Tip Review Chapter 5, "Creating Hyperlinks and Anchors," if you need a refresher on anchor points and how they work.

- **Create New Document** This hyperlink type generates a new document of the type you specify. This type is not frequently used.

- **E-Mail Address** This type inserts a hyperlink that opens the default email application and begins composing a message.

In the following exercise, you will add text hyperlinks and navigation buttons.

Insert Text and Graphical Hyperlinks

1. In Expression Web, switch the index.htm main editing window back to Split view if it is not already there.

2. In the Design pane, click the Domestic Travel button to select it.

3. Choose Insert | Hyperlink.

    The Insert Hyperlink dialog box displays.

4. In the Address box, type **domestic.htm**.

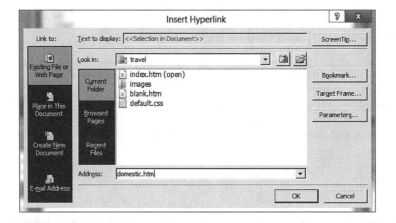

Note The *tips.htm* file is not in your webpage yet, but that's okay. You can create hyperlinks that refer to files you will add later.

5. Click the ScreenTip button to display the Hyperlink ScreenTip dialog box. Type **Domestic Travel** and then click OK.

6. Click OK.

7. In the Code pane, check the code that has been added for the hyperlink.

```
<a href="domestic.htm" title="Domestic Travel">
<img alt="Domestic navigation button" height="23" src="images/domestic.png"
width="150" class="autostyle2">
</a>
```

Tip You should recognize these tags from Chapter 6; the *<a>* tag is the hyperlink itself and it contains the title attribute with the ScreenTip text. The *<img>* tag shows the button. It is contained within the double-sided *<a>* tag.

8. In the Toolbox pane, locate the Paragraph tag on the Tags list and then drag-and-drop it into the Code pane after the *<div id="footer">* tag.

   In the code pane, it now looks like this:

```
<div id="footer">
<p></p>
</div>
```

9. Inside the *<p>* tag, type the following:

   `<p>Site Map   Contact Us   Legal Information</p>`

10. Select the Contact Us text in the Design pane and then click Insert | Hyperlink.

    The Insert Hyperlink dialog box displays.

11. Click E-Mail Address.

12. In the E-mail Address box, type **margie@margiestravel.com**. The application adds mailto: in front of the address you type automatically.

13. In the Subject box, type **Question about the site.**

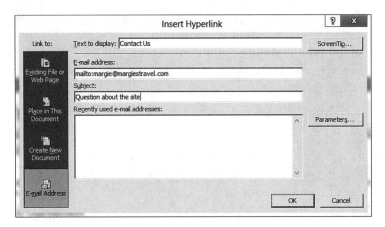

14. Click OK.

The hyperlink is applied to the text, which appears underlined in the Design pane.

15. Look at the code in the Code pane to see the hyperlink that was created.

```
<a href="mailto:margie@margiestravel.com?subject=Question about
site">Contact Us</a>
```

16. Save your changes to all files and then close Expression Web.

Key Points

- Expression Web is an application for creating webpages in a graphical, what-you-see-is-what-you-get interface.

- The Expression Web interface can show your page in Design view, in Code view, or in Split view (which shows half of each).

- To work with web sites, use the Site menu. From there you can create a new site or open an existing ones.

- When creating a new page, use the Page Editor Options dialog box to specify that you want to create HTML5-compliant code.

- Expression Web includes many CSS templates for creating page layouts. Click File | New | Page and then click CSS Layouts.

- To insert graphics, drag them from the Folder List pane onto the page in Design view.

- To add a background to a division, set its Background property in the CSS Properties pane to include a reference to a graphic file.

- You can format text directly using Expression Web's toolbar buttons. The code for the formatting is placed either in the individual tags or in the CSS, depending on the type of formatting.

- You can change a division's size by dragging its border in Design view.

- Use the Insert | Hyperlink command to insert hyperlinks.

Appendices

Designing for Usability

Although there is a certain amount of artistic freedom when creating a website, there are also well-established "best practices" among professional web designers. Have you ever visited a webpage that was hard to navigate, difficult to understand, or just plain ugly? A good web designer can look at these pages and offer suggestions for improvement.

In this guide, you'll learn some techniques for making your website as usable as possible. By making your website easy and fun for your visitors to navigate, you increase the time people will spend at your site and the number of times they will return.

Note Want a laugh or two along with your learning? Visit "Vincent Flanders's Web Pages That Suck" at *http://www.webpagesthatsuck.com*. This site contains hundreds of examples of what not to do on your site!

Understanding Usability

Usability refers to the experience visitors have when they view your website. It includes these qualities, summarized from *Usability.gov* (a U.S. Government guide to web usability):

- **Ease of learning**   How quickly do people understand how the site navigation works? Can people who have never before seen the interface learn it well enough to find their way around without a steep learning curve?

- **Ease of use**   After people have figured out how to navigate the site, how easy is it for them to actually find the information they need? A highly usable site puts information at the visitors' fingertips, with flexible and powerful searching and browsing tools.

- **Memorability**   How much will a typical repeat visitor remember about your site? A highly usable site sticks in visitors' minds.

- **Error-handling** How often do visitors make mistakes in navigating your site, and how easy is it for them to get back on track? A highly usable site provides helpful error messages when problems occur, complete with hyperlinks that help users do what they intended.

- **Subjective satisfaction** How much do people enjoy visiting your site? A highly usable site is just fun to explore.

> **Tip** For more in-depth exploration of these usability issues, see *http://www.usability.gov/ basics*.

Usability is extremely important in generating loyal, repeat visitors to your site. An advertising campaign can drive visitors to your site initially, but if the site is not easy to use, most of them will never return. According to website design expert Jakob Nielson:

> *Studies of user behavior on the Web find a low tolerance for difficult designs or slow sites. People don't want to wait. And they don't want to learn how to use a home page. There's no such thing as a training class or a manual for a website. People have to be able to grasp the functioning of the site immediately after scanning the home page—for a few seconds at most.*

Planning for Usability

Usability planning should begin before you create the first page of your website because your answers to key questions about purpose and audience will shape the overall organization and layout of your site.

First of all, why do you want a website? What do you hope to achieve with it? A website designed for selling products online will probably look very different from one that is mostly for sharing information. Clarifying your goals before you begin designing your site makes it easier to define and create the site you want. For example, the goal of the Margie's Travel site (the website featured in the examples in this book) was to provide information about tours and destinations and to encourage people to sign up for the company's guided tours.

Try to make your goals specific and tie them to your business or organization's objectives. Margie's Travel's goals might have been, for example, to reduce phone calls from customers wanting general information about tours, to make people feel more confident about traveling in foreign countries, and to encourage customers to dream about the vacations they would like to take.

Next, what audience are you targeting? "Everyone" is a poor answer to that question. You can't please everyone, and if you try, you'll end up pleasing no one. A store that sells live plants, for example, might be specifically interested in people who live near one of its brick-and-mortar stores. With that audience in mind, the company might want to provide local maps showing their stores' locations, directions from major highways, and printable coupons. Think about the characteristics of the people you are targeting and what they are looking for in a website. For example, a plant store's customers might turn to the website to get information about a specific problem they are having; making troubleshooting information easy to find would attract customers and keep them interested in the site.

Sketching the Site Organization

The next step is to sketch out a chart showing how users will access content, starting with your home page (start page) at the top. Any pages that will be directly accessible from the home page will display at the first level and pages that are subordinate to those will display at lower levels.

Here are some tips for planning the site organization:

- **Decide what links will be in the navigation bar** Arrange the links in order of importance from top to bottom (or left to right). The home page should always be the topmost or leftmost link on the navigation bar.

- **Decide what content you will deliver on each page** Eliminate any pages that visitors won't want or that don't deliver information that supports your business or organization's goal for the site.

- **Plan ways to reduce the number of clicks the average user needs to make** One way to do this is to put a direct link on the home page to the most popular content.

Designing a Consistent Page Template

For ease of navigation, the entire site should have a consistent layout, with common elements such as the navigation bar and the page title in the same place on each page. The simplest way to accomplish this is to create a template page and then base all other pages upon it. Your template page can use tables, frames, or divisions for layout.

Here are some tips for the layout of your template page:

- Place a masthead across the top of the page containing your organization's logo and name.

- Place the navigation bar at the right, left, or top of the page. Left and top bars are the most common, but many usability experts say that a navigation bar at the right is actually more intuitive for a visitor to use.

- If you have a very information-rich site, consider having multiple navigation barsone at the top of the page to include the overall main categories and one at the left or right with a longer list of subcategories.

- Make the navigation bar stand out somehow. It can be a different color, have a different background, or be surrounded by a box, for example.

- Place a text-only navigation bar at the bottom of the page so people do not need to scroll back up to the top again to navigate to other pages.

- If you decide to use frames, be very careful. It is very easy to create a frameset in which a frame is too small and cuts off the content placed within it. Ensure that each frame is adequately sized not only for the default content it starts with, but for every page that might appear in each frame throughout the user's entire visit to your site.

- When possible, make the page size flexible (for example, by leaving one table column or one vertical division to fill the remaining space in the window). If you are specifying a fixed width for the page content, make it no more than 800 pixels wide. That way, even people with low-resolution screens will be able to view it without scrolling.

- Select colors that reflect the content and identity of the site. Reds and yellows build excitement; blues and greens are calming. Body text should be dark letters on a light-colored background.

- Tailor color choices to your target audience. Researcher Natalia Khouw reports, for example, that men prefer blue and orange; women prefer yellow and red. Young people like bright primary colors; people middle-aged and older like subdued colors such as silver, gray-blue, and pale yellow.

- Select a simple, readable font as the default, such as Arial (Helvetica, Sans Serif), at a size that's adequate for your audience.

Designing the Content of Individual Pages

After creating the template that will form the structure of each page, start thinking about the unique content for the individual pages. Here are some tips for creating effective webpages:

- Use short sentences (20 words or fewer) and short paragraphs (five sentences or fewer).

- Ensure that there is some vertical space between each paragraph. By default the <p> tag leaves a good amount of space, but some people remove or lessen the vertical space by modifying the style.

- Whenever possible, break up information into bulleted or numbered lists for easier skimming. (Isn't it easier to find information in this bulleted list you're now reading than if it were in plain paragraph form?)

- Match the page's length to its purpose. Pages that summarize or provide navigation should be short; pages that provide detailed information on a subject can be as long as needed.

- Keep articles on one page. Do not split up the text of an article onto multiple pages just because a page seems long. Visitors who want to print the article will find it much easier to do so if it is all on one page, and they will appreciate not having to click a link to see the rest of the article.

- Break up long articles by using many descriptive headings. If the article is longer than a few pages, include bookmark hyperlinks at the top of the page that point to the major headings.

- If content goes more than one level deep on your site, use   to help users find their way back to where they came from. Breadcrumbs are a trail of hyperlinks that enable the user to back up one or more levels in the structure, like this:

  Home > Jazz > John Coltrane

- Limit the size of the graphics files you use on a page so that the page doesn't take a long time to download on a slow connection. The total file size of all the graphics on a page should ideally not exceed 30 KB. If you need to show larger, higher-resolution graphics, consider using thumbnails.

- Look for ways of reducing unused space. On a page that has a great deal of empty space at the right, for example, consider adding a text box containing information. One way to do this is to use a division with absolute positioning.

Performing Usability Testing

Big businesses spend big money on usability testing for their products and websites, but you can test your small business or hobby site much more simply and economically.

Friends and relatives make good usability testers. Sit down next to someone who has never seen your website before, and ask him to start exploring and commenting on whatever he notices. Don't explain anything—let him discover it. Pay attention to what catches his interest and what doesn't. Does he view the pages in the order you expected? How much time does he spend on each page? Are there any pages that he doesn't visit or can't find? Run through this process with as many people as you can round up; the more information the better! Then make changes to your site based on what you learn, and try another round of testing.

Designing for Accessibility

Accessibility, a subset of usability, refers to a website's suitability for use by anyone, regardless of age or disability. Designing for accessibility is not only a nice thing to do, but a smart thing. An estimated 18.7 percent of the population of the United States has some form of disability, and as the Baby Boomer generation continues to age, that number will only increase. Nobody would intentionally alienate 18.7 percent of his or her potential audience, but that's exactly what creators of non-accessible websites do. A certain level of accessibility might even be required by law if your organization is required to comply with the Americans with Disabilities Act (ADA).

> **Note** Many resources are available online to help web designers make their sites more accessible. One of the best known is the W3C Web Accessibility Initiative, found at *http://www.w3.org/WAI*. On the WAI site you will find more complete coverage of each of the guidelines presented here, as well as a working draft for a newer version of these guidelines, Web Content Accessibility Guidelines (WCAG) 2.0.

If you have normal sight, vision, and mobility, perhaps you have never thought about the web surfing challenges faced by people who have difficulty in any of those areas. Here are some of the most common accessibility issues:

- Mobility limitations
- Users might be limited to keyboard or mouse use only
- Users might be using voice recognition software to navigate
- Visual limitations
- Users might have difficulty reading on-screen text, especially at its default size
- Users might be color-blind or have trouble reading colored text on a colored background

- Users might be relying on a program that reads the content of the page aloud

- Hearing limitations

- Users might not hear music or narration being played

To plan for these limitations, W3C has compiled a list of accessibility guidelines for web designers to follow. The following sections summarize these guidelines; for more complete information about the guidelines, see *http://www.w3.org/TR/WCAG*.

Guideline 1: Provide Equivalent Alternatives to Auditory and Visual Content

Provide content that, when presented to the user, conveys essentially the same function or purpose as auditory or visual content.

You don't have to avoid graphics, audio clips, and video clips altogether; they add interest and excitement to your pages, and the majority of visitors can enjoy them. However, you should not deliver any content exclusively in those forms. Here are some ways to satisfy this guideline:

- Include an *alt=* argument for each picture, describing its content and purpose.

- For complex content where the description would be too long to display in an *alt=* argument, use an accompanying text note.

- Provide a transcript of audio and video clips. It doesn't have to be on the page itself; you could create a hyperlink that connects to a separate page containing the transcript.

- Use client-side image maps with *alt=* arguments for each area. Or, for a server-side image map, provide text hyperlink alternatives.

- In a visually based multimedia presentation, provide an audio track that reads or describes any essential information. Ensure that the audio is synchronized with the video.

Guideline 2: Don't Rely on Color Alone

Ensure 9that text and graphics are understandable when viewed without color.

Use color freely, but don't use it to convey information without providing an alternative method of conveying the same information. In addition, ensure that foreground and background colors contrast sufficiently so that someone with limited ability to distinguish colors (such as someone who is color-blind) can easily read the information provided.

Guideline 3: Use Markup and Style Sheets, and Do So Properly

Mark up documents by using the proper structural elements. Control presentation with style sheets rather than with presentation elements and attributes.

More web designers have been moving toward using division-based layouts that separate the page's content from its formatting, as you learned in Chapter 13. This approach has many advantages, such as ease of making formatting changes, but one of the best benefits is greater accessibility. Accessibility experts recommend using only style sheet-based layout (that is, a layout with divisions), and not tables or frames. They maintain that tables must be used only for true tabular information, and frames should not be used at all.

Separating the content from the formatting has the side benefit of being able to offer different style sheets for the same content. In "old school" HTML, specific formatting was applied directly to each tag, limiting the way site visitors could modify it in their browsers. In HTML based on cascading style sheets, however, the content and the formatting are independent, so you can provide multiple style sheets and allow site visitors to choose among them by providing buttons that, when clicked, switch to a different version of the page. You might have a regular style sheet applied by default, for example, but also have one with extra-large fonts and high color contrast available for users who can benefit from that.

Here are the guidelines for ensuring that your code is accessible from a structural perspective:

- Use HTML tags and text rather than graphics wherever possible. For example, for a math formula, use text rather than a graphic of it.

- Use document type declarations at the beginning of the HTML file, as you learned to do in Chapter 2, and ensure that the type you declare is valid.

- Use style sheets rather than formatting tags to control layout and presentation.

- Use relative rather than absolute units of measurement when describing the formatting properties of an item or class. For example, you might use percentages rather than inches or centimeters to describe an item.

- Nest headings, starting with *<h1>* for the top-level headings, *<h2>* for headings within an H1 section, and so on. Do not choose a heading style simply because you like its default formatting; instead, use the next logical heading level and then format it in the style sheet to look like you want.

- Ensure that nested lists are properly marked. For example, if you have an *<ol>* within a *<ul>*, ensure you close the *<ol>* before you close the *<ul>*.

- Format quotations by using the *<q>* or *<blockquote>* tag, not simply by italicizing or indenting them.

Guideline 4: Clarify Natural Language Usage

Use markup that facilitates pronunciation or interpretation of abbreviated or foreign text.

When a visitor is using a screen-reading program to read a page, the software that reads the text aloud can have difficulty reading foreign words and abbreviations.

> **Note** *Markup* in this context means *HTML code.*

Sometimes such software can switch to a different mode if you alert it to the change in language by using the *lang=* argument. If there's no existing tag where the language changes, surround the word with a *<span>* tag. You can also identify the primary natural language of the document in the opening *<html>* tag, but if the language is English, most reader software will assume it is even if you don't declare it.

You can use the *<abbr>* tag to mark an abbreviation. Even though Microsoft Internet Explorer does not fully support those tags (in that it doesn't display a dotted underline under it or pop up balloon help, as some browsers do), the screen reader recognizes it and signals its presence to the user. At the first usage of an abbreviation, you should spell out the full word or phrase, and use the shortened version only for subsequent occurrences on the same page.

> **Note** Text marked as *<abbr>* is spelled out with the individual letters, so a screen reader would read *<abbr>SOAP</abbr>* as S-O-A-P.

Guideline 5: Create Tables that Transform Gracefully

Ensure that tables have necessary markup to be transformed by accessible browsers and other user agents.

This guideline states that tables should be used only for tabular information and not for layout because tables are difficult for screen-reading software to interpret.

When you do use tables, it suggests using some additional tags that you didn't learn in this book to clarify the purposes of various cells. For example, use *<td>* for data cells, but use *<th>* for headers. In addition, for tables with two or more logical levels of row and column headers, use column groups to organize them.

If you do use tables for layout, ensure that the information would still make sense if the table tags were stripped out and the information was presented as plain text. It's really hard to design a page to meet that requirement using a table layout, and many web designers avoid using tables for layout altogether for this reason.

Avoid using table elements strictly for visual formatting; for example, the *<th>* tag makes the text in a table cell centered and bold, but do not use *<th>* simply to achieve that formatting.

Guideline 6: Ensure Pages that Feature New Technologies Transform Gracefully

Ensure that pages are accessible even when newer technologies are not supported or are turned off.

This guideline states that pages must not rely on new technologies, such as cascading style sheets, XML, JavaScript, Flash, Shockwave, and so on, to deliver their content. It's okay to use those techniques, as long as you provide alternatives, such as the following:

- Ensure that all pages are still readable when the style sheets are not available.

- Make text-only equivalents available for dynamic content, and ensure that the text is updated when the dynamic content changes.

- Ensure that pages still load even when scripts, applets, or other programmatic objects are turned off or not supported. If that's not possible, provide equivalent information on an alternative accessible page.

Guideline 7: Ensure User Control of Time-Sensitive Content Changes

Ensure that moving, blinking, scrolling, or auto-updating objects or pages may be paused or stopped.

This guideline states that whenever there is sound or movement on a page, the visitor should be able to control it. Here are some tips:

- Don't use background sounds that the visitors can't control. For example, don't use the *<bgsound>* tag, which you learned about in Chapter 15.

- Provide controls for all audio and video clips, so the visitor can pause, stop, and restart the clip.

- Avoid flickering, scrolling, or blinking elements. For example, do not use the blink or marquee elements (which are both non-standard and deprecated anyway). Blinking and flickering elements have even been known to induce photosensitive epileptic seizures.

- Don't allow pages to automatically refresh themselves unless there is a way for the visitor to stop the page from refreshing.

- If possible, do not use HTML to redirect pages automatically; instead configure the server to perform redirection.

Guideline 8: Ensure Direct Accessibility of Embedded User Interfaces

Ensure that the user interface follows the principles of accessible design: device-independent access to functionality, keyboard operability, self-voicing, and so on.

When an embedded object has its own interface, such as a Java applet that plays a game or performs a test, the interface must be accessible, just like the page itself. If this is not possible, provide an alternative, accessible page.

Guideline 9: Design for Device Independence

Use features that enable activation of page elements through a variety of input devices.

Device independence means that visitors can interact with the page by using whatever input device they are most comfortable with: keyboard, mouse, voice, and so on. Someone with a movement-related disability might be limited to only one of those inputs.

Device independence can be an issue with non-text elements on a page, such as embedded user interfaces and image maps. Client-side image maps are better than server-side ones because they are easier to navigate without a mouse.

HTML forms can be made more device-independent by the use of keyboard shortcuts (*accesskey=* argument) and by setting a logical tab order for links, form controls, and objects. For example, you can add a *tabindex=* argument for each form control and set its value to a number representing the order in which the tab key should move a user through the fields.

Guideline 10: Use Interim Solutions

Use interim accessibility solutions so that assistive technologies and older browsers will operate correctly.

User agents and other assistive technologies are being developed to enable users with disabilities to more easily view webpages that employ the newest features, but until user agents are widely available to all visitors who need them, web designers must be creative and employ interim accessibility solutions basically, workarounds ensuring that the pages are accessible to all.

Here are some tips for avoiding web design elements that cause problems for many users:

- Don't cause pop-up windows or other windows to appear automatically. For example, avoid using a frame whose target is a new window.

- Don't change the current window without informing the user.

- For all form fields, ensure that the text label describing the field is positioned to the left of the field, so that a screen reader would first read the label, and then move on to the field immediately afterward. Do not position the field labels above the fields (in a previous row of a table, for example) or to the right of the field.

- Include place-holding characters in empty text areas and input form controls. (The most popular one is the non-breaking space: * *.) Some older browsers do not allow users to navigate to empty edit boxes.

- Include non-link, printable characters between adjacent hyperlinks, surrounded by spaces. Some older screen readers read lists of consecutive lines as one link.

Guideline 11: Use W3C Technologies and Guidelines

Use W3C technologies (according to specification), and follow accessibility guidelines. Where it is not possible to use a W3C technology, or doing so results in material that does not transform gracefully, provide an alternative version of the content that is accessible.

The current guidelines recommend the use of standardized HTML coding wherever possible; that's the type of coding you've learned about in this book. Some non-W3C formats, such as PDF and Shockwave, require plug-ins or stand-alone external applications, and these formats sometimes cannot be viewed or navigated easily with screen readers and other assistive technologies.

Guideline 12: Provide Context and Orientation Information

Provide context and orientation information to help users understand complex pages or elements.

When a page has a complex structure, it can be difficult for users to understand it using screen readers or other assistive technologies. Here are some ways to help:

- If you are using a frameset, ensure that each frame has a title. (Use the *title=* argument.)

- For each frame, if it is not obvious what the frame's purpose is and how it relates to the other frames, include a *longdesc=* argument containing that information.

- Divide blocks of information into manageable groups where natural and appropriate. For example, you can create option groups to organize options.

- Associate labels with form controls by using the *label=* argument.

Guideline 13: Provide Clear Navigation Mechanisms

Provide clear and consistent navigation mechanisms orientation information, navigation bars, a site map, and so onto increase the likelihood that a person will find what they are looking for at a site.

Throughout the book, I have encouraged you to use clear and consistent navigational aids, but these are especially critical for visitors with disabilities. Here are some tips for making your site easier to navigate:

- Ensure that each hyperlink's target is clearly identifiable. The underlined text in a hyperlink should describe the target page, not simply be an instruction such as "Click here".

- Keep hyperlink text brief—a few words at most.

- Provide metadata to add semantic information to pages and sites. For example, you can use the Resource Description Framework (RDF) to identify a document's author and content type. (For more information about RDF, see *http://www.w3.org/RDF.*)

- Provide a site map or table of contents. Include a description of the available accessibility features.

- Ensure that navigational elements are consistent among pages.

- Use navigation bars.

- Group related items together.

- If you provide a search function, enable different types of searches for different skill levels and preferences (for example, a basic search and an advanced search).

- Place descriptive information at the beginning of headings, paragraphs, lists, and so on.

- Provide a means of skipping over multi-line ASCII art.

Guideline 14: Ensure that Documents are Clear and Simple

Ensure that documents are clear and simple so they can be more easily understood.

This guideline is fairly self-explanatory: keep it simple. Use consistent page layout, recognizable graphics, and easy-to-understand language. All users appreciate this, not just those with disabilities. Use the clearest and simplest language possible, and supplement it with graphics or audio clips only when they help users understand the site better.

Appendix C

Quick Reference

HTML5 adds over 20 new tags to the web developer's toolbox. Some of these new tags are semantic tags used for defining different types of divisions, like footer and header. Others pertain to audio and video clips and user forms.

Here is a list of the new tags with chapter cross-references where applicable. Because this book is intended for beginners, many of these new tags are not covered, as they are primarily for the use of more advanced web developers.

Tags Added in HTML 5

Tag	Description	Covered in Chapter
<article>	Defines an article	11
<audio>	Defines sound content	15
<canvas>	Defines graphics	
<command>	Defines a command button	14
<datagrid>	Defines data in a tree-list	14
<datalist>	Defines a dropdown list	14
<datatemplate>	Defines a data template	
<details>	Defines details of an element	
<dialog>	Defines a dialog (conversation)	
<embed>	Defines external interactive content or plugin	
<eventsource>	Defines a target for events sent by a server	
<figure>	Defines a group of media content, and their caption	9
<footer>	Defines a footer for a section or page	11
<header>	Defines a header for a section or page	11
<mark>	Defines marked text	

<meter>	Defines measurement within a predefined range	
<nav>	Defines navigation links	10
<nest>	Defines a nesting point in a data template	
<output>	Defines some types of output	
<progress>	Defines progress of a task of any kind	
<rule>	Defines the rules for updating a template	
<section>	Defines a section	11
<source>	Defines media resources	15
<time>	Defines a date/time	
<video>	Defines a video	15

HTML5 has also removed certain tags. These tags had already been deprecated (that is, recommended for phasing out) previously, but HTML5 discontinues their support entirely.

Tags Removed in HTML 5

Tag	Description
<acronym>	Defines an acronym
<applet>	Defines an applet
<basefont>	Defines the base font
<big>	Defines big text
<center>	Defines centered text
<dir>	Defines a directory list
<frame>	Defines a sub window (a frame)
<frameset>	Defines a set of frames
<isindex>	Defines a single-line input field
<noframes>	Defines a noframe section
<s>	Defines strikethrough text
<strike>	Defines strikethrough text
<tt>	Defines teletype text
<u>	Defines underlined text
<xmp>	Defines preformatted text

Glossary

A

absolute path Paths that contain a complete address that anyone could use to get to a webpage. (See also *relative path*.)

accessibility A subset of usability that refers to a website's suitability for use by anyone, regardless of age or disability. (See also *usability*.)

alignment The horizontal placement of a paragraph, specified by using the text-align attribute.

anchor A marker within an HTML document, roughly analogous to a bookmark in a Microsoft Word document.

argument See *attribute*

attribute Text within a tag that contains information about how the tag should behave. Sometimes called *argument*.

B

background image An image that displays behind the text on a webpage. By default, the image is tiled to fill the page, and scrolls with the page.

baseline The imaginary line on which text rests.

block-level element An element that occupies a complete paragraph or more.

body The section of an HTML document defined by the two-sided *<body>* tag. It contains all the information that displays in the web browser when the page is viewed.

breadcrumbs A trail of hyperlinks that enable the user to back up one or more levels in the structure of a website.

button-creation program A program used to generate buttons for webpages.

C

cascading style sheet (CSS) A document that specifies formatting for particular tags and then can be applied to multiple webpages.

cell A distinct area of a table, into which you can place text, graphics, or even other tables.

child folder A subfolder of a parent folder.

class A category of content, defined by the web developer, used to apply consistent formatting among all items in that category. Similar to an ID, but multiple elements can have the same class within a document.

codec Compression/decompression. A helper file that works with your media player program to play a compressed video file.

command button A button that executes a function.

compiled A compiled programming language that runs the human-readable programming through a utility that converts it to an executable file (usually with an *.exe* or a *.com* extension), which is then distributed to users.

D

definition description Uses the *<dd>* tag; a paragraph that defines a definition term.

definition list Uses the *<dl>* tag; contains the complete list of headings and definition paragraphs.

definition term Uses the *<dt>* tag; a word or phrase to be defined in a definition list.

deprecated A tag that should be avoided as it is in the process of being phased out or is no longer supported in the most recent version of the HTML standard.

descriptive tag A tag that describes the function of the text, rather than providing directions for formatting. Also called a *logical tag*.

dithered A color formed by a cross-hatch pattern of two colors blended together.

E

em A multiplier of the base font size.

entities Special characters in HTML that are created by using codes beginning with ampersand (&), followed by an entity name or entity number, and then ending with a semicolon (;).

entity name A name that defines a special character.

entity number A number that defines a special character.

extended name Another way to express color values. Extended names are similar to basic color names, but there are more of them. Not all colors named in the extended set are web-safe.

Extensible Markup Language (XML) A language closely related to HTML that programmers use to create custom tags.

external style sheet A plain-text file with a *.css* extension that defines styles to be applied to webpages.

F

file size The number of bytes a file takes up on the disk.

font family A set of fonts listed in order of preference.

foreground color The default color for a webpage that can be set with the *style="color: color"* argument.

frame A section of a browser window in which a webpage loads.

frameset A container file that describes how many frames the browser window will be divided into and what sizes and shapes they will be.

H

hanging Bullets and numbers that "hang" off the left edge of the paragraph.

Head The section of an HTML document defined by the two-sided *<head>* tag. The Head section contains the page title and information about the document that is not displayed, such as its meta tags. It can also include lines of code that run scripts.

header A friendly or descriptive title that displays in the title bar of Microsoft Internet Explorer. The text is specified in a *<title>* tag placed in the *<head>* section.

HTML document See *webpage*.

hyperlink Text or a graphic that you can click to go to a different location on a webpage, open a different webpage, start an email message, download a file, view a movie, listen to an audio clip, activate a web-based program, and more.

Hypertext Markup Language (HTML) The basic programming language of the World Wide Web.

I

ID An identifier for a unique element in a document. Similar to a class, except there can be multiple elements assigned to the same class within a document but each ID can be assigned only once per document.

image map An overlay for a graphic that assigns hyperlinks to certain defined areas (hot spots) on the image. The hot spots can be rectangular, circular, or irregularly shaped (called a *poly* hot spot).

indentation An indentation offsets text from the usual position, either to the right or to the left. In HTML, the three types of indentation you can set are first-line indent, padding, and margin.

inline span A shell into which you can place any arguments you need.

interpreted A program that is distributed in human-readable format to users, and the program in which it is opened takes care of running it.

L

leading The amount of space between each line. Also referred to as line height.

list item Uses the *<li>* tag; an item within a numbered or bulleted list.

logical tag See *descriptive tag*.

M

metatag A type of header tag that provides information about the document, such as keywords.

monospace font A font in which each letter occupies the same amount of horizontal space, regardless of its actual size and shape.

N

navigation bar A set of hyperlinks that connect to the major pages of a website.

nested A term referring to embedding within, as when a list is embedded within a list.

O

one-sided tag A tag that does not have a closing tag and that takes arguments.

ordered list Uses the *<ol>* tag; a numbered list.

P

page title The text in an HTML document's Head section that displays in the title bar of the web browser and on the Microsoft Windows taskbar button.

paragraph formatting Formatting that is applicable only to entire paragraphs; it's not applied to individual characters.

parent folder A folder one level above a child folder (or subfolder).

player An external program that plays an audio or video file in a separate window.

plug-in A helper file that allows content that a browser does not natively support to open in a browser window.

proportional font A font in which the characters take up various amounts of space horizontally depending on their sizes.

pseudo-class A class that uses a variable to determine membership.

Q

quirks mode The mode used to process HTML pages when the browser doesn't encounter a *DOCTYPE* tag.

R

redirect A redirect sets up an old webpage to automatically display a new webpage.

relative path A path that uses just the file name rather than the complete address. A relative path looks for the destination file in the same folder as the current file's location. (See also *absolute path*.)

resolution The size of a graphic, determined by the number of pixels that comprise it. Resolution is expressed in width and height.

rule An argument, especially when applied within a style tag or section.

S

samples A series of audio "snapshots" that are taken per second when an audio clip is digitized.

sampling rate The number of samples taken per second.

semantic tag A tag where the name is based on its usage, such as *<aside>* or *<article>*.

spam Junk email.

special characters Characters that are not included on a standard English keyboard.

standards mode The mode used to process HTML pages when the browser encounters a *DOCTYPE* tag.

style A formatting rule that can be applied to an individual tag, to all instances of a certain tag within a document, or to all instances of a certain tag across a group of documents.

T

table A grid of rows and columns, the intersections of which form cells.

tags In HTML, tags indicate where the formatting should be applied, how the layout should display, what pictures should be placed in certain locations, and more.

themes Formatting templates in Word that can be applied to any document.

two-sided tag Tags that enclose text between their opening and closing tags.

U

unordered list Uses the *<ul>* tag; a bulleted list.

usability A term referring to the experience a user has when they visit a website. Qualities included in usability are ease of learning, ease of use, memorability, error-handling, and subjective satisfaction.

V

visited hyperlink A hyperlink to a page that has already been visited.

W

webpage A plain text file that has been encoded using Hypertext Markup Language (HTML) so that it appears nicely formatted in a web browser.

web-safe color A color that exactly matches one of the colors in a standard 8-bit display.

World Wide Web Consortium (W3C) The organization that oversees HTML specifications and is the governing body for most web standards.

Index

Symbols

A

About the Author

 FAITHE WEMPEN, M.A., is a Microsoft Office Master Instructor, an A+ certified PC technician, and the author of over 120 books on computer hardware and software. She is an adjunct instructor of Computer Technology at Indiana University/Purdue University at Indianapolis (IUPUI), and in her spare time owns and operates a small bed and breakfast in rural Indiana.

What do you think of this book?

We want to hear from you!
To participate in a brief online survey, please visit:

microsoft.com/learning/booksurvey

Tell us how well this book meets your needs—what works effectively, and what we can do better. Your feedback will help us continually improve our books and learning resources for you.

Thank you in advance for your input!